MW00781863

Sin • a • gogue

SIN AND FAILURE IN JEWISH THOUGHT

CHERRY
ORCHARD
BOOKS

Sin • a • gogue

SIN AND FAILURE IN JEWISH THOUGHT

DAVID BASHEVKIN

BOSTON
2019

Library of Congress Cataloging-in-Publication Data

Names: Bashevkin, David, 1985- author.
Title: Sin.a.gogue : sin and failure in Jewish thought / David Bashevkin.
Description: Boston : Cherry Orchard Books, 2019. | Includes bibliographical
   references and index.
Identifiers: LCCN 2018023281 (print) | LCCN 2018023521 (ebook) | ISBN
   9781618117984 (ebook) | ISBN 9781618117960 (hardcover) | ISBN
   9781618117977 (pbk.)
Subjects: LCSH: Sin--Judaism. | Repentance--Judaism.
Classification: LCC BM630 (ebook) | LCC BM630 .B38 2018 (print) | DDC
   296.3/2--dc23
LC record available at https://lccn.loc.gov/2018023281

ISBN 9781618117960 (hardcover)
ISBN 9781618117984 (ebook)
ISBN 9781618117977 (paperback)
©Academic Studies Press, 2019

Book design by Lapiz Digital Services
On the cover: photograph by Menahem Kahana, reproduced by the author's permission.

Published by Cherry Orchard Books, imprint of Academic Studies Press.
28 Montfern Avenue
Brighton, MA 02135, USA
press@academicstudiespress.com
www.academicstudiespress.com

CONTENTS

A WORD ABOUT THE COVER

The photograph on the cover was taken by Menachem Kahana, an Israeli photographer who was given unprecedented access to the Israeli *Haredi* community. His photographs were later published in a volume called *Haredim* (Tel Aviv, Israel: Eretz Israel Museum, 2009).

This photograph was taken from behind the Hasidic Rebbe of Belz as he was conducting a ceremonial meal known as a *tisch*. Next to the back of the Rebbe is his trusted assistant, known as a *shamish*. Flanked on both sides are hundreds of Hasidim watching carefully at the Rebbe's moves and utterances.

But that's not why I love the photograph.

Underneath the table where the Rebbe sits is a lone child, patiently and quietly hiding and listening to the Rebbe. If you look at the picture quickly, you may not even notice the child underneath the table. I like to think that each section of the photograph depicts a different element of the Jewish community. You have your leader, the Rebbe. Each leader has his right-hand men, the proverbial "number two." And of course, the followers who anxiously wait for direction. But the person that interests me most is the one who is not at the table. The child hiding underneath. The people on the periphery. Such people inspire me, and I think this picture aptly portrays many of the feelings this book will hopefully describe. It's not enough to connect with leaders and their loyalists—you also need to check who is not at the table.

בְּרֹגֶז רַחֵם תִּזְכּוֹר.
כִּי הוּא יָדַע יִצְרֵנוּ.

סדר תחנון—

In wrath, remember mercy.
For he knows our nature.

—Tahanun

FOREWORD

Let's face it, most modern Jews have a problem with sin. It's not that we don't do it, often even enjoy it, and also repent for doing it, but we don't like to talk about it much, we don't like our Judaism to be infused with talk of sin. From Modern Orthodoxy to Reform, Reconstructionism, and Renewal, we like our Judaism positive. Of course, Scripture basically begins with sin and failure and to one degree or another, as David Hartman once said, the Hebrew Bible is a book of Jewish failure. We only get to the third chapter of Genesis when Adam and Eve sin against God. In chapter four, Cain kills his brother Abel, in chapter six it seems like all of humanity is mired in sin except Noah, and in chapter eleven the people rebel and build the Tower of Babel. Then of course, Abraham lies to save his own skin, Jacob lies to get his father's blessing, Joseph's brothers throw him in a pit and sell him down to Egypt, and we're still in Genesis!

The kabbalist Isaac Luria reads creation as an act of divine failure, of rupture and devastation that is our world. Works like the medieval *Sefer Hasidim* and the dark world of the Zohar are obsessed with sin, failure, and evil, and the modern Musar Movement's focus on *"tikun ha-midot"* (repairing one's ethical traits) impels a state of failure that pervades its view of human nature.

The reasons modern Jews are made uncomfortable with sin and failure are varied. In part it may be an attempt to distinguish itself from Christianity, in part simply the produce of a world that chooses to focus on light instead of darkness, part of the American ethos of "morning in America." In any case, what David Bashevkin shows us in this wonderful book is that sin and failure are not only embedded in the Jewish tradition but that the tradition has fascinating and compelling things to say about the sinfulness of the Jews, and human beings in general, and he examines the ways such insights can contribute to contemporary analyses of questions of human vulnerability and failure in our overly psychologized society.

By weaving together classical Judaic sources that exhibit Bashevkin's broad and deep knowledge of the tradition with contemporary discussions from ethicists, scientists, social scientists, literary figures, and philosophers, Bashevkin brings alive material the secular world had no access to, and material the "yeshiva" world did not know existed. There is something daring in "equaling the playing field" in comparing a comment by George Orwell to the Hazon Ish, but that is precisely Bashevkin's point: to humanize lionized figures in order to truly enter the world of struggle and failure that each experienced and continued to struggle with as part of their human greatness. This is an exercise in intellectual and spiritual war against the genre of hagiography, the fantasized depiction of great figures used so often today to shield such figures from the sins and failures that helped make them great.

When we look more closely, argues Bashevkin, we find that when we give voice to many Jewish heroes, often through correspondence, what we find is that they undermine their own sense of grandeur and are more concerned with confronting their weaknesses than overlooking them. There are certain obvious cases such as the Hasidic master Nahman of Bratslav, whose homiletic writings are replete with allusions to his own desires and failures. But even in more temperate figures, Bashevkin shows us in intricate detail how they never shied away from the challenges of their humanness and engaged deeply with questions of sin and failure in their own lives.

This book is a synthetic exercise of modern discomfort with sin and traditional engagements with the challenges of being human that are too often whitewashed because of our desire to see our heroes as figures not burdened by the same desires as we are. Or, because we want our religion to be uplifting and not depressing. In addition, Bashevkin's comparative perspective enables us to narrow the divide that separates one religious tradition from another, and to see them all as exemplars of the sheer passion and desire to live with the fragility of human existence. This book will make some readers uncomfortable, some because of its iconoclastic temperament, and some because it all strikes too close to the broken human heart we all share. But there is little doubt that *Sin-a-gogue: Sin and Failure in Jewish Thought* is a work of deep Judaic learning and creative and refreshing modern interpretation. "Human. All-too-human."

Shaul Magid
Hanover, New Hampshire

INTRODUCTION:
THE STORIES WE TELL

To pay for my father's funeral
I borrowed money from people
He already owed money to.
One called him a nobody.
No, I said, he was a failure.
You can't remember
A nobody's name, that's why
They're called nobodies.
Failures are unforgettable.

—**Philip Schultz, "Failure"**

A man of genius makes no mistakes; his errors are volitional and are the portals
of discovery.

—**James Joyce,** *Ulysses*

Jews, said Rabbi Nahman of Bratslav, as opposed to other cultures, do not tell stories to lull children to sleep but rather to wake them up. But what are those stories, in fact, that wake us up? Typically, Jewish storytelling is associated with lofty tales of hagiographic piety that recount the greatness and righteous deeds of religious leaders. This, however, is not one of those stories. This is a story of sin and failure and its place within Jewish thought and life. It is not a racy exposé or tell-all but a frank and honest discussion of some of the lesser known aspects of sin and failure and their place within Judaism. Ultimately it is a story that I hope wakes up some who seem to be drifting asleep.

Judaism has a complex relationship with failure and sin, particularly as it relates to storytelling. In 2002 Rabbi Nathan Kaminetsky published a book entitled *Making of a Godol*. The book was intended to be a multi-volume biography of his father, Rabbi Yaakov Kaminetsky (1891–1986). Only one volume, which covered the first two decades of his father's life, was published. As a book it is nearly unreadable. There are a little more than sixty pages covering the sequential life of Rabbi Yaakov's early years; the other twelve hundred pages or so comprise confusing footnotes and excurses delving into each detailed aspect of his life. When it was first published, hardly anyone cared to read it. And then it was banned.[1] A group of rabbis in Israel felt that the book was disparaging of the Jewish leaders of previous generations. Their claim was not without merit. *Making of a Godol* is certainly not your typical religious storybook. For outsiders to the Orthodox community the offending passages seem entirely innocuous. But for those who were raised listening to their parents read saintly tales of rabbis from previous generations, it was certainly jarring to discover that Rabbi Aharon Kotler wrote love letters to his fiancée. Or that the famed Rabbi Yisrael Meir Kagan, known as the Hafetz Hayyim, struggled with depression. Or that Rabbi Yisrael Salanter smoked cigarettes. These were not the stories that mothers told their children. Jewish stories, it seemed, should be carefully sanitized to avoid sullying the reputation of their protagonists or, more dreadfully, the ears of the reader.

Sanitized stories and ideas are certainly an important part of Jewish education. Rabbi Shimon Schwab admirably defended the importance of sanitized storytelling. He writes:

> What ethical purpose is served by preserving a realistic historic picture? Nothing but the satisfaction of curiosity. We should tell ourselves and our children the good memories of the good people, their unshakeable faith, their staunch defense of tradition, their life of truth, their impeccable honesty, their boundless charity and their great reverence for Torah and Torah sages. What is gained by pointing out their inadequacies and their contradictions? We want to be inspired by their example and learn from their experience.[2]

He is not wrong. I, for one, am glad that my mother did not tuck me in at night reading to me the litany of mistakes and infractions committed by rabbis throughout history. It does not bother me when I read a rabbinic biography that exclusively recounts the piety and holiness of leaders from previous generations. In fact I find it inspiring. Others may find that sanitized stories are left with a hospital-like, uncomfortable odor when they are stripped of their more historical—and often borderline-heretical—aspects. I don't. So why spend so much time discussing sin and failure?

The Stories We Tell

An Emory University study illuminates the importance of discussing sin and failure. Dr. Marshall Duke, along with his Emory colleagues Robyn Fivush and Jennifer G. Bohanek, designed a survey called "Do You Know," which asks children questions about their family narrative.[3] Do you know how your parents met? Do you know where your grandparents grew up? Which person in the family do you act most like? They formed a list of twenty questions about family narrative and discovered that the more children knew about their family, the better they thrived when faced with adversity. Based on these questions, they then explored the different sorts of narratives that shape families. As recounted by Bruce Feiler in his *New York Times* column "The Stories That Bind Us," they found there are essentially three thematic narratives that families tell. Feiler writes:

> First, the ascending family narrative: "Son, when we came to this country, we had nothing. Our family worked. We opened a store. Your grandfather went to high school. Your father went to college. And now you. . . . Second is the descending narrative: "Sweetheart, we used to have it all. Then we lost everything."[4]

The narrative, however, that cultivated the most resilience and strength among families was the third type, which Duke calls "the oscillating family narrative." This form of family narrative integrates moments of success—wealth, marriages, promotions—with moments of failure such as illness, layoffs, and death. When children hear their family's oscillating narrative and know that nonetheless their family persevered, a sense of courage and resilience is conveyed that will allow them to transcend their own moments of tribulation. "The bottom line," writes Feiler, "if you want a happier family, create, refine, and retell the story of your family's positive moments and your ability to bounce back from the difficult ones. That act alone may increase the odds that your family will thrive for many generations to come."

Like family, religion is also a story. It begins with biblical stories but is perpetuated with the continued traditions each family tells. Moments of

doubt, moments of inspiration, transitions toward observance and jour-
neys away—our religious practice is informed by different forms of narrative. The Bible itself compares life to a book, each life containing a different
story.[5]

What stories, then, does Judaism tell? For many it is an ascending narrative with a secular beginning and a religious destination. Others follow
a descending narrative in which religious life was primarily an exit door
from behavioral constraints and theological frustration. I hope this book,
with its candid look at sin and failure, helps others develop an oscillating
narrative about their Judaism. Granted, sin and failure cannot be the only
stories we tell, and this book thus shouldn't be the only book on anyone's
shelf. But a book about sin still serves a purpose of sorts and its presence on
our shelf helps ensure we tell the right stories.

Rabbi Yitzhak Hutner (1906–80) was no stranger to oscillating narratives. Born in Warsaw, he narrowly missed the 1929 massacre in Hevron.
He spent time studying at the University of Berlin before eventually set-
tling in the United States, where he led Yeshivat Rabbeinu Chaim Berlin in
Brooklyn. In September 1970, while traveling with his daughter, her husband, and a student, his plane was hijacked by the Popular Front for the
Liberation of Palestine. Throughout the harrowing ordeal he managed to
maintain his dignity. When offered a can of soda by one of the terrorists,
Rabbi Hutner, known for his sharp wit and humor, reminded the terror-
ist that he prefers his Pepsi cold. While he survived the ordeal, a finished
manuscript of his book on Shavuot was lost and had to be rewritten from
scratch. Aside from the theologically complex and sophisticated volumes
of writing he left, Rabbi Hutner also stands out as a moving advocate for
the oscillating narrative, particularly in his published correspondence.

"Everyone is in awe of the Hafetz Hayyim," writes Rabbi Hutner, referring to Rabbi Yisrael Meir Kagan of Radin (1838–1933), who wrote a famed
compendium on proper speech in Jewish law.[6] But who actually considers,
he asks, how many struggles, difficulties, and battles the Hafetz Hayyim had
to wage in order to develop his famed meticulousness with language? This
is likely the most oft-cited letter of Rabbi Hutner and for good reason. The
letter, which begins by lamenting the hagiographic nature of rabbinic narratives, reminds a student that greatness does not emerge from the serenity
of our good inclinations but from our struggles with our baser tendencies.
The verse in Proverbs (24:16), "the righteous fall seven times and stand up,"
has been perennially misunderstood. It is not despite this failure that the

righteous stand up—it is *because* of the fall that the righteous are able to stand confidently. Greatness does not emerge despite failure; it is a product of failure.

But our narratives, both personal and religious, have become warped. We think of success as a sequential line that over the course of time points upwards. Instead, success in any endeavor is a winding, meandering journey with many false starts, unfulfilled promises, and public failures. The distinction between the straight, sequential narratives we tell and those more winding and twisted stories we actually live are reflected in the Hebrew words for song. Throughout Psalms, the words *shir* [שיר] and *mizmor* [מזמור] frequently appear as synonyms for hymns. What is the difference between the words *shir* and *mizmor*? A *shir* shares the same root as the word *shura* [שורה], the Hebrew word for straight line. *Shirah* are our songs of appreciation for those sequential moments of accomplishment in our life as well as prayers that the trajectory of our life should proceed accordingly. The root of the word *mizmor* is *zemer* [זמר]—the Hebrew word for a vine. Vines loop, twist, and curve. During moments of setback and failure, *mizmor* is a reminder that those moments are part of our song as well. Life surely will be comprised of lines and vines, moments of *shir* and *mizmor*—both, however, must be sung.

Our Story, in Blurbs

Nothing highlights our complicated relationship with religious narrative better than the narratives we tell about ourselves. But when, honestly, are we ever telling our narrative truthfully? The culprit for our narrative neurosis is the typical structure of our bio blurbs. You may have seen a bio blurb for an author or a scholar-in-residence. They look something like this:[7]

After graduating from Harvard University, John Leiner received the prestigious MacArthur Genius Grant. A gifted teacher who has lectured throughout the world, Dr. Leiner is currently the CEO of the Leiner Foundation. His daily insights can be found at JohnLeiner.com.

Sound familiar?

I find bio blurbs very eerie, like looking at a photoshopped family photo. Vague phrases are always used like "sought-after speaker" and "internationally-renowned" that would seem narcissistic if spoken but are strangely accepted practice in bio blurb writing etiquette.

The absurdity of the bio blurb is only fully realized after writing one's own. The first realization that immediately descends is that everyone writes his own bio blurb. Granted, we collectively suspend disbelief and pretend it came from our personal PR department, but privately we all smirk as we imagine our friends and mentors struggling over which superlatives they could convincingly describe themselves with.

As Orwell noted, "Autobiography is only to be trusted when it reveals something disgraceful. A man who gives a good account of himself is probably lying."[8] If good biographies tell a proper story of nonsequential success, bio blurbs are the fun house mirrors that portray success as a pristine linear progression without the blemish of failure. But a bio blurb that is merely successes—our own ESPN highlight reel—sends the wrong message to others and paints a stilted portrait of ourselves.

Rabbi Menachem Mendel Morgenstern, the famed rabbi of Kotzk, once said, "I like to keep my good deeds private and my failures public." Of course we should be proud of our successes, but both for a more honest reflection of life and as a sign of encouragement and solidarity to anyone who has just received a first (or fiftieth) thin envelope, perhaps we can do a better job of integrating life's failures within our typically self-obsessed bio blurbs. It's great to list all of your successes in three to five short sentences, but maybe if one of those sentences were a failed project, rejected application, or unexpected difficulty, even our successes would seem more lively. It may only take one sentence to remind yourself that you can laugh at yourself. It's only one sentence to tell others that life will always have its disappointments. It's a one sentence tribute to one of the thin envelopes you have received in your life.

I am not suggesting a major revolution, just a cute little ploy that might help paint a more accurate picture of your life's oscillating narrative.[9]

In fact, I'll start with mine.

David Bashevkin is the Director of Education for National NCSY and is pursuing a doctorate in public policy and management at The New School's Milano School of International Affairs. He was rejected from the Wexner Graduate Fellowship. Twice.

SECTION I

THE NATURE OF SIN

1

WHAT WE TALK ABOUT WHEN WE TALK ABOUT SIN

"Say what you want to, but I know he loved me," Terri said. "I know he did. It may sound crazy to you, but it's true just the same. People are different, Herb. Sure, sometimes he may have acted crazy. O.K. But he loved me. In his own way, maybe, but he loved me. There was love there, Herb. Don't deny me that."

—Raymond Carver, "The Beginners"

Eskimos and Jews

Franz Boas, the nineteenth-century anthropologist, was the first to suggest why Eskimos, given the Arctic climate in which they live, have an inordinate number of words to describe snow. He pointed to the distinctions within Inuit, the language predominantly spoken by Eskimos, for snow of the ground, snow that is still falling, and drifting snow.[10] Boas was demonstrating how our environment and worldview affect the subtleties of our languages. One word cannot suffice to describe snow if it covers your entire world. This assertion—since questioned, if not entirely discredited—is still instructive in considering the many words for sin in the Hebrew language. Sin for Jews may be the linguistic equivalent of snow for Eskimos. Among the many words for sin in Hebrew, we have the biblical words *het* [חטא], *avon* [עון], *pesha* [פשע], and the later more generic rabbinic term *aveirah* [עבירה]. What do these different words tell us about the Jewish concept of sin and what, indeed, are Jews really talking about when they talk about sin?

Gary Anderson, a Bible professor at the University of Notre Dame, wrote an intriguing analysis of the etymology of sin in his work, aptly titled *Sin: A History*. Anderson, based on the biblical usage of the term *nosa avon* [נשא עון], meaning "to carry iniquity," focuses on the biblical imagery of sin as a burden. The implied weight of a burden, explains Anderson, reinforces the physicality of sin, or what he terms the "thingness" of sin.[11] Joseph Lam, a professor of Religious Studies at the University of North Carolina at Chapel Hill, also wrote a seminal volume on the different metaphors conveyed by biblical words for sin. Similar to Anderson, Lam explains that much of the imagery of sin is meant to depict sin as a burden. Such imagery, writes Lam, "lends itself potentially to this portrayal of the psychological effects of conscious culpability."[12]

After presenting proof texts for the metaphor of sin as a burden, Anderson turns to another common analogy for sin found in Scripture, namely sin as debt. As found in Isaiah's consolation of the Jewish people (40:2), sin is a debt that can be accrued or, if merited, forgiven. Anderson gives the "sin as debt" metaphor the bulk of his attention as part of his ancillary agenda to reemphasize among his readers a sense of personal obligation toward tithing and almsgiving. If sin is a debt, he reasons, charity is the best way to repay it.

The analysis of Anderson underscores a more important point about sin: metaphors matter. In other words, the way we talk about sin tells us a lot about sin itself. Anderson couches this emphasis in the philosophy of Paul Ricoeur, whose oft-cited aphorism states that "the symbol gives rise to thought." Whether sin is seen as a debt or a burden, the way we see errors and attempts to rectify our errors tells us much about ourselves. Or as Lam writes, "metaphor is a way of imposing order on the world around us, or of grasping the world by means of the ideas available to us."[13]

Sin as debt can be seen as a potentially dangerous description. As Anderson cautions, some have pointed to the metaphor of sin as a debt to "draw an unflattering picture of rabbinic Judaism." The financial metaphor, he writes, "seems to conjure the notion that God sits in heaven with his account books open and scrutinizes every human action with an eye toward properly recording it as either a debit or a credit."[14] This, Anderson reminds us, is a distortion:

> To be sure, God could be depicted as an imperious lending officer who
> would demand every penny he had coming. But he could just as easily be

portrayed as a soft-hearted aunt who was prone to forget the money she had lent a favorite nephew.[15]

The rigidity of the imagery of debt depends on the context. The great Hasidic thinker Rabbi Nahman of Bratslav employed the imagery of sin as a debt to validate his own spiritual activism. Unlike many other spiritual leaders, Rabbi Nahman was quite candid about his own struggles with sin. He used a story to address the inadequacy a rabbi preaching spiritual betterment may feel while himself struggling with sin. The story was about a rich man who loaned money to whoever was in need. After lending thousands of rubles, the wealthy man sought to be repaid, but none of his debtors appeared. Eventually, one remorseful individual stepped forward. He acknowledged the debt he owed his creditor while admitting that all the money he borrowed was gone. Dejected, the borrower did not know how he would ever repay the rubles he owed. The creditor, seeing how forlorn the borrower was, explained that the sum of money he owed as an individual was a pittance compared to all the money everyone else still owed him. "Forget about the money I loaned you," advised the lender, "but help me recover the other moneys I am owed. That will be a far greater repayment of your individual debt."[16]

This story highlights the spiritual leverage created by imagining sin as debt. As Arthur Green explained in his classic biography about Rabbi Nahman, *Tormented Master*:

> Here the personal meaning of the parable is quite transparent. How can one who is himself a sinner assume the mantle of God's representative to others? Being a *rebbe* is nothing more than the way this poor sinner pays off his own debt to God, atoning for his own sins by bringing others to repentance.[17]

If sin is a debt, then like a debt it can be collateralized and collectively repaid.

Sin can be something carried, but it can also be something else. The word *het* [חטא] appears in Judges 20:16 to describe a stone missing its mark.[18] Although the term *nosa avon* [נשא עון] describes the heaviness of sin, the word *het* describes sin as a missed opportunity. Here sin serves as a foil for a target, likely man's own self-actualization. If self-development and actualization are the objective, sin is when that objective remains unmet.

As instructive as metaphors can be in the analysis of sin, it is also important to keep in mind that the range of metaphors does not necessarily represent the collective scope of the meaning of sin. As Lam correctly notes, "The idea of sin in biblical Hebrew is no more encapsulated by the metaphors of *sin is a burden* and *sin is an account* than the notion of *love is a journey, love is a physical force, love is madness*."[19] A metaphor is a window to understanding, but it is important not to fixate on windows and to consider the words for sin from other vantage points.

Defining Sin's Severity

Aside from the metaphors which emerge from a consideration of the biblical words for sin, the Talmud also considers its meaning. As mentioned, there are three primary biblical words for sin: *het*, *avon*, and *pesha*. For the casual reader of the Bible these words appear nearly synonymous. Ronald Youngblood, one of the original translators of the *New International Version of the Bible*, summarized the overarching meaning of these words as follows:

> The widespread use of our three roots for *sin* in connection with numerous
> roots relating to walking along a particular way or turning from a certain
> path serves to stress the fact that sin is comprehensively viewed in the Old
> Testament as the deliberate act of veering off the road that God wants people
> to travel.[20]

There is certainly truth to Youngblood's assertion, but he seems to have painted with too wide a brush. All the words for sin certainly connote some aspect of deviation, but how do they differ? If they all essentially mean the same thing, shouldn't one word suffice? It is certainly easier to approach these three words like a Californian approaches snow, but for a more sophisticated understanding of sin in the biblical context, we will have to think like Eskimos and study the Talmudic explanation for sin as well.

On Yom Kippur, when the Temple still stood in Jerusalem, there was a special service performed by the High Priest. Throughout the Day of Atonement, the High Priest confessed three times—twice on his personal sacrifice and once on the communal scapegoat. The confession began with a plea: "Please God!" The remainder of the confession, however, is subject to a Tannaitic dispute. Everyone agrees to the basic text of the confession, but the dispute surrounds the order of three important words: *het*, *avon*, and *pesha*. According to Rabbi Meir, the confession concludes as follows:

> Please, God, I have sinned [עויתי], I have done wrong [פשעתי], I have rebelled
> [חטאתי] before You, I and my family. Please, God, grant atonement, please,

for the sins [לעונות], and for the wrongs [ולפשעים], and for the rebellions [ולחטאים] that I have sinned, and done wrong, and rebelled before You, I and my family.[21]

According to Rabbi Meir, throughout the confession the synonyms for sin are ordered *avon*, *pesha*, and *het*. This, the Talmud points out, is a rational order given that it is the very same order found in the Bible's thirteen attributes of God (see Ex. 34:7).

The Rabbis of the Mishnah insist that the order is different: first *het*, then *avon*, followed by *pesha*. Their reasoning is that each of these words for sin connotes varying degrees of intent. A *het* is a sin committed inadvertently. An *avon*, explain the Rabbis, is an intentional sin. *Pesha* is a sin that is not only committed deliberately but also as an act of rebellion against God. As each word for sin represents a different degree of rebellious intent, it makes sense that they should be ordered in ascending order of severity.

To summarize, Rabbi Meir and the Rabbis both agree that the various words for sin indicate different levels of severity.[22] Their argument surrounds the order of the High Priest's confession. According to Rabbi Meir the order of the confession is based upon the order as presented in the Bible.[23] According to the Rabbis the order of the Priest's confession is based upon which sins have the most pernicious intent.

The linguistic distinctions presented by the Talmud are telling. Intuitively, we may have already assumed that not all sins are created equal, but how do we differentiate between sins of differing severity? We have categories that distinguish some sins. Idolatry, adultery, and murder are singled out by the Talmud as sins that require Jews to succumb to martyrdom rather than commit any one of the three. But such sins, while certainly severe, do not factor into the Talmudic classification of the different names for sin. Rather, the names for the different sins are based upon the motivation of the sinner. An otherwise minor infraction can be classified as a *pesha* if the sinner committed such an act as a marked act of rebellion against God. Conversely, an egregious sin can be characterized as a *het* if the sin was unintentional. If beauty is in the eye of the beholder, the severity of sin, according to the Talmud, is in the mind of the transgressor.

Contrast the Talmudic approach to the different categories of sin to the different categories of crime in American law: infractions, misdemeanors, and felonies. Most people have committed an infraction at one point or another, usually resulting in a ticket or minor fine. Misdemeanors are usually defined as crimes that are punishable by up to a year in jail. Felonies, the most severe, are crimes that are punishable by jail sentences exceeding a year or even, in certain states, death. Blurring the distinction between crime—categorized by the punishment assigned to it—with sin, which is gradated by the intention of the perpetrator, has warped our view of sin and crime. Dr. Karl Menninger, in his classic work *Whatever Became of Sin,* notes that in the public's mind sin and crime have become nearly indistinguishable. "Many former sins have become crimes," he writes, while some "former crimes have becomes sins." The sociological shift that emerges from this confusion is that "[t]he policeman replaced the priest."[24] In replacing the priest or rabbi with a policeman, our understanding of sin has deteriorated. When sin and crime are confused we place a disproportionate emphasis on the role of punishment in evaluating the severity of sin. The proverbial lightning bolt from heaven is not what characterizes the most heinous sins. Crime, as immortalized by Dostoevsky, is measured by punishment. Sin, however, is measured by purpose. Of course, as we will consider later, the actual action associated with sin is of serious consequence, but in the Talmudic reading the heart of defining the different gradations of sin is not the commensurate punishment—it is the mindset.[25]

A Word on the Rabbinic Word for Sin

The Bible and later rabbinic works such as the Mishnah and Talmud do not always speak the same language. There are a host of Hebrew words that are frequently used in Mishnaic literature that are not mentioned anywhere in the biblical canon. Regarding sin, one word frequently used in Mishnaic literature is completely absent in the Bible—*aveirah* [עבירה].[26] For instance, when the Mishnah in *Pirkei Avot* instructs its students to flee from sin[27] it does not use any of the more familiar biblical terms such as *het, avon,* or *pesha*. Instead, the Mishnah uses the term *aveirah*. Similarly, when describing sins between man and God [עבירות בין אדם למקום] and interpersonal sins [עבירות בין אדם לחברו], the Mishnah uses the term *aveirah*. The term *aveirah* does not appear in this context anywhere in the Bible. What does this rabbinic neologism tell us about the rabbinic concept of sin?

The word *aveirah* is clearly derived from the biblical word *la-avor* [לעבר], to transgress. Although we do not find the noun *aveirah* in the Bible, we frequently find the term *la-avor* as a verb indicting that a sin has been committed. The absence of the word *aveirah* in biblical literature may be part of a larger biblical trend that avoids abstract nouns in biblical writing. For instance, in the Bible we find the term *sho'khain* [שכן], a verb denoting God's dwelling, but only in later rabbinic literature do we find the conceptualized noun *shekhinah* [שכינה], meaning the presence of God. Steven Fraade, Judaic Studies professor at Yale, develops the idea that many biblical verbs later emerged within Mishnaic literature as conceptualized nouns. He writes:

> My thesis at first appears to be simple: that nominalized verbs, that is, verbal nouns that follow from each verbal conjugation by fixed morphological patterns, often appear for the first time in early rabbinic literature (here focusing on the Tannaitic corpora) to denote newly concretized, or hypostatized abstract concepts, which previously could only be inferred from their verbal usages. I will argue that such morphological innovations may signal a conceptual innovation, or shift, that needs to be understood in its broader historical context. However, since the increased nominalization of verbs is a broader development both within biblical Hebrew and between it and its successors, and that the shift to more abstract meanings inhering in both verbs and their nominalized forms proceeds abreast, we might ask to what extent the linguistic innovations facilitate the conceptual changes, or to what extend the conceptual changes serve to accelerate the linguistic developments.[28]

According to Fraade, Mishnaic times marked a shift towards conceptualization of many biblical terms as evident by the new conjugation of many words. From the verb לעבור—to transgress, emerged the conceptualized noun עבירה—a transgression. Sin, with this new word, was no longer an action; suddenly sinning had become a concept.

It is not entirely clear why Mishnaic literature felt it was necessary to add another word for sin to the already robust catalogue of חטא, עון, and פשע—but the word *aveirah* has certainly become a common term referring to sin.[29] Grossman, in his exhaustive study of the word *aveirah* in rabbinic literature, thinks the word was used as a euphemism for sexual sins. He does not explain why this term became more popular and what its imagery represents.[30] Certainly, it remains a curious question: why did the word *aveirah*, without any mention in biblical literature, become such a common term for sin in rabbinic literature? What additional conceptual imagery does this word convey about sin? Perhaps two new dimensions can be suggested.

First, the word *aveirah* adds a clear spatial dimension to the act of sin. As mentioned, the word *aveirah* derives from the word *la-avor* [לעבור], meaning to cross over. The physical imagery of overstepping presupposes clear boundaries that demarcate where one is and is not permitted to trespass. Perhaps sin was conceptualized in this manner, specifically in Mishnaic literature, to underscore the clear legal borders that were structured within the texts of rabbinic Judaism. As the rabbinic codifiers of the Mishnah and Talmud hewed the corpus of Jewish law, legal boundaries became clearer as well. Once the parameters were codified and canonized,[31] violations of such laws could more aptly be described as an *aveirah*—a transgression.

Second, the word *aveirah* relates to the word *avar*, meaning "the past."[32] While this etymological connection is certainly more tenuous, the conceptual connection between sin and time is actually a much discussed theme in more modern rabbinic works. Rabbi Elijah of Vilna, known as the Vilna Gaon, posits a fascinating connection between time and failure. He notes that when God informs Avraham of the future exile in Egypt, God stipulates that the children of Avraham will be slaves for "four hundred years." However, when promising the ordained redemption from Egypt, God affirms that it will occur in "the fourth generation." Exile is foretold as a measure of time—four hundred years—while the redemption is expressed in terms of subsequent generations. Based on this distinction, Rabbi Elijah of Vilna states the following:

הקלקולים נתלים בזמן, והתיקונים באדם

> Destructiveness is a product of time—and constructiveness is from within mankind.[33]

Time, according to this construct, arches towards failure. The course of the world's affairs can only be corrected towards redemption through the acts of people. Only mankind can correct the entropy of time.

Time's connection to failure can be expressed in two ways. Maimonides in his *Laws of Repentance* describes those who are mired in sin and ignore the call to repent since "they forget the truth due to the vanities of time." Time's perpetual march forward obscures man's locus of control. If someone decides to be totally passive, time will still continue making decisions for them. Failure naturally emerges from a passive approach to time. Mankind needs to assert its creative control over time in order to assure it is redeemed. When the absurd vanities of time eclipse man's locus of control, entropy becomes the guiding force forward.

Another association of time with failure is the effect of the past on the present. Namely, past experiences can inform, enlighten, and educate, but they also contain a halting force. The memories of yesterday can distract from the responsibilities of today. In *Sefer ha-Hinukh*, an anonymous work about the Jewish commandments, the author warns that an overemphasis on past experiences can be a catalyst for a spiritually absent present. In the work, written as an educational curriculum for the author's son, *Sefer ha-Hinukh* explains that many people living in the tenth through thirteenth centuries did not don *tefillin* (phylacteries) due to a misconception about sin; some believed that previous misdeeds precluded them from performing the mitzvah of *tefillin*.[34] *Sefer ha-Hinukh* teaches that abstaining from *tefillin* because of other misdeeds is both an incorrect assumption about *tefillin* as well as a dangerous misconception about the observance of commandments in general. The author writes, "In truth this prevents many people from observance and is a great evil."[35] Past mistakes do not preclude present spiritual actions:

ולא כן ביתי אני עם האל, כי ידעתי שאין צדיק בארץ אשר יעשה טוב ולא יחטא, ועם כל זה לא נמנעהו מהתעסק במצוה בעת רוח אלהים טובה תלבשהו לעשות טוב, כי מי יודע אם אולי ימשך בדרכו הטובה עד עת מותו והמות פתאום תבוא.

> This is not how I operate with God in my home for I know that there is no one so righteous who does good and never sins. Nonetheless, they should never be inhibited from getting involved in a *mitzvah* in the moment that the spirit of God adorns them to do good. Who knows if perhaps they will continue on their path of goodness until death. And death comes fast.[36]

The *Sefer ha-Hinukh* warns people that ruminating about mistakes and failures can distract a person from performing *mitzvot* in the current moment. Guilt, shame, or spiritual malaise about the past easily misdirects a person's present positive trajectory. Since dwelling on the past can discourage change, it is no wonder that the Jewish concept of repentance focuses so prominently on the future. Of the four legal qualifications for repentance, committing oneself to a proper future is the final step.[37] If sin is becoming mired in the past, repentance is seizing control of the future.

Alan Lightman, an MIT professor, wrote a remarkable book on the varying concepts of time entitled *Einstein's Dreams*. This work of fiction imagines how life would function with different conceptions of time. Lightman describes a town where time repeats itself. Another chapter envisions a world without time—only images. One story invites the reader to consider a world where everyone lives forever—infinite time. The small book contains many of the most profound perspectives on how time shapes our lives. One story describes a world where the passage of time brings increased order. In such a world, he writes: "Desks become neat by the end of the day. Clothes on the floor in the evening lie on chairs in the morning. Missing socks reappear."[38]

Like all of the stories in Lightman's book, this story presents an interesting thought experiment. How would people live if time, instead of being entropic, curved towards order? In many ways this description of time is the inverse of the idea suggested by Rabbi Elijah of Vilna's conception of time as a destructive, exilic force in the world. When time is the force that creates order, there is far less pressure on man to be proactive in life. As Lightman describes in this story:

> In such a world, people with untidy houses lie in their beds and wait for the forces of nature to jostle the dust from their windowsills and straighten the shoes in their closets. People with untidy affairs may picnic while their calendars become organized, their appointments arranged, their accounts balanced.[39]

Such a world, he explains, would also negate the meaning of much of man's involvement in the world. By contrast, in the world described by Rabbi Elijah of Vilna, time increases disorder. The chaos and torment of time make failure more likely but also place added significance on human efforts. More socks may be missing, but they'll never be found if we don't search.

As discussed earlier, one of the metaphorical descriptions of sin is as a burden. Perhaps the term *aveirah* with its shared root with the term *avar*, meaning "past," is a subtle reminder that our past sinful experiences must not hinder our will to repent. Sin at its worst warps our sense of time and burdens our ability to correct our future.

Sins as White as Snow

Franz Boas' conjecture about Eskimo words for snow has long been discredited. Nonetheless, his idea still offers insight about how we think about language. Granted, the number of words for snow or sin may not be significant in one language or another, but the nature of the linguistic distinctions within each language is worth considering. As he writes:

> Thus it happens that each language, from the point of view of another language, may be arbitrary in its classifications; that what appears as a single idea in one language may be characterized by a series of distinct phonetic groups in another.[40]

So it is with sin. Each word in biblical and rabbinic language for sin tells a different story about the nature of sin itself. Both the imagery of each term and the distinctions among them offer insight into how sin and failure should be considered in Jewish thought.

One of the most iconic rituals of Yom Kippur, the Day of Atonement, is the scapegoat that is sent off a cliff to atone for the sins of the Jewish people. A Mishnah in *Yoma* (6:8) records that before offering the scapegoat the High Priest tied a strip of red wool around the animal's horns. If the Jewish people were indeed forgiven, the red wool would turn white. This ritual, the Mishnah explains, was based upon a verse in Isaiah (1:18), "If your sins will be like crimson, they will become white as snow." However many words Eskimos have for snow, we pray that our sins will eventually be described with one of them.

2

SIN'S ORIGINS AND ORIGINAL SIN

They could find no flaw
In all of Eden: this was the first omen.

—Donald Justice, "The Wall"

The mind is its own place, and in itself can make a heaven of hell, a hell of heaven...

—John Milton, *Paradise Lost*

When Sin Happens

The origin of sin occupies just twenty-five verses in the bible.[41] Here is the basic synopsis: Following the story of creation, which includes nearly the entire first two chapters, the Bible presents the story of Adam's sin. Adam's sin begins in the final verse of the second chapter, "They (Adam and Eve) were both naked, the man and his wife, and they were not ashamed." Enter the snake. Despite God's earlier warning that eating from the Tree of Good and Evil will surely cause death, the snake reasons to Eve that God is just trying to prevent Eve from becoming like God. Eve eats from the Tree and proceeds to feed Adam as well. Immediately afterwards, Adam and Eve's "eyes are opened" and they realize they are naked. After fashioning clothes for themselves, Adam and Eve hear the sound of God "walking through the Garden." He calls out to Adam and Eve, "Where are you?" They hide. Eventually they acknowledge their sin and God curses Adam and Eve each respectively with the pains of labor and the difficulty of child labor. The story concludes with Adam and Eve banished from Eden.

The only thing obvious about the story of Adam and Eve's sin is how perplexing it is. Clearly, there are a host of questions that immediately present themselves to the reader. Firstly, what was Adam's sin? Knowledge of good and evil seems like a helpful thing to possess, so why was it prohibited? Secondly, aside from what, how could Adam have sinned? Isn't knowledge of good and evil a prerequisite for sin? How could he have sinned before eating from the Tree that gave him powers of discernment? These questions are of course just added to the myriad narrative riddles that appear throughout: Why did Adam try to hide? What was the nature of God's punishment? What's with all the nudity?

As intriguing as all of these questions are, there is another question, often overlooked, that may be even more central to understanding the nature of sin's origin. Namely, *when.* When did the story of Adam and Eve take place? A cursory reading of the Bible would suggest that the story occurs immediately following creation. Structurally, the order of Genesis certainly would suggest that the story of the Tree occurs immediately following the conclusion of God's seven days of creation. The creation story ends on Saturday with the creation of Shabbat, so it wouldn't be far-fetched to assume Adam and Eve ate from the Tree sometime after the completion of creation. Perhaps Sunday morning brunch?

The importance of this question seems to be unknown to most scholars and thinkers. Christian chronology for the sin of Adam and Eve varies, though most scholars ignore this question altogether. Some depictions have the temptation to eat from the Tree lingering for an agonizingly long amount of time.[42] One scholar, Archbishop James Ussher, was more specific. He dated Adam and Eve's residence in Eden to be just short of two weeks. According to Ussher's calculation, man was created on October 28 and expelled on November 10.[43] The Jewish answer to when Adam and Eve sinned is actually quite clear. The Talmud (*Sanhedrin* 38b) presents the following chronology for the creation and eventual sin of Adam:

> The day is divided into twelve hours—starting with sunrise and ending with sunset. The first five hours of the day were occupied with the formation and creation of Adam. During the sixth hour he named all the animals. During the seventh hour, Eve was created. Cain and Abel were born during the eighth hour. During the ninth hour Adam was commanded not to eat from the Tree, and during the tenth hour they all transgressed. During the eleventh hour they were judged, and during the twelfth hour—immediately before Shabbat—they were banished from the Garden.[44]

The Talmud's chronology is startling. We are used to thinking about the sin of Adam and Eve as a perversion of God's pristine creation—a post-creation act. That is how the Bible situates the story of sin. Creation is complete—sin destroys the perfect world. The Talmud's chronology tells a very different story. The story of Adam and Eve's sin was a part of the seven days of creation. Sin was an act of creation. What, however, did sin create?

The Creation of Sin

Imagine, for a moment, Adam and Eve moments after they were created. The creation process still not even complete, they stand in Eden as witnesses to God's hand in the world. In such a world, creations and their Creator still remain tethered. Many descriptions of Adam prior to his sin go to great lengths in describing the lofty state of his connection to God. Milton poetically describes how Adam struggles in such a world even to conceive of the very concept of death:

> So neer grows Death to Life, what ere death is,
> Som dreadful thing no doubt; for well thou knowst
> God hath pronounc't it death to taste that Tree.[45]

According to Nachmanides, prior to the sin, Adam naturally reflected the will of God, like all His other creations:

> ...he (Adam) did whatever was proper for him to do naturally, just as the heavens and all their hosts do—"faithful workers whose work is truth, and who do not change from their prescribed course."[46]

Adam, prior to sinning, was not autonomous. Rather, like the stars and moon, he innately reflected God.

The state of Adam prior to the sin, however, poses a problem. If Adam before sinning naturally followed the will of God, what possessed him to sin? In other words, how could Adam sin before he was given free will? This question has been addressed by many Jewish thinkers but can perhaps be best understood through an analogous lens of contemporary political debate. William Safire, who ran a brilliant linguistic column entitled "On Language" for The New York Times, discussed the difficulty of framing the two sides of the debate in the abortion battles of the 1970s.[47] Those who opposed abortion aptly described themselves as pro-life. Their opponents were then faced with the dilemma. What should those who advocate for abortion rights call themselves? To simply take the inverse side of their pro-life opponents would leave them in the politically indefensible camp of anti-life. To describe themselves as pro-abortion also would be misleading. They were not advocating that people get abortions. Rather, as they eventually came to be known, they were pro-choice. Many members of the pro-choice camp in fact thought abortions were an upsetting solution; still, they reasoned, women should have the right to choose. Adam was not pro-sin, he was pro-choice. A world completely subsumed by Godliness, while sublime, would be missing a crucial component—a visceral sense of choice.

Herein lies the crucial importance of the question of "when." A plain reading of the Bible presents the story of Adam as happening after the creation story. Such a reading suggests that sin was a corruption of creation. However, based on the aforementioned, seemingly undisputed view of the Jewish tradition, Adam's sin occurred during creation. Sin was an act of creation. What did sin create? Sin created Adam's sense of self. Following his sin, Adam emerged as an autonomous being with free will and capable of choice. No longer simply an extension of God, Adam emerged with an independent sense of self.

Sin and Self-Creation

Sin as an act of creation is most emphatically presented within the commentaries of the Hasidic school of Izbica-Radzyn. The Hasidic school of Izbica-Radzyn, no strangers to controversy, explain that the sin of Adam was an essential act in the process of God's creation of the world. Here is Rabbi Mordekhai Yosef, the founder of the Izbica-Radzyn school:

> Creation came into this world through the sin. As the Zohar says, "The First Man had nothing at all of this world." And in the writings of the Holy Ari, before the sin, "he was barely anchored in this world." After the sin, he became firmly placed in this world. That was God's will, so that goodness could be attributed to the work of human hands.[48]

Rabbi Yaakov Leiner, the son of Rabbi Mordekhai Yosef, elaborates on the perspective established by his father. Adam's sin was always a part of God's creation plan. He writes:

> There was profound wisdom in God's design [eitzah 'amukah be-ratzon Hashem]. How could shame [bushah] be placed into the human heart, to

become an integral part of them? Indeed, the world itself is founded on that quality [of shame and awe]. At this point, Adam, the creation of God's own hand, still saw manifestly that nothing can happen without God's willing it. Profound wisdom, then, was needed to invest him with shame. That came about, by God's will, through the episode of the Tree of knowledge.[49]

This approach highlights the term *bushah*, shame, which appears in the introductory verse to the biblical story of Adam's sin:

וַיִּהְיוּ שְׁנֵיהֶם עֲרוּמִּים, הָאָדָם וְאִשְׁתּוֹ; וְלֹא יִתְבֹּשָׁשׁוּ.

And they were both naked, the man and his wife, and were not ashamed.

Adam and Eve's lack of shame is the pretext for the entire story of the sin. The goal of Adam's sin was creating within man a sense of shame.

It is important to note that the term *bushah* is featured prominently in another biblical story of sin. In the thirty-second chapter of Exodus, we are introduced to the story of the golden calf. Following Moshe's ascent to God on Mount Sinai to receive the Torah, the Jewish people begin to become restless. Moshe was only supposed to be gone for forty days, but according to the faulty count of the Jewish people, they believed that Moshe was still absent on the forty-first day. Moshe was late. Believing that their leader had abandoned them, the Jewish people fashion a new leader in the form of a golden calf.

This story, as presented by several sources, is a reenactment of Adam's original sin. As Shaul Magid explains, "…the story of the exodus and Sinai is not only a story of failure but a story whose failure is prefigured from the beginning."[50] The Talmud, explains that initially revelation at Sinai cured the effects of Adam's sin. That cure, however, would only be momentary. The golden calf recreated the repercussions from Adam's sin.

When describing the concern of the Jewish people for Moshe's delay, the term *bushah* reappears, albeit in a different form. The verse recalls:

וַיַּרְא הָעָם, כִּי-בֹשֵׁשׁ מֹשֶׁה לָרֶדֶת מִן-הָהָר; וַיִּקָּהֵל הָעָם עַל-אַהֲרֹן, וַיֹּאמְרוּ אֵלָיו קוּם עֲשֵׂה-לָנוּ אֱלֹהִים אֲשֶׁר יֵלְכוּ לְפָנֵינוּ--כִּי-זֶה מֹשֶׁה הָאִישׁ אֲשֶׁר הֶעֱלָנוּ מֵאֶרֶץ מִצְרַיִם, לֹא יָדַעְנוּ מֶה-הָיָה לוֹ.

And when the people saw that Moshe delayed coming down from the mount, the people gathered themselves together unto Aaron, and said unto him: "Up, make us a god who shall go before us; for as for this Moshe, the man that brought us up out of the land of Egypt, we know not what has become of him." (Ex. 32:1)

In this context, the term *bushah* means delay. Though the usage is different, the appearance and meaning of the term in the stories of Moshe and Adam are significant. How does the term for lateness relate to the sin of Adam?

Lateness connotes dissonance. You were supposed to arrive by now, but you are late. There is a disconnect between where you are and where you are supposed to be. *Bushah*, both lateness and shame, describes a conflict between expectations and reality. Adam prior to the sin was not capable of such dissonance. When God is suffused in all of reality, then whatever is present must have been God's intention. For man to experience such dissonance, he must first have his own expectations and sense of self. It is man's capacity to fashion personal expectations, ambitions, and aspirations that allow for experiential "lateness" when such hopes do not materialize. The product of Adam's sin was the capacity to experience the shame of personal delay. Following the sin, now with his own will, wants, and desires, Adam could encounter the pain of missing the mark of his personal objectives. Indeed, as discussed earlier, the Hebrew word חטא—sin, means to miss the mark. Adam's sin created the possibility for man to form his own expectations, and along with that ability, came the possibility of failure.[51]

Hermann Cohen, the great Jewish neo-Kantian philosopher, argued that much of what separates religion from systematic philosophy is the former's emphasis on sin through which there is a unique capacity for self-discovery.[52] Philosophical ethics, Cohen explains, is concerned with the laws and norms that regulate collective societies and communities whereas religion is concerned with the individual. Religion, according to Cohen, is especially suited to facilitate individual discovery because of its emphasis on self-discovery as a product of moral failures. While philosophical ethics emphasizes ideals for the collective community, the individual can only be found through his moral failures. Some have compared Cohen's approach to religion to Tolstoy's remark, "All happy families are alike; each unhappy family is unhappy in its own way":

> The crux of his account of religion's distinctiveness seems to be the vaguely
> Tolstoyan assumption that insofar as individuals are moral, they are alike,
> but every individual is immoral in his or her own way.[53]

In Cohen's words, "In myself, I have to study sin, and through sin I must learn to know myself."[54] In other words, religion for Cohen is the vehicle through which each person confronts *bushah*, each individual's own unique "lateness." Religion focuses on man's moral lapses and there it finds the individual. Human individuality emerges through the friction of moral failure and aspiration. The process of failure and atonement as a medium for individual discovery is the province of religion alone. Systemic philosophy gave us societal norms; only through the sin and strivings provided by religion are individuals created. As Cohen emphatically writes, "the discovery of humanity through sin is the source from which every religious development flows."[55]

Failure as self-discovery has been considered by other modern thinkers. In Brian Christian's 2011 book *The Most Human Human*, the author uses a fascinating strategy to discover the essence of what makes us human. In 1950 computer scientist Alan Turing proposed using a test to differentiate between human thought and machine calculation.[56] A judge should have a conversation via text with two individuals—one actual human and one computer. If, proposed Turing, a computer could convince a judge that he was in fact conversing with a human being, such a computer could be considered to be capable of thought. Though some thinkers argue with Turing's suggestion, each year a modern-day Turing competition is arranged with the grand prize, known as the Loebner Prize, awarded to the most human computer. Brian Christian, he describes in his book, entered the competition for a different prize. Aside from the award given to the most human computer, the judges also reward the human whose conversation is most human. Mr. Christian's work offers a fascinating lens into the signals and tools with which humans express their humanity. Of course, as the modern era progresses and computers become more sophisticated, the distinguishing characteristics of human beings become more and more elusive as well. As he writes:

> Harvard psychologist Daniel Gilbert says that every psychologist must, at some point in his or her career, write a version of "The Sentence." Specifically, The Sentence reads like this: "The human being is the only animal that _____." Indeed, it seems that philosophers, psychologists, and scientists have been writing and rewriting this sentence since the beginning of recorded history.[57]

Likely, Hermann Cohen would have completed "The Sentence" with the word "sins." Similarly, those in the Izbica-Radzyn School would likely have completed "The Sentence" with a tribute to man's capacity to experience shame. Both, however, reflect the centrality of Adam's sin to their conception of Adam's essence. Of course, whether it is Turing's Test or Gilbert's

Sentence, humans will continue to angst over their individuality. In fact, when asked in an interview how he would complete "The Sentence," Mr. Christian offered the following clever suggestion: "One can always turn the sentence on itself: humans appear to be the only things anxious about what makes them unique."[58] Indeed as we have seen, it is not man's arrival and fulfillment that sets him apart. Rather, lateness, sin, failure, and shame are the crucial components that make humans human.

The Other After Sin

Adam just realizes he has sinned. His eyes are open. What does he see? First, the Bible mentions that he recognizes he and Eve are not dressed, a biblical allusion to the prominent role of sexuality in sin. Immediately afterwards Adam and Eve hear a noise:

> And they heard the voice of God walking in the Garden toward the cool of day; and the man and his wife hid themselves from the presence of the Lord among the trees of the garden. (Gen. 3:8)

The Bible's description of God following Adam's sin is quite telling. God is now an Other—someone who can be avoided and evaded. The creation of self is now complete. No longer does Adam look at himself as an extension of God—God is now an Other strolling through the Garden. In the space created for self, there is now room for failure, growth, shame, and anxiety. As Wiskind-Elper explains in her brilliant presentation of Izbica-Radzyn thought:

> The Face (of God) is hidden. In the vacant space of absence that gapes before them, humans first taste the freedom to choose. Anxiety and an unfamiliar dimension of self-consciousness quickly crowd into these moments.[59]

Godly immanence has become more transcendent in order to leave space for the self. There was always uncertainty with how that space would be filled—but that was precisely the choice Adam advocated for.

The dual implications of the biblical versus Talmudic chronology of Adam's sin reflect the dual nature of sin and free-will. On the one hand, like the biblical implication, sin is avoidable. As reflected in the biblical introduction of sin, only following the creation story, Adam's sin corrupts an otherwise pristine world. In this reading sin is not a part of creation but a rebellion against it. Here a fully developed Adam commits the sin.

The Talmudic reading, as elaborated upon by the aforementioned later approaches, presents sin as part of creation. Here sin, self, and free will are just as much a part of the creation story as light, water, and the stars. Whether sin, and by extension man's capacity for choice, is pre-ordained or a product of human agency may depend upon which reading you prefer. This duality—sin as a part of creation or a corruption of creation—remains a central theme throughout Jewish philosophy. Is all of creation, sin included, suffused with God or are there limits to His immanence? The tension between Divine immanence and Divine transcendence and its relation to the question of God's presence in acts of sin, which has been debated throughout Jewish history, has its root in the very origin story of sin. Ultimately the guiding question behind the nature of sin is not just what or why, but it may be a matter of when.

Original Sin's Legacy

Sin's origins were embedded in creation, but what of original sin? The Christian doctrine of original sin has a long and fascinating history on which several volumes have already been written.[60] Basing himself on the teaching of Paul (Rom. 5:12–19), Augustine brought the doctrine to the mainstream attention of the Christian public. According to Augustine, the sin of Adam created an indelible and permanent stain on mankind that could only be removed through the sacrament of baptism. Thus the doctrine of original sin, as developed by Augustine, had two innovative components. Firstly, the sin of Adam affected all of mankind for future generations. Secondly, the only way to remove the stain of original sin was through the rite of baptism.

The latter point, it turned out, created much more controversy—even within the Christian world. If baptism were needed to redeem the effects of original sin, what about infants who die without such rites? According to Augustine, such infants, with the stain of original sin still apparent, would be doomed to eternal damnation. This helpless account of human salvation was rejected by Pelagious, a British monk who refused to accept that man could only be redeemed through God's grace. According to Pelagianism, original sin did not remove man's capacity to live a decent and ethical life. It is through man's decisions and free will that human redemption is achieved.[61]

During the wave of Jewish–Christian polemics of the Middle Ages, original sin became a frequent target of Jewish criticism. Much like the Pelagian objection, Jewish polemicists objected to the implications that those who did not receive baptism—included in which are the Forefathers—would suffer damnation. This objection was coupled with the legal difficulty based upon Deuteronomy 24:16 that "Fathers will not be put to death for their children, nor children for their fathers; a man shall be put to death only for his own sins." Surely, the doctrine of original sin contradicted the Torah's assurance of no ancestral punishment.

Joel Rembaum, in his comprehensive survey of Medieval Jewish arguments against the Christian doctrine of original sin, summarizes the mainstream Jewish reaction as follows:

> They contended that this concept led to a number of absurd and blasphemous conclusions regarding God and divine justice. Given the Jewish concept of the evil inclination, Jews were generally willing to admit that the effects of Adam's sin were physically transmitted to all of Adam's descendants. They categorically denied, however, that Adam's sin generated a permanent spiritual corruption that was transmitted to the souls of all humans.[62]

The backlash of medieval Jewish polemicists to the doctrine of original sin should not be accepted at face value. Generally, polemical works are poor sources for actual Jewish doctrine. Daniel Lasker, in the introduction to his work on Jewish–Christian polemics, notes the healthy skepticism deserved by extrapolation of theological truth from polemical tracts:

> Polemical compositions were intended as polemics, a genre for which objective truth is one of the first casualties. . . . If one wants to know a particular author's true view on a subject, a polemical treatise is the last place one would look to determine it. When this literature is analyzed without due recognition of "polemical license," the research runs the risk of reading too much into the texts. Drawing historical, theological, social, or intellectual conclusions from polemical literature should be attempted only in a restrained manner.[63]

Given this warning, it is not surprising that the vehemence with which the doctrine of original sin was opposed within polemic literature may not actually reflect its patent rejection within Jewish sources. In fact, as pointed out by Lasker, the doctrine of original sin "was not entirely foreign to Judaism" as some polemics would otherwise suggest.[64]

The Talmud (*Shabbat* 146a) seems to acknowledge the effects of original sin but asserts that the collective revelation of Sinai countered its effects for the Jewish people. It writes:

> Why are the idolaters polluted? Because they did not stand at Sinai. When the serpent copulated with Eve, he imposed pollution in her. The Jews who stood at Sinai—their pollution has ceased; the idolaters who did not stand at Sinai—their pollution has not ceased.

Presumably, the pollution referred to here is the lingering poison of the original sin. Of course, the antidote in the Jewish view is not baptism but rather the revelation at Sinai. In fact, Rabbi Avraham Ibn David of Posquières, known by the acronym Raavad, uses this Talmudic passage as a prooftext to explain a difficult passage in the *Passover Haggadah*. In the hymn *Dayenu*, we praise God's beneficence by saying, "If He had brought us to Mount Sinai and not given us the Torah it still would have been sufficient." The statement is puzzling—what would be gained by standing at Sinai had we not received the Torah? Raavad explains, based on the aforementioned passage, that the aftereffects of Adam's "original sin" were in fact cleansed by our collective presence at Sinai.[65]

While certainly rejecting the role of Jesus and Christian salvation, nonetheless the contradiction between Judaism and the doctrine of original sin is smaller than Jewish polemics would suggest. Aside from the Raavad and among many others, both Rabbi Ephraim Luntschitz in his famed biblical commentary *Kli Yakar* and Rabbi Isaiah Horowitz, known as the Shelah, make use of this Talmudic passage to suggest a broader notion of original sin than is presented in polemics.[66]

Aside from the Talmudic reference, many more mystically influenced commentators, particularly within the school of Lurianic Kabbalah, were more receptive to a broader conception of the effects of original sin that more closely align with Christian presentations.[67] Lasker explains their approach as follows:

> Certain kabbalists taught a doctrine of original sin in that Adam's transgression gave evil an active existence in the world. The entire creation became flawed by this first sin. Unlike the Christian, however, the kabbalists taught that every man had the power to overcome the state of corruption by his own efforts with divine aid. There was no implication here, as there was in Christianity, that salvation could be achieved only by the sacrifice of a God-man.[68]

Indeed, the prominence of Adam's sin in Lurianic mysticism, particularly the subsequent notion of *tikun*-rectification, attracted many Christians to Lurianic mysticism. In her groundbreaking study on the impact of kabbalah on the scientific revolution, Allison Coudert details an entire community of Christian scholars and thinkers that became enchanted with kabbalistic thought.[69] Led by Francis Mercury van Helmot and Christian Knorr von Rosenroth,[70] kabbalistic texts were translated into Latin, collected into the work known as *Kabbala denudata*, and disseminated to many emerging thinkers in Christian circles, most notably Wilhelm Leibniz.[71] Normally the emphasis on the repercussions of Adam's sin are seen as a Christian idea, but within the esoteric world of Lurianic thought, Adam's sin and the subsequent struggle for restitution became markedly Jewish.[72] In fact this is what attracted Christian mystics to kabbalah. Whereas Augustine's presentation of original sin, against the Pelagian objections, minimized man's ability for redemption without Christian rites of sacrament, the Lurianic reading highlighted man's singular power and responsibility to attain redemption. As Coudert writes:

> The Lurianic Kabbalist could not retreat into his own private world. He had to participate in a cosmic millennial drama in which his every action counted. The Lurianic Kabbalah was the first Jewish theology which envisioned perfection in terms of a future state, not in terms of a forfeited ideal past, and as such it contributed to the idea of progress emerging in the West.[73]

Lurianic mysticism recast the narrative of original sin into a recurring contemporary notion of redemption. Yes, original sin had grave repercussions. But the magnitude of the sin was overshadowed by the capacity for redemption.

Returning to Eden after Eden

A common refrain within the liturgy of the High Holidays is a prayer from the book of Lamentations (5:21): השיבנו ה' אליך ונשובה חדש ימינו כקדם—Bring us back to You, O Lord, and we shall return, renew our days as of old.

To "renew our days as of old" is a somewhat contradictory request. Days presumably can either be old or renewed—how can we ask for both? Based on this seeming contradiction, the Midrash reinterprets the term *kedem*—קדם; it is not referring to an antiquated time but rather a place. The term *kedem*, explains the Midrash, refers to the Garden of Eden, which in the Torah is referred to on two occasions as *kedem*. Curiously, when demonstrating the association between the word *kedem* and the Garden of Eden, the Midrash ignores the first reference in the Torah, which reads, "God planted a garden in Eden, to the east" and instead chooses the second reference to the Garden of Eden as *kedem*. The latter reference, "and having driven out the man, he stationed east of the Garden of Eden," does not refer to Adam's idyllic residence in the Garden but rather his exile. Why does the Midrash when interpreting our plea to "renew our days of old" skip the first reference to the Garden and instead read our prayer as a reference to Adam's exile?

A dear friend, Rabbi Dr. Simcha Willig, showed me a remarkable interpretation of our prayer to "renew our days of old" from Rabbi Rob Scheinberg. His words:

> The word *kedem* in Genesis 3:24 is not a word associated with the Garden of Eden itself, but a word associated with the EXILE from the Garden. The decision to quote the word *kedem* from this verse, rather than from 2:8, indicates that, from the perspective of this quotation from Eikhah Rabbah, "hadesh yameinu ke-kedem" does NOT mean "renew our lives as they were in the Garden of Eden."
>
> Rather, it means, "Renew our lives, as you renewed our lives after we were exiled from the Garden of Eden." "Hadesh yameinu ke-kedem" is then not a plea for restoration of a formerly perfect condition, but rather it is a plea for resilience, a plea for the ability to renew ourselves after future crises and dislocations, just as our lives have been renewed before.
>
> As Elie Wiesel said, "God gave Adam a secret—and that secret was not how to begin, but how to begin again."[74]

Similar to the Lurianic shift in perspective, the focus on Adam's sin is not about reclaiming a utopian past but having the resilience and grit to create a more perfect future. We did not forfeit perfection with Adam's sin but assumed the responsibility to create it ourselves.

3

SICK, SICK THOUGHTS: INTENTION AND ACTION IN SIN

Nothing was your own except the few cubic centimeters inside your skull.
—**George Orwell,** *1984*

By all accounts Gilberto Valle had sick, sick thoughts. In September of 2012, after growing suspicious, his wife installed spyware to monitor his online activities. What she found was horrifying. Her husband was having descriptive chats online about the kidnapping, rape, torture, and murder of her and several of her friends. Most shocking—he planned to cook and eat his victims. After being indicted on five counts of conspiracy to commit kidnapping, Mr. Valle, a member of the NYPD, was soon dubbed the "Cannibal Cop" by the media. At his trial Mr. Valle insisted that his online discussions, however detailed, were mere fantasy and did not constitute illegal activity. The prosecutor pointed to actual steps taken by Mr. Valle to commit crimes, including searching for victim information on a police database. Though the Cannibal Cop was initially found guilty in 2013, the ruling against him was overturned in 2014, and the 2014 ruling was subsequently upheld by the United States Court of Appeals for the Second Circuit in 2015. In the Second Circuit ruling, which upheld the district court's dismissal of the case, the judge explained his ruling:

> This is a case about the line between fantasy and criminal intent. . . . We are loath to give the government the power to punish us for our thoughts and not our actions. That includes the power to criminalize an individual's expression of sexual fantasies, no matter how perverse or disturbing. Fantasizing about

> committing a crime, even a crime of violence against a real person whom you
> know, is not a crime. This does not mean that fantasies are harmless. To the
> contrary, fantasies of violence against women are both a symptom of and a
> contributor to a culture of exploitation, a massive social harm that demeans
> women. Yet we must not forget that in a free and functioning society, not
> every harm is meant to be addressed with the federal criminal law.[75]

The court was clear: thoughts, however heinous, are not a crime.

Edward Coke (1552–1634), the famed English jurist, created the phrase from which most contemporary legal considerations of criminality still derive: *actus reus non facit reum nisi mens sit rea*—an act does not make a person guilty unless the mind is also guilty.[76] Nowadays legal scholars and lawyers evaluate culpability based on both the presence of *actus reus*, meaning an action, and *mens rea*, the mental component of criminality. Mr. Valle, of course, had *mens rea* of the worst sort, but those alone could not convict him. Without meaningful *actus reus*, his thoughts remained legally inscrutable.

How would Jewish law approach the case of the Cannibal Cop? When considering the parameters of thought and action in determining religious criminality a few important distinctions must be made. First, not every divine sin is necessarily prosecuted in *Beit Din*, the Jewish court system. There are many religious prohibitions and sins that can corrupt religiously but are nonetheless unable to be prosecuted or punished in *Beit Din*. For instance, negative speech, known as *lashon hara*, is a Torah prohibition but is not prosecuted or punished in the Jewish court system. Secondly, much like American law, whatever combination of thought and action is required only constitutes one necessary criterion for punishment in court and is not sufficient to merit punishment on its own. Aside from committing a sinful act, there are a host of other requirements necessary to qualify for punishment in religious court. Among the conditions are warning, proper witnesses, and being of sufficient age for accountability for punishment. Lastly, the question of thought crimes in Jewish law must be distinguished from the question of whether thought has consequence in Jewish law. Thought, in the sense of conscience intention, frequently carries legal consequences in certain areas of Jewish law such as tithing, withdrawing ownership, and the nullification of *hametz* on Passover.[77] Our discussion will remain focused on the role of thought and action when evaluating culpability for sin in Jewish law.

Alone With Your Thoughts

There shouldn't be much to think about. The Talmud (*Kiddushin* 39b) states quite clearly—except for thoughts about committing idolatry—God does not punish for thoughts about committing sins. No conceptual idea or rationale is presented to justify the exclusion of thoughts from culpability; rather the Talmud cites verses to support its claim:

> But the Holy One, Blessed be He, does not link an evil thought to an action, as it is stated: "If I had regarded iniquity in my heart, the Lord would not hear" (Psalms 66:18). But how do I realize the meaning of the verse: "Behold I will bring upon these people evil, even the fruit of their thoughts" (Jeremiah 6:19)? In the case of an evil thought that produces fruit, i.e., that leads to an action, the Holy One, Blessed be He, links it to the action and one is punished for the thought as well. If it is a thought that does not produce fruit, the Holy One, Blessed be He, does not link it to the action.

Similarly, the exclusion of idolatry from this rule is also derived scripturally by the Talmud.[78] Aside from the exception of idolatry, the Talmud seems to establish as a general rule that God does not deem thoughts without action a religious crime.

This of course is not the whole story on thought. Another Talmudic passage (*Yoma* 29b) states, "thoughts (*hirhurei*) of sin are worse than the sin itself." This passage seems to indicate that thoughts *are* accounted when assessing sin.[79] In fact, even without this passage the aforementioned passage of Talmud that excludes thought from culpability seems to be contradicted by a host of religious prohibitions. Some commentaries include the verse "and be not stiff-necked" (Deut. 10:16) as a general prohibition, even though it is apparently only a violation that can be transgressed with thought.[80] Similarly, the prohibition not to covet a neighbor's possessions (Deuteronomy 5:18), which is included in the second recording of the Ten Commandments, is according to some a prohibition of covetous thoughts.[81] So when is the principle excluding thoughts from religious liability operative, as found in the passage in *Kiddushin*, and when are thoughts indeed considered to be sins?

Oddly, most commentaries do not address this apparent contradiction. Rabbi Yehudah Loew (1512–1609), the rabbi of Prague known as the Maharal, does however suggest a simple distinction.[82] He explains that when the initial formulation of a sin requires action, such prohibitions cannot be violated with thought alone. However, thought can still be considered a sin when the thought is the action—the very definition of the particular sin includes thought. This means a prohibition such as murder, which clearly includes an action, cannot be violated by mere thought, but if thoughts by dint of their formulation are the subject of the prohibition—then they are sufficient to be considered a sin. As such, our earlier assumption that Jewish law does not prosecute thoughts alone must be qualified. Thoughts can in fact be prohibited. But the prohibition must by definition require thought alone. If, however, an action is needed to violate a given prohibition, then thought alone will not be sufficient to be considered a transgression.[83]

Attempted Sin

Thought alone—unless it is the essence of the sin itself—is not considered a sin. Just beyond the threshold of thought crime lies a different form of crime known as attempt. Whereas thought crimes only possess *mens rea*, a criminal thought, attempt introduces elements of *actus reus* (albeit unsuccessful) as well. Common law has long distinguished between a thought crime and an attempted criminal act.[84] Thinking about murder is legal while attempting murder is illegal. Why such a distinction exists is less clear. In other words, what is the nature of criminality for an attempted crime? If the crime is unsuccessful why should the perpetrator nonetheless be punished? Aside from thinking, nothing else has been accomplished.

Gideon Yaffe has spent much of his career attempting to define the criminality of attempt. Dr. Yaffe, a Yale Law professor, wrote a masterful work on attempted crime, aptly entitled *Attempts*. His work and approach reflect his academic background as a philosopher as opposed to a lawyer, giving much of his analysis a much needed conceptual approach. There are several core philosophical problems in the conception of attempt, but the one that is most relevant to our discussion is the nature of criminality for attempt. Namely, if no harm was done why is an attempted crime considered a crime at all—what happened to "no harm, no foul"? If no damage is incurred from an attempted crime, what distinguishes it from a thought crime? Yaffe presents three schools of thought in explaining the criminality of attempt.[85]

Subjectivists posit that attempt is indeed a thought crime, but its criminality derives from the fact that it is a "special species of thought that is acceptable to criminalize (such as resolute intentions)." This view concedes that thought crimes generally should not be punished but explains that attempt—while a form of thought crime—should be an exception to that principle. As Yaffe notes, "The fundamental challenge for subjectivists, then, is to explain why it is not monstrous for a liberal society to punish attempts." Objectivists, on the other hand, presume that attempt cannot be a form of thought crime, since punishment for a thought crime is simply inconceivable. Instead, they explain, that attempt must involve some sort of action that is punishable. For objectivists, the criminality of attempt rests more on the *actus reus* than the *mens rea*. Their challenge, as Yaffe explains, is how to "explain what it is about the conduct involved in attempt thanks to which it is punishable despite its harmlessness."[86] A final approach to the criminality of attempt, developed and preferred by Yaffe, is called the Guiding Commitment View. This view doesn't distinguish attempt based upon either bad thoughts or bad conduct; instead the Guiding Commitment View proposes that the act of trying can be defined as a criminal act. According to Yaffe there is an overarching rule in the criminalization of attempt called the Transfer Principle, which assumes that "if a particular form of conduct is legitimately criminalized, then the attempt to engage in that form of conduct is also legitimately criminalized."[87] Based on the Transfer Principle, the Guiding Commitment View establishes the criminality of attempt by setting clear guidelines for what is considered trying. Attempted murder is not prohibited because of the thoughts it necessarily contains or the act that it entails—it is illegal because it is an act of trying that is prohibited under the Transfer Principle. Yaffe defines the criminality of trying as follows:

> To try to act, in the sense of relevance to the criminal law, is to have an intention that commits one to each of the conditions involved in completion, and for one's behavior to be guided by that intention.[88]

Each of the three aforementioned approaches to the criminality of attempt draws different conceptual lines between thought crime and attempt. The courts as well have developed different tests to demarcate when plans and fantasies enter criminal territory. One important test, developed by Justice Oliver Wendell Holmes, focuses on how much planning still needs to be carried out in order for the crime to be successfully committed. Known as the "dangerous proximity" test, planning for a crime is deemed criminal when the likelihood of its completion, commensurate with the severity of the act, is considered dangerously close.

In a way, an attempted crime is an ironic form of failure given that any crime is really a failure to obey the law—so, an attempted crime is really a failed attempted at failure. Of course, why an attempt fails successfully to break the law is an important legal facet when considering the criminality of attempt. Why a crime was not realized is an important factor in deeming whether the attempt was criminal. Many pages of legal literature have been written considering the question of impossibility—crimes that were attempted but that were not realized because they were never possible to execute.[89] For instance, someone attempted to conceal stolen property, but it was later revealed that the property in question was never even stolen.[90] Or imagine someone who kills someone—but claims that when the bullet was fired the victim was already dead.[91] Recently, impossibility has been a frequent feature of law enforcement stings, such as in setups that involve fake narcotics or in nabbing pedophiles with adults who present themselves as underage minors.[92] Applications of impossibility are usually divided into two categories: factual impossibility and legal impossibility. Regarding the former, factual impossibility occurs when unbeknownst to the defendant, the basic facts of an attempted crime make it impossible to have been successfully committed. For instance, a group of men were convicted of rape even though unbeknownst to them, the woman was already deceased at the time of the crime.[93] Courts do not look at factual impossibility as a favorable excuse and consider such attempts criminal. Alternatively, legal impossibility occurs "when unbeknownst to the actor, what the actor planned to do had not been made criminal."[94] Cases of legal impossibility, such as someone who attempts to kill someone but the target turns out to be something else entirely like a tree stump or a branch, are considered by courts as lacking the elements necessary for criminal liability. Of course as many note, the entire difference between factual and legal impossibility is quite murky. The imaginary line dividing factual impossibility, which is deemed criminal, from legal impossibility, which is considered a valid defense, has rightly been criticized as "an illusionary test leading to contradictory, and sometimes absurd, results."[95]

So much for crime, but our topic is sin. Does Jewish law criminalize attempted sin? And does Jewish law consider aborted actions to be sins when they are legally or factually impossible to complete?

A conceptual category of attempt, as is found in common law, does not seem to exist in Jewish law. Someone who attempts murder but is unsuccessful cannot be found liable for attempted murder—such a concept is not found in the Talmud. The closest example of a Talmudic ruling regarding attempted sin is based on a story in Exodus 2:13. Moshe finds two people arguing. Just as one lifts his hand to strike the other, the text reads, "And he (Moshe) said to the wicked man, why do you hit your friend?" Although no blow has landed Moshe already refers to the attempted assailant as a wicked person. Based on this biblical story, the Talmud cites the opinion of Reish Lakish that "he who lifts (raises) his hand to strike his friend, even though he did not hit him, is called wicked."[96] Later legal codifiers debate whether the "wicked" status would disqualify such a person from serving as a witness in Jewish court.[97] Regardless, the attempted assault clearly has legal ramifications. This ruling, however, seems to be more localized—a similar status of "wickedness" is not found regarding other attempted sins. Indeed Jacob Bazak, the Israeli Supreme Court Judge, notes that "[i]t is not at all clear whether it is safe to deduce from that single Talmudic source a general conclusion that Jewish law considers an attempt to commit a crime to be a crime in itself."[98] Most likely this is a localized stringency regarding attempted assault rather than a general principle that criminalizes attempt.

Interestingly, the form of attempt which does receive quite a bit of attention in Talmudic literature is the impossible attempt. As defined earlier, an impossible attempt is an attempt to commit a crime which for either legal reasons or factual reasons could never have been completed. Regarding what seems to be an evaluation of the criminality of impossible attempts, the Talmud (*Kiddushin* 81b) records the following:

> Rabbi Hiyya bar Ashi was accustomed to say, whenever he would fall on his face in prayer: May the Merciful One save us from the evil inclination. One day his wife heard him saying this prayer. She said: After all, it has been several years since he has withdrawn from engaging in intercourse with me due to his advanced years. What is the reason that he says this prayer, as there is no concern that he will engage in sinful sexual behavior?
>
> One day, while he was studying in his garden, she adorned herself and repeatedly walked past him. He said: Who are you? She said: I am Haruta, a well-known prostitute, returning from my day at work. He propositioned her. She said to him: Give me that pomegranate from the top of the tree as payment. He leapt up, went, and brought it to her, and they engaged in intercourse.
>
> When he came home, his wife was lighting a fire in the oven. He went and sat inside it. She said to him: What is this? He said to her: Such and

such an incident occurred; he told her that he engaged in intercourse with a prostitute. She said to him: It was I. He paid no attention to her, thinking she was merely trying to comfort him, until she gave him signs that it was indeed she. He said to her: I, in any event, intended to transgress. All the days of that righteous man he would fast for the transgression he intended to commit, until he died by that death in his misery.

(The Talmud proceeds to explain the source of the idea that one who intended to transgress is punished even though he did not actually sin.) As it is taught in a *baraita* concerning a husband who nullified the vow of his wife: "Her husband has made them null; and the Lord will forgive her" (Numbers 30:13). With regard to what case is the verse speaking? Why would the woman require forgiveness if her husband has nullified her vow? It is referring to a woman who vowed to be a nazirite, and her husband heard and nullified her vow. And she did not know that her husband had nullified her vow, and she drank wine and contracted impurity from a corpse, violating her presumed vow.[99]

Here the Talmud records two cases of impossible attempts. First, attempted adultery with the rabbi's actual wife; second, an attempt to violate a vow which had already been annulled. This passage of Talmud concludes with the somber reaction of Rabbi Akiva to these attempts. When Rabbi Akiva would consider the case of the woman who attempts to violate her vow, he would cry.

He said: And if with regard to one who intended to eat pork, and kosher lamb came up in his hand, like this woman who intended to violate her vow but in fact did not, the Torah nevertheless says: She requires atonement and forgiveness, all the more so does one who intended to eat pork and pork came up in his hand require atonement and forgiveness.

Both of these Talmudic cases of legally impossible sin involve *mens rea*, the intention to violate the law—whether a marriage or a vow—and *actus reus*, a completed action. It is only a failed attempt because the attempted sinner was not aware of all of the contextual circumstances of the crime. Much like a drug deal with artificial cocaine, a sufficient amount of both action and intention must exist to move the crime from the realm of thought and innocence to the domain of sin and liability.

The Talmud seems to conclude the impossible attempts of sin are inculpating. This conclusion is complicated by comments of Rabbi Hayyim Ibn

Attar (1696–1743) in his famed biblical commentary *Ohr ha-Hayyim*.[100] At the end of the book of Genesis, Joseph reconciles with his brothers. After being sold as a slave by his siblings and subsequently rising to political power in Egypt, Joseph addresses his brothers (Gen. 50:20), "And Joseph said unto them: 'Fear not; for am I in the place of God? And as for you, ye meant evil against me; but God meant it for good, to bring to pass, as it is this day, to keep a great populace alive.'" Joseph assures his brothers that although they intended to kill him, their plot had fortuitous results since it led to Joseph's rise to power.[101] So Joseph forgives his brothers. On Joseph's assertion of his brother's innocence, Rabbi Hayyim Ibn Attar comments:

> And you meant evil against me; but God meant it for Good, this is comparable
> to someone who intends to poison a friend, but instead (unknowingly) gives
> them wine—such as person is not liable anything. And they are exempt and
> innocent even in Heavenly Judgment.

This brief comment raised considerable controversy regarding the parameters of the liability for attempt. If the aforementioned passage of Talmud held the woman who attempted to transgress her vow and the man who attempted to commit adultery as guilty, then how can the *Ohr ha-Hayyim* claim that Joseph's brothers are innocent? The principle of guilt for impossible attempts of sin, derived from the verse "Her Husband has made them void and the Lord forgave her," (Numbers 13:30), should seemingly apply to the brothers of Joseph as well.[102]

Several answers are suggested in order to resolve the apparent contradiction between the *Ohr ha-Hayyim's* comments and the Talmudic conception of attempt thwarted by legal impossibility. Rabbi Meir Dan Plotsky (1866–1928) in his brilliant work *Kli Hemdah* suggests that impossible attempts at sin are only inculpating when the sin in question is primarily between man and God.[103] Since intent and action are equivalent in the eyes of God, impossible attempts are inculpating when the sin is an abrogation of a commandment against God. While God does not punish for thought alone, when it is coupled with action, as in the cases cited in the Talmud, there is liability. In contrast, sins that are primarily interpersonal, like the sibling feud between Joseph and his brothers, are only assessed based on the actual outcome. So in the case of Joseph and his brothers, since their attempt was not only unsuccessful but actually resulted in Joseph's political elevation, the brothers were innocent. This approach establishes an important distinction in the rules of attempted sin whereby the target of the sin—man or God—drastically alters the underlying principles of liability.

Another suggested resolution for the comments of the *Ohr ha-Hayyim* was proposed by Rabbi Yosef Pazanavski (1875–1942) in his work *Pardes Yosef* where he explains that the case of Joseph's brothers was not a typical case of impossible attempt. He contends that Joseph's brothers had convened a formal court and sentenced Joseph to punishment.[104] Their actions were not an intended sin but rather a reflection of their genuine conviction that Joseph deserved to be punished. This approach, which is more of a reflection of a particular form of Talmudic biblical interpretation, does not really change the way we think about attempt—just the way we think about Joseph's brothers.

Four principles emerge from our discussion: (1) Thoughts alone are not inculpating as sins unless the very definition of the sin is one of thought. (2) Attempted sin which does not result in damage is not inculpating, though the localized case of attempted assault may be an exception. (3) Impossible attempts that involve both intent and a completed action do require atonement. (4) There may be a distinction between the target of the sin—namely man or God—when evaluating the liability of an impossible attempt.

Action Packed Crimes

The case of the Cannibal Cop raised important questions regarding the parameters of liability for attempted sin. To complete our discussion of sin in Jewish law, we must briefly consider one additional topic: intent. Namely, how much intent is necessary to find one liable for a properly executed sin? We have considered the attempted violation of sin without any outcome, but what of acts of sins without serious intent? In other words, how much thought—*mens rea*—is necessary to be culpable for a sinful act in Jewish law?

Like most Talmudic questions, intent is a complex issue. *Halakhah* makes several nuanced distinctions when considering different levels of intentionality for criminal acts. Talmudic terminology is abounding as well. Terms such as *meizid* [מזיד], *mitasek* [מתעסק], *shogeg* [שוגג], and *oness* [אונס] all contribute to the complexity of this legal question, making it all the more inaccessible to the layperson.

In Stephen Hawking's introduction to his 1988 classic *A Brief History of Time*, he was faced with a similar dilemma. "Someone told me that each equation I included in the book would halve the sales," he writes. So, he explains, "I therefore resolved not to have any equations at all. In the end, however, I did put in one equation, Einstein's famous equation $E = mc^2$. I hope that this will not scare off half of my potential readers."[105] Like equations, Talmudic terminology does not win one a wide readership. Our discussion, however, will require more than just one famous equation or term. Nonetheless we will strive for clarity—hopefully without having to resort to simplicity or losing half of this book's readers.

The role of intention in assessing sin in Jewish law could be its own dissertation. In fact, it has been. At least twice. In 1927 Michael Higger completed his dissertation "Intention in Talmudic Law" from Columbia University.[106] Over eighty years later, Shana Strauch-Schick completed her dissertation from Yeshiva University on the subject, "Intention in the Babylonian Talmud: An Intellectual History."[107] In fact, Strauch-Schick was the first woman to be awarded a PhD in Talmud from the Orthodox institution. Together their works comprise over 300 pages on the subject. Both studies focus nearly exclusively on Talmudic law and do not discuss in great detail later rabbinic contributions to the subject. Our discussion will be extremely condensed while still including some later rabbinic opinions on the subject.

Sinning Like You Mean It: The Category of *Meizid*

Sinning with intention is called *meizid* (מזיד). The term is related to the term *nazid*, which is a form of cooking. Much like the American idiom "what are you cooking up?" the Talmudic term also suggests deliberate and sinister preparation.[108] How does Jewish law define sinister purposefulness? Frequently, discussions of intention are characterized by a negative theology of sorts—the act is defined by describing ways of behaving without intention. We understand intention by carefully defining what it is not. This isn't just lazy scholarship; it is a problem acknowledged in Talmudic law. The Talmud explains that the only way we are able to distinguish between whether a sin was committed intentionally or unintentionally is by warning the potential sinner. As far as Jewish courts are concerned, sins are only considered intentional if, prior to committing the sin, the perpetrator is warned and clearly informed that the action about to be committed is against Jewish law.[109] In the Jewish court system, sins are not subject to capital punishment unless they are committed following a proper warning. Of course, God knows whether a sin was intentional or accidental, but as far as the court is concerned a proper warning is necessary to ascertain intentionality definitively.

Oops, I Sinned: The Categories of *Shogeg* and *Mitasek*:

The categories of sin are not binary. It is not innocence versus guilt—rather there are a host of categories and gradations in assessing the severity of sin. As we have seen, in order to be strictly liable and punished for a sin, the person first must be warned by proper witnesses that the action he is about to commit is prohibited—and then proceed to violate that prohibition nonetheless. That is called sinning *b-meizid*—intentionally. Absent an actual warning, there are still several other categories of awareness that are necessary to assess a person's liability for sin.

The term *shogeg* appears in the fourth chapter of Leviticus, "נפש כי תחטא בשגגה"—"if anyone shall sin through error." If someone commits a sin *b-shogeg*, he is obligated to bring a sacrificial offering. What is the precise definition of an action done *b-shogeg*? The word means to go astray. Legally, however, a sin performed *b-shogeg* is one in which the action of sin was intended, but the action was not intended to be sinful. This is in contrast to an act that was not intended at all, which is referred to in Talmudic literature as *mitasek* [מתעסק]. This is how Higger explains the definitions:

> ..."*shogeg*," regarding sin in general, is not ignorance of law but rather an error of the understanding. . . . [I]n cases of "*shogeg*," intent of the act does exist. The individual, due to an erroneous assumption, performs the act he has intended; but he has not intended to sin. In the cases of "*mitasek*" on the other hand, the individual has not at all performed the action he intended.[110]

As mentioned, a sin violated *b-shogeg* requires a sacrificial offering—a *hatat*—while a sin performed while *mitasek* is exempt from sacrificial obligation. Given that an action performed while *mitasek* was unintended, some rabbinic authorities question whether such actions can be considered sins at all.[111] Sin or not, what emerges from these distinctions is the emphasis Jewish law places on even slight variations of *mens rea*—intentionality.

Each varying gradation of intentionality in sin requires a different process of penance.

CoerSIN: The Category of *Oness*

Aside from the previous categories of sin, which include deficiencies in *mens rea* and *actus reus*, there is a final categorical exception to the culpability of sin worth considering—duress. Sins committed while under duress are different from the previous categories since the act done under coercion does ostensibly include both an action and intention. Nonetheless, the Talmud provides a broad exclusion for coerced sins based on the verses in Deuteronomy (22:25–27), which excludes a betrothed woman from punishment if she were raped while married.[112]

The exemption of coercion is fairly straightforward; what is more complex is defining what constitutes an act performed under coercion. The source of the exemption of coercion involves someone's being physically forced to sin, but what about someone who is just threatened with death or financial ruin? Most Halakhic decisors include actions done to prevent a threat of death within the exemption of coercion.[113] However, most do not include an action done in order to avoid financial ruin within the exemption of duress.[114] Maimonides is adamant that in order for an action to qualify for the categorical exemption of coercion, the person must first do everything possible to avoid the sin. He writes:

> One who could, however, escape and flee from under the power of a wicked king and fails to do so is like a dog who returns to [lick] his vomit. He is considered as one who worships false gods willingly. He will be prevented from reaching the world to come and will descend to the lowest levels of *Gehinnom*.[115]

Maimonides' strong language here is likely in response to the growing epidemic during his time of Jews' being forced to convert to other religions in order to save their lives. Maimonides famously comforted the Moroccan Jewish community, who had converted to Islam in order to avoid death at the hand of the Almohad caliphate.[116] In the passage cited above, Maimonides reminds that those faced with the prospect of coercion should first do everything possible to avoid sin rather than merely submitting due to the fact that an element of coercion is present.

Most earlier debates about the parameters of the definition of conversion involved Jews who faced pressure to convert by other religious entities, most commonly Christian and Muslim forces. In modern times, of course, such cases—while not entirely inconceivable—are exceedingly rare. Nonetheless the definition of coercion and its concomitant exemption from punishment is still a relevant topic in the Jewish community. In particular, the question of defining someone's internal impulses, sexual or otherwise, as being so strong as to be considered coercion has important implications for those with homosexual orientations.[117] While male sexual relations may be excluded from the exemption of coercion for other reasons,[118] the concept of an internal impulse qualifying as Halakhic coercion is a topic still relevant and closely debated.

A Silver Lining for Our Thoughts

Mens rea matters. Every slight variation in the level and focus of intentionality while sinning can have drastic changes in the categorical consequences of the sin. Thought not only provides context but can be the very sin itself, as seen earlier in the Talmudic passage "[t]houghts of sin are worse than the sin itself." While this passage was qualified to be legally applicable to only a limited set of sins, it can still be understood more broadly as a note of caution of the severity and power of thought alone. Thoughts can quickly morph into fantasies and preoccupations. Thoughts may not bear any legal consequences, but they can have dire experiential effects. The experiential effects of thought, however, need not be negative. In a playful repurposing of the Talmudic warning to be wary of thought about sin, Rabbi Hutner points out that a person's preoccupations with aspirational holiness may have a greater impact on the individual than the actions of holiness itself. In his words:

וכשם שציורים ודמיונות של חטא נאמר הרהורי עבירה קשים מעבירה כמו כן שפיר יתכן לומר שיש אשר לפעמים דמיונות של קדושה עדיפים ממעשה של קדושה.

And just as (regarding) the thoughts and imaginations of sin it is said (*Yoma* 29b) the thoughts of sin are worse than sin itself, similarly it seems reasonable to say that there are instances where our imaginations of holiness are greater than our very actions of holiness.

Thoughts of sin may be in some respects worse than sin itself, but our thoughts and aspirations of holiness may speak louder than the very acts of holiness to which we aspire. Thoughts matter. Our thoughts reflect deeper values and aspirations. When thoughts are sick, the diagnosis can be grave. But when thoughts are positive, they reveal something about ourselves that our actions may yet achieve.

4

WHAT TO WEAR TO A SIN: NEGOTIATING WITH SIN

There is no virtue if there is no immorality.
—**Fyodor Dostoevsky**, *The Brothers Karamazov*

Negotiating with Sin

Imagine the following scenario. A train is barreling down the tracks while up ahead five men are working on the tracks. The trolley can be diverted to avoid hitting the workers, but the diversion would result in one person's death. Should the train be diverted? This thought experiment, known as the Trolley Problem,[119] was introduced by Philippa Foot, a renowned ethicist and granddaughter of President Grover Cleveland. This deceptively simple thought experiment inspired an entire discipline known as trolleyology. What if the only way to divert the train from hitting the five workers is to actively throw a fat man in front of the train? Such are the questions and scenarios contemplated by modern day trolleyologists. One philosopher joked that the host of variations and commentaries to the Trolley Problem "makes the Talmud look like CliffsNotes."[120]

Aside from being an interesting thought experiment, the Trolley Problem also highlights some of the more interesting issues that arise regarding sin. Sin is most commonly thought of as a binary proposition. Either sin or don't sin. It is a decision that can either be made or avoided. The Trolley Problem is a stark reminder that decisions related to sin are not always so simple.[121] Morality is not always a choice between good and bad but, perhaps most frequently, it is a decision between two evils. The difficulty is only compounded when it is unclear which of the evils is worse. Jewish law is replete with situations that require similar negotiations. Of course, like in any legal system the best course is to avoid sin altogether. But Judaism's worldview is not quite so simplistic. As will be discussed, there are a variety of considerations and negotiations in the Jewish approach to sin.

Kosher Conundrums

If illness requires someone to eat non-kosher food, the Talmud (*Yoma* 83a) instructs that the person should eat the food with the smallest relative prohibition. Rabbi Moshe ibn Habib, the seventeenth-century Sefardic Chief Rabbi, was puzzled.[122] What is the novelty of this Talmudic passage? Isn't it obvious that even someone who is gravely ill should try to minimize the prohibitions being violated? His answer has important implications for the Jewish approach to sin. Rabbi ibn Habib explains that the Talmud is teaching that sin is not binary. Had it not been for this teaching, one might have presumed that once illness allowed consumption of a prohibited food, the level of prohibition was no longer relevant. Instead, the Talmud is teaching that sin is not binary—there are gradations. Even when circumstances allow the violation of certain prohibitions, that does not mean that now all prohibitions become moot. When possible, we always seek to minimize the gravity of sin. Certainly, as the Talmud allows, there are moments where violations are necessary—but even in such situations the differentiations between discrete orders of sin still remain relevant.

The Talmudic principle presented in *Yoma* is an example of how law still informs even when it is being broken. Law is not limited to proscribing actions; it even guides when and how we are supposed to violate normative law. To some degree this is analogous to statutes in American law such as the necessity doctrine in tort law[123] which, while allowing instances where a private citizen can damage another's property, still insists that care is taken to minimize those damages. The analogy is certainly not perfect, since in the case of Jewish law we are negotiating with entirely different prohibitions while in the case of the necessity doctrine we are just dealing with minimizing the cost of damages, but both are important examples of how the law even addresses the way in which the law, in certain contexts, should be broken.[124]

Jewish law understands that people are not perfect. And there are different kinds of imperfection addressed in Jewish law. In the case of an ill individual's eating, the law was not addressing a sinner but someone whose health leaves no recourse other than to eat non-kosher food. The scope of the law, however, addresses those who break the law due to sin as well. Jewish law understands that a religious person who sins is not an oxymoron but a part of reality as it has been from time immemorial. Imperfection does not exclude us from Jewish law. Jewish law speaks to everyone—saints and sinners. Indeed, as the wisest of men said, "there is no one righteous in the land who does good without sinning" (Eccl. 7:20). The Talmud (*Bava Batra* 165a) in fact says that everyone succumbs to "*avak lashon hara*" (a form of defamation rabbinically prohibited). Jewish law is not oblivious to imperfection—it anticipates and addresses our imperfections and failures.

What to Wear to a Sin

On Shabbat we wear special clothes. Dress codes help us align emotionally with whatever occasion or event we attend. School, weddings, graduations, and vacations all have their own dress codes—whether implicit or explicit. It seems silly to consider, but does sinning have suggested attire? Of course for sinning to have a dress code, one would have already have had to resign themselves to the idea that they were in fact committing a sin. But do unavoidable sins of such magnitude even exist? And if one finds oneself in a situation of grave sin (for instance, in a house of ill repute) should he take off his *yarmulke* or other identifying religious objects?

If only such a scenario were actually so outlandish. It does not take a very active imagination to think of places of sin where one would want to remove any religious markers. But aside from the question of removing religious markers, to which we will return, the Talmud actually considers whether an entirely different dress code is recommended. The Talmud (*Kiddushin* 40a and *Hagigah* 16a) states:

> R. Ilai the Elder said: If a person sees he is overcome with illicit desire, he should go to a place where he is not recognized, don black clothes and do what his heart desires rather than desecrate God's name in public.

This surprising text seems to permit the commission of sin. Can it be? Commentators dispute whether this statement is meant as a strategy to avoid sin or instructions for how to minimize sin's damage. Rabbeinu Hananel (*Hagigah* ibid.) explains that Rabbi Ilai is not offering any dispensation for someone who succumbs to temptation. Rather, the statement is a strategy to avoid sin. He understands this opinion in the Talmud as describing someone who has not yet succumbed to sin and, through the process of donning somber clothes and traveling to a distant location, will hopefully abate his desires. By delaying and complicating sin, Rabbi Ilai hopes to prevent it.

The Tosafists (*Kiddushin* and *Hagigah* ibid.), however, disagree. The language of the passage, according to the Tosafists, indicates a more literal dispensation. Someone who is going to sin should indeed just ensure it is done privately, where he will not be recognized. This is not permission to sin but advice to minimize it. The recommended dress code is not a way to avoid sin but to avoid the recognition of the sinner. Sin, but better not to be recognized so as to avoid additional desecration of God's name.

Rabbi Yitzhak Alfasi in his Talmudic commentary (*Kiddushin* ibid.) as well as Rabbi Asher ben Yehi'el (*Moed Katan* 3:11) seem to side with Tosafot's understanding. In explaining why they rule against the statement of Rabbi Ilai, they cite the Talmudic passage (*Berakhot* 33b) that "all is in the hands of heaven except the fear of heaven." Clearly, Rabbi Alfasi and Rabbi Asher ben Yehi'el understand Rabbi Ilai's statement to be predicated on the fact that some sins are simply outside of one's con-trol. Since as they understand, the Talmud in *Berakhot* does not allow for any circumstance of sin to transcend a person's "fear of heaven," they reject Rabbi Ilai's opinion as a minority view. Rabbi Ilai allows for some sins to exist outside of man's control and squarely within the confines of the "hands of heaven."

Interestingly, Rabbi Elchanan Wasserman (1874–1941) is baffled by the interpretation of Rabbis Alfasi and Asher ben Yehi'el.[125] How can it be, Rabbi Wasserman questions, that they were even willing to consider that an opinion in the Talmud disagrees with the statement that "all is in the hands of heaven except the fear of heaven"? In his words, "It is the foundation of the entire Torah that man was given the ability to choose between right and wrong." How could it be, he asks, that any opinion allows for some sins to transcend free will? He leaves this question unresolved—but it is an issue that others have addressed. The existence of sins that transcend free will may have concerned Rabbi Wasserman, but it is an idea that was very familiar in the Hasidic world of Izbica.

The Alleged Heresies of the Hasidic School of Izbica

Izbica Hasidut has a controversial history. The Hasidic court of Izbica was established on Simhat Torah in 1839 when, dramatically and mysteriously, Rabbi Mordekhai Yosef Leiner (1801–54) left Kotzk to establish his own community. A range of explanations have been posed as to why Rabbi Mordekhai Yosef left Kotzk, but the eschatological import of the year was likely a factor.[126] Rabbi Mordekhai Yosef led the Hasidic community of Izbica until his passing in 1854. A reformation from the individualistic revolution perpetuated in Kotzk, which in turn was a response to the initial leader-centric Hasidut, Izbica Hasidut continues to have innovative and radical implications within the Jewish community.

Aside from its founder Rabbi Mordekhai Yosef, who are the primary personalities who fashioned the theology of Izbica? There are three leaders who merit special attention: Rabbi Yaakov Leiner (1818–78),[127] Rabbi Gershon Henokh Leiner (1839–91),[128] and Rabbi Zadok of Lublin (1823–1900).[129] Following the passing of Rabbi Mordekhai Yosef, the court of Izbica amicably divided into two parts. One community remained in Izbica and was led by Rabbi Mordekhai Yosef's son Rabbi Yaakov, and afterwards by Rabbi Yaakov's son Rabbi Gershon Henokh, who moved the Hasidut to Radzyn. The other community, initially led by Rabbi Leible Eiger (1816–88),[130] respective son and grandson of famed rabbinic leaders Rabbi Shlomo and Rabbi Akiva Eiger, moved to Lublin where, following Rabbi Leible's passing, it was led by Rabbi Zadok Ha-Kohen Rabinowitz. Though each of the aforementioned leaders certainly had his own unique style and approach to the radical elements of Izbician theology, together they constitute the essential intellectual legacy of this profound Hasidic movement.

Explaining the essential source of controversy within Izbica-Lublin Hasidut is fairly simple; the complexity lies in how these controversial ideas should be applied. The controversy stems from the repurposing of the Talmudic phrase "All is in the hands of heaven, except for the fear of heaven" in Izbica Hasidut, wherein the refrain is decidedly found "All is in the hands of heaven, including the fear of heaven."[131] This raises the old problem, both in general philosophy and specifically in Hasidic thought, of determinism. The reason this seemingly deterministic formulation is so controversial is because it can be understood to pave the way towards antinomianism, the abrogation of the law. As neatly presented by Morris Fairstein:

> There is an inherent danger in Mordecai Joseph's teaching that the purpose of the mitzvoth is to bring man to an awareness that all is in the hands of God. For example, is the person who has already attained this level of understanding still required to fulfill the obligations imposed by the commandments?[132]

Or as presented by Rabbi Herzl Hefter, a contemporary scholar of Izbica, "[B]eyond a doubt, from the Orthodox perspective, we have here a potentially dangerous doctrine of radical Divine immanence which at times justifies antinomian behavior."[133] If all action and thought derives from God, can sin be deemed an appropriate religious expression?

The allure of antinomianism within Izbician thought was acknowledged by its leaders. Several biblical and Talmudic personalities are explained within Izbica Hasidut as mistaking the doctrine of divine immanence with an allowance (or even encouragement) of antinomian behavior. Of note are the stories of Adam and Eve, Korah, the death of the sons of Aaron, the nation of Amalek, Pinhas' confrontation with Zimri, and the heresy of the Talmudic sage *Aher*,[134] all of which are stories that are reimagined as cautionary tales in properly negotiating between a personal spiritual intuition invested with divine significance and the antinomian tendencies that can arise from such an intuition. Each of these personalities was left to grapple with the question that if indeed the personal revelations I experience are also part of God's will, then how should I respond when my intuition conflicts with God's will as expressed by the Torah?

While the theological rationale for positing such a radical conception of divine immanence varies among the different leaders within Izbica-Lublin, with Rabbi Mordekhai Yosef Leiner's appealing to internal religious phenomenology[135] and Rabbi Zadok's grounding this conception in Lurianic kabbalistic doctrine,[136] the normative world they construct is still decidedly Halakhic. In fact no one, scholar or Hasid, disputes the Halakhic nature of Izbician life, giving cause for many writers to wonder why this radical theology gave rise to such a traditional community.

Coping with Sin outside of Our Control: The Floor and the Ceiling

The Izbician concept of sin outside of our control rightfully raises some serious concerns. Rabbi Wasserman's initial reaction that such a view undermines the entire Torah system is not without merit. True, his reaction may not have considered the Izbica school, but how should those with Izbician inclinations integrate this radical view practically within their own lives? How did the adherents of Izbica prevent their deterministic notion of sin from devolving into an antinomian conception of Judaism?

Shaul Magid emphasizes the importance of this question in his seminal study of Izbica, though he admits that it remains unresolved:

> The question that looms large above all of the previous scholarly studies in Hasidism in general and Izbica/Radzin in particular is how and why these radical thinkers were able to remain within the halakhic tradition and not take the route of Sabbateans, who either repudiated the radical antinomian doctrines of Sabbatei Sevi and Nathan of Gaza and became reabsorbed into traditional communities or, like the Frankists, abandoned Judaism altogether.[137]

Rabbi Hefter, suggests two considerations.[138] The first assumes that the conservative lifestyle within Izbica Hasidut was a public policy consideration. As Rabbi Hefter writes, "The mass awareness of 'All is in the hands of Heaven' would be detrimental to the stability of the community, which requires normative behavior by its members." This "conspiracy theory" approach is belied in most respects by the first publication of Izbician theology, *Mei ha-Shiloah,* which Rabbi Gershon Henokh published based on the teachings of his grandfather. Even given its introductory cautionary note, to which we will return, if the leaders of Izbica wanted to withhold these ideas from the masses they surely should not have published them. Censorship in order to prevent misinterpretation was actually employed in the publication of Rabbi Zadok's works,[139] but the Izbician notion of "All is in the Hands of Heaven" was nonetheless still cleared for publication.

A second consideration presented by Rabbi Hefter, quoting Magid, attributes cognitive dissonance to Rabbi Mordekhai Yosef Leiner. Rabbi Hefter writes, "Perhaps the [*Mei ha-Shiloah]* was simply 'too frum,' that is to say, in the end he was emotionally unwilling to countenance in practice the far-reaching ramifications of his doctrines."[140] This suggestion also seems untenable. Aside from casting Rabbi Mordekhai Yosef as lacking the courage of his convictions, it doesn't seem to have a historical basis. Rabbi Mordekhai Yosef had already been ostracized by much of mainstream Polish Hasidic leadership for his theology. Why would he shy away from embracing the full implications of his beliefs? It seems more likely that the radical interpretations which seem to create a contradiction between Rabbi

Mordekhai Yosef's actions and his beliefs are the creation of the modern reader.

Instead, I would like to present other frameworks for considering the question of the divide between Izbician theology and practice. My chief concern is not resolving this particular historical question but rather how addressing this question can provide some perspective on incorporating the theologically rich and oftentimes radical aspects of Izbica Hasidut into the contemporary Jewish community.

Religious life has both a floor and a ceiling. The ceiling is built upon the ideals and values we reach towards, which we may never attain. The floor, however, is the framework and perspective from which we deal with failure and those still mired in sin. Much of religious life is spent vacillating somewhere in the middle. The more radical deterministic elements of Izbica-Lublin can provide cushions and comfort on the floor of Judaism without altering the ceiling. Sometimes, when religious life feels closer to the floor, there may be a feeling that Godliness and spiritual meaning are unattainable. It is here that Izbician theology is most instructive, reminding us that "[w]herever a Jew may fall, he falls into the lap of God."[141]

Applying a deterministic theology as a retrospective means of making spiritual sense of religious failure can be done without insisting on a deterministic perspective that undermines the ideals we are working towards.[142] For instance, the encouragement and strategies we develop for someone struggling with the Halakhic observance of Shabbat need not become the ideal way in which we present Shabbat observance. Failure and sin may indeed both be intractable parts of religious life, but the theological means with which we soften our "floor" don't have to become the theological ends with which we secure our "ceiling." The communal world of Izbica-Lublin likely remained traditional because they adapted this distinction in applying their radical theology.

A fascinating presentation on the need for an aspirational ceiling in Judaism despite the failures and inconsistencies of those on the floor is given by Rabbi Elliot Cosgrove. Rabbi Cosgrove, a Conservative rabbi, presents Chabad Hasidut as a model for Conservative Jewry to focus less on Halakhic accommodation and instead realize that part of the allure of religion is that its aspirational ideals make people uncomfortable. His words, which I will quote in full, may give pause to those calling for ritual innovation in more progressive factions in the Orthodox community. He writes:

There is, and we shall explore this a bit further, a theory that people come to religion to feel the comfort of home, to see their values given expression in prayer, ritual and community. By this formulation, religion is a form of self-affirmation in that religion must accommodate the values we hold dear. There is, however, another side of the discussion, a side that says that when people come to religion, whether it is here in the sanctuary, in their homes or elsewhere, they do so not to affirm the familiar, but just the opposite. People come to religion because it engages a totally different muscle group and set of expectations. The rites and rituals of any faith tradition are supposed to be a bit irrational, they are intended to make us feel out of place. After all, what is the point of religion if not to give expression to the sacred, the unfamiliar, or to use the technical term—the numinous.[143]

Dr. Jennie Rosenfeld's 2008 dissertation on sexuality in the Modern Orthodox community serves as a fine example of the contemporary application of Izbica-Lublin theology, balancing its more radical elements with traditional ideals. Her presentation of the thought of Izbica-Lublin, which relies heavily on Brill's scholarship, provides a paradigm for the application of Izbician thought to address a contemporary struggle without jeopardizing the communal ideal. She addresses those who are struggling with Halakhic ideals in the areas of sexuality and, through the work of Rabbi Zadok, provides encouragement in dealing with the guilt and shame that can result from such shortcomings. What she doesn't do is say that Rabbi Zadok abrogates the need to continue to make an effort towards living a sexually pure life. She writes:

> R. Zadok's message of teshuvah—what repentance is and how it can reframe a person's life—is critically important for those who are at a point where they can hear this message. For those who are at a place in which repentance and return to full halakhic observance in the sexual realm is not an option at this point, R. Zadok's message must at least stand in the background, as a hope for the future if not the present.[144]

What is most notable about her work is not her analysis of Hasidic thought but rather the maturity and discipline of her application. Izbica-Lublin thought is not used to replace the aspirational notions of sexual purity and holiness but rather is artfully used to address those who are already struggling. As she notes, Rabbi Zadok couches much of his approach to sin in the Talmudic phrase, "A person cannot stand on words of Torah until they have caused him to stumble."[145] In some contemporary applications of Hasidic thought, not even exclusively as it relates to matters of sexuality, the idealized notion of "standing" becomes obscured in the effort to validate the preliminary falls.[146] Such interpretations, however, ignore how the theology was applied within the community of Izbica-Lublin; in Izbica-Lublin, radical theology did not beget radical communal innovation. The floor was carpeted, but the ceiling remained in place.

"Intimates who understand their true value": On Divorcing Theology from Community

In 1994 Dr. Haym Soloveitchik published his renowned article "Rupture and Reconstruction: The Transformation of Contemporary Orthodoxy," which addressed many of the sociological changes in the Orthodox community in the second half of the twentieth century.[147] Soloveitchik describes a community that has shifted from a mimetic tradition, one that "is not learned but rather absorbed,"[148] to a text based tradition. As it relates to the *mitnagdic* community, which by his own admission is Soloveitchik's focus, the mimetic and textual traditions are considered in terms of the community's Halakhic observance. Among other communal innovations, Soloveitchik notes how the over-reliance on text has contributed to the development of a more radicalized Orthodox community. He writes:

> Fundamentally, all of the above—stringency, "maximum position compliance," and the proliferation of complications and demands—simply reflect the essential change in the nature of religious performance that occurs in a text culture. Books cannot demonstrate conduct; they can only state its requirements. One then seeks to act in a way that meets those demands.[149]

Aside from the descriptivist elements within the article, it also serves as a lament. Soloveitchik is concerned that the "new and controlling role that texts now play in contemporary religious life"[150] has irrevocably altered Jewish life itself. The article concludes with a haunting epitaph on the direction of the Jewish community:

> It is this rupture in the traditional religious sensibilities that underlies much of the transformation of contemporary Orthodoxy. Zealous to continue traditional Judaism unimpaired, religious Jews seek to ground their new emerging spirituality less on a now unattainable intimacy with Him, than

on an intimacy with His Will, avidly eliciting Its intricate demands and saturating their daily lives with Its exactions. Having lost the touch of His presence, they now seek solace in the pressure of His yoke.[151]

If discarding the mimetic tradition in favor of textuality, as it relates to *Halakhah*, has such a broad-range of communal results, what lessons can be extracted from such a bifurcation in the realm of theology? If accessing *Halakhah* through text alone without the accompaniment of a mimetic tradition created such radical results, should we not be suspicious of theological textual interpretation wholly divorced from the immersive tradition within the community that created it? Therein lies the danger of communal innovation based on the radical theology of Izbica-Lublin.

Yes, there were elements of the theology within Izbica-Lublin that were radical. But as recognized, the community remained consistently traditional. Is that a contradiction? The answer is, to echo Soloveitchik, "at times, yes; at times no." But what is certain is that whatever radical elements existed in the textual tradition of Izbica, they were not given precedence in dictating the overall lifestyle. Izbica-Lublin was not radicalized because like any tradition, there were simultaneous traditional values imparted that tempered the radical components of the theology. This means the perceived dissonance between Izbica-Lublin's textual tradition and their communal lifestyle is a product of our overreliance on text as the arbiter of communal values. If Soloveitchik is to be believed, a community's environment can provide an equally rich and oftentimes more powerful repository of tradition than that which emerges from their texts alone.

Mei ha-Shiloah begins with a cryptic caution. The ideas contained within, cautioned Rabbi Gershon Henokh, are only published "for the sake of our intimates who understand their true value." Based on the lessons from Soloveitchik's "Rupture and Reconstruction," this preface is given added significance. What was Rabbi Gershon Henokh's concern? Some understand this warning, including Rabbi Hefter, as relating mostly to theological misunderstanding; however, its true intention may also be directed at theological misapplication. Namely, without the accompanying immersive experience of being an "intimate" within the traditional Izbica-Lublin community, the texts will inevitably become radicalized. Like *Halakhah*, when transmitted exclusively through text, theology cannot be transferred without some sort of rupture from its original intent.

Interestingly, while the separation of text from experience in Halakhic tradition has cultivated some extreme tendencies in the *Haredi* world, the

opposite seems to be true regarding Hasidic theology. When Hasidic theology is extricated exclusively from text, divorced from its communal context and ambiance, radical suggestions suddenly become more plausible in
some circles. Without the tempering effect of the communal environment,
Hasidic texts can seem deceptively radical. However, it cannot be forgot-
ten that whatever textual radicalism existed in Izbica-Lublin, there was
a concomitant experiential tradition among the "intimates" that assured
communal radicalism did not develop. Still, the ambiguities in the theologically pregnant texts of Izbica-Lublin have led others to advocate for more
innovation in Jewish communal practice. It seems that having cast off the
pressure of His yoke, they now seek solace just in the touch of His presence.
Oftentimes, however, both are needed for sound communal policy.

Navigating the Inevitable

As Izbica explicitly articulates, some sin is inevitable. But as discussed, the
inevitability of sin does not mean law is no longer relevant and applicable.
Like generations of Izbica students, a radical theology need not uproot a
traditional community.

Rabbi Yitzhak Hutner, though not technically a student of Izbica, was
very much influenced by its Hasidic approach.[152] In a moving letter, Rabbi
Hutner allows for the existence of certain sins that transcend man's free
will but cautions that one can never know for certain which are unavoidable. He writes:

> …Know this my beloved, those sins which in truth are only committed due
> to the fact that "there is no righteous man in the land who does not sin"
> (Ecclesiastes 7:20), nevertheless it is beyond man's comprehension to decide
> which sins are in fact committed out of his free volition and which can by
> tallied on account that [some sin is inevitable]. And therefore, he remains
> obligated to develop for himself a plan of *teshuvah* for all of his sins. And if
> a person does not do *teshuvah* for all sins, on account that he assumes they
> were only committed since some sin is inevitable, then, even if such sins
> were inevitable, he is still going to be punished for them. For the lack of
> *teshuvah* on all sins, including those that were inevitable, is an indication of
> this individual's lack of seriousness regarding sin.[153]

Given that we do not know which temptations in our lives are truly
insurmountable, a person must approach all sins as if they are in his control

and attempt *teshuvah* (repentance) for any transgressions. Though there is solace in knowing that some spiritual failure is unavoidable, Rabbi Hutner cautions that dismissing our shortcomings as simply unavoidable is a sin unto itself.

Practically speaking, in a situation where a person is overcome with a seemingly unavoidable sin, should their *yarmulke* be removed? Rabbi Moshe Feinstein addresses this question in regard to someone who plans on going to the movies or theater. Rabbi Feinstein seems to invoke Tosafot's approach, calling taking off one's *yarmulke* in such a situation a "*sevara gedolah*" (a substantial consideration).[154] However, he ultimately dismisses this approach. Allowing a person to take off his *yarmulke* in such a situation, according to Rabbi Feinstein, is just an excuse to denigrate another aspect of Judaism, namely the wearing of a *yarmulke*. Only someone who genuinely is concerned about desecrating God's name could be allowed such a dispensation. Such a person, says Rabbi Feinstein, is not likely to be someone who is overcome with sin.[155]

In the fifteenth century, Rabbi Yitzhak of Arama (1420–1494) was posed a disturbing question by leaders in his community. Apparently, in their community adultery had become rampant, particularly among many communal leaders. A group of men approached Rabbi Yitzhak and proposed that the community should advocate for prostitution as a less deleterious option than adultery, which was tearing apart families. Rabbi Yitzhak was adamant that such a consideration was out of the question. "It is an outrageous perversion and sin," he responded, "it is a sin for an entire community and it cannot be forgiven."[156] Our collective imperfection is not cause for collective allowance or encouragement of our imperfections. Sin and failure, no matter how common, can never be communally condoned or publicly institutionalized. As Jews have intuited for centuries, the existence of sin cannot obscure our aspirations.

5

CAN SINNING BE HOLY?

===

To live outside the law, you must be honest.

—Bob Dylan, Absolutely Sweet Mary

Sin as Sweet as Honey

There is a sensational legend about Emperor Rudolf II (1552–1612) that is most certainly false but nevertheless worth repeating. As the legend goes, Emperor Rudolf was puzzled. On the one hand, he was an established anti-semite. On the other hand, however, he also found himself being very kind and compassionate towards the Jews he met. Emperor Rudolf, confused by these conflicting emotions towards Jews, visited the famed Maharal of Prague, Rabbi Yehudah Loew. The Maharal revealed to the Emperor the source of his conflicting attitudes towards Jews. The parents of Emperor Rudolf, the Maharal explained, were having difficulty conceiving children. Rudolph's father assumed that not he but his wife, the Queen, was infertile. In order to bear a child, Rudolph's mother the Queen accosted a Jewish woman and insisted she have a child with her husband. If the Jewish woman did not agree to bear the King's child, the Queen threatened to terrorize all the Jews who lived in their kingdom. The Jewish woman consulted with a Jewish tribunal of rabbis who gave her written permission to live with this King in order to prevent the tragedy that would surely befall the Jewish community if she refused. This story, explained the Maharal to the Emperor, is the reason for Emperor Rudolf's ambiguous feelings towards the Jews—he had a Jewish mother![157]

This tale, of course, never happened. Those with discriminating ears will immediately detect that it is essentially a dramatized retelling of the Purim story with medieval personalities. Still, like the Purim story, the Rudolph legend raises some important questions. To what extent is one permitted to go in order to save Jewish lives? Can the means of sinning be repurposed for a justified end? Essentially, are there situations where sinning can be holy?

Of course, there are situations where it is permissible, and even required, to transgress a sin. For instance, in life-threatening situations all sins should be violated with the exceptions of idolatry, adultery, and murder—any of those three one must even give up their life to avoid violating.[158] The status of adultery as one of three inviolable sins is the subject of rich Talmudic debate—especially concerning the Purim story. If adultery does in fact have such a status, how could Esther of the Purim story live with King Ahashverosh when she was already married to Mordekhai? Shouldn't Esther have sacrificed her life rather than commit adultery with Ahashverosh? The Talmud (Sanhedrin 74b) presents two opinions to explain the Halakhic rationale for Esther's relationship with Ahashverosh. According to Abaya, Esther was permitted to sleep with Ahashverosh because she was a passive participant in the relationship. Rava explains that Ahashverosh was motivated by lust, not religious persecution, so Esther was only obligated to give up her life to avoid a religiously motivated sin. Rabbi Moshe Isserles codifies an interpretation of Abaye's opinion as Jewish law.[159] Accordingly, so long as a sin is only violated passively–even if it is one of the three cardinal sins that normally require martyrdom—there is no obligation to give up a life. Since Esther remained passive in her relationship with Ahashverosh, she was not obligated to give up her life to avoid violating the prohibition.

Still, the legal grounding of the farcical tale we began with remains unresolved. In the story of the Emperor Rudolf, the woman actively offered herself in sin in order to save the lives of others. Is such an offer permissible or perhaps even required? Moreover, later in the Purim story Esther approaches the king voluntarily, albeit to save the lives of her people. Certainly she was not acting passively, so what was the Halakhic rationale for allowing her active approach to the king? Sometime at the turn of the eighteenth century this question came to the fore. A group of travelers were accosted by a band of outlaws, who threatened to kill them all. Considering the situation, one of the married female travelers offered to have relations with one of the outlaws in exchange for the group's safety. Though she did save the group's life, a Halakhic question was posed to Rabbi Yaakov Reischer (1661–1733), inquiring whether she had acted permissibly. After all, Esther was only permitted to sleep with Ahashverosh when she was forced, but was it also acceptable to actively offer oneself to avoid being killed? In his response Rabbi Reischer ruled that the woman had acted correctly. Normally a woman would be forbidden to initiate an inappropriate sexual relationship even if she remained passive, but since many people's lives were at stake in this situation, it was permissible.[160]

Rabbi Yehezkel Landau (1713–1793) disagreed with Rabbi Reischer's comparison of the case of kidnapped travelers to the story of Esther. A central difference, he explains, is that in the case of Esther she offered herself in order to save the entire Jewish people, who were potentially threatened by the decree of Haman. In the situation presented to Rabbi Reischer, however, it was only a small group of people whose lives were at stake. It is only when the lives of the entire Jewish people are jeopardized that proactively engaging in an inappropriate relationship can be justified.[161]

The privileged status of sins committed in order to save the entire Jewish people became especially relevant following the formation of the State of Israel. Some Halakhic authorities equated the population of the Jews in Israel as the legal equivalent of saving all Jews.[162] As such, based on the distinction of Rabbi Landau, if the lives of the Jews in Israel were threatened it would be permissible to engage actively in a sexually prohibited relationship if this would save the lives. Incredibly, this far-flung scenario became a reality. In 1986 Israel's nuclear secrets were compromised by a nuclear technician named Mordechai Vanunu. Mr. Vanunu offered details of the as-yet unconfirmed Israeli nuclear program to British news outlets, including *The London Sunday Times*. Before he completed the transaction, however, he was captured by the Israeli Mossad after being seduced by an undercover agent, known as a honeypot, who brought him back to Israel to stand trial.[163] Any Halakhic ground for Vanunu's capture must be based upon the consideration of the applicability of Esther's actions. Whether it was the fanciful story of Emperor Rudolf or the very real capture of Mordechai Vanunu, there certainly seem to be situations where sin can serve a holier purpose.

For Sin's Sake

Esther may be the most prolific biblical figure who seemingly violated a prohibition in the service of a higher purpose, but she certainly was not the first woman to do so. In fact, several hundred years before the story of Esther the Book of Judges records a story that became the Talmudic model for sinning for a loftier purpose. In the fourth chapter of the Book of Judges, the Canaanite general Sisera fled the battleground after failing to attack the Jewish people at Mount Tabor. Looking for a place to hide from the Jewish soldiers who were trying to capture him, Sisera entered the tent of Yael. We don't know a great deal about Yael. She was likely not even Jewish.[164] But once alone with Sisera, Yael (according to the Talmud's interpretation) seduced him and then promptly killed him by driving the stake of her tent through his skull.

On the one hand she actively seduced Sisera—a sin. On the other hand she vanquished a notorious enemy of the Jewish people. Should her actions be praised or condemned? In the next chapter of Judges she is praised by Deborah, one of the leaders of the Jewish people at the time. "Most blessed of women is Yael, wife of Hever the Kenite," said Deborah in a poetic song, "by women in the tent she will be blessed" (Judg. 5:24). Based on this praise the Talmud introduces a seemingly paradoxical concept—an *aveirah l-shmah*, literally translated as "a sin for a purpose." The Talmud writes as follows:

> Rav Nahman bar Yitzhak said: Greater is a transgression committed for its own sake, than a *mitzvah* performed not for its own sake.
>
> But didn't Rav Yehudah say that Rav said: A person should always occupy himself with Torah and *mitzvot* even not for their own sake, as it is through acts performed not for their own sake that good deeds for their own sake come about?
>
> Rather, a transgression for the sake of Heaven is equivalent to a *mitzvah* not for its own sake. The proof is as it is written: "Most blessed of women is Yael, wife of Hever the Kenite, by women in the tent she will be blessed" (Judg. 5:24), and it is taught: Who are these "women in the tent?" They are Sarah, Rebeccah, Rachel, and Leah. Yael's forbidden intercourse with Sisera for the sake of Heaven is compared to the sexual intercourse in which the Matriarchs engaged (*Nazir* 23b).

The Talmudic term *aveirah l-shmah* is vague. The term *l-shmah* in Talmudic literature can mean a lot of things. It certainly connotes some sort of intention, but what type of intention is less clear. Dr. Yuval Blankovsky, an Israeli scholar, wrote his dissertation on this Talmudic concept. In his book *Sin for the Sake of God: A Tale of a Radical Idea in the Talmudic Literature*, which is based on his doctoral work, he presents several different connotations for the word *l-shmah*.[165] It may mean doing a sin for the sake of God or perhaps for the sake of a fulfilling a future commandment. Blankovsky argues that its definition may in fact depend on how you understand this Talmudic concept.

Blankovsky explains there are three ways to understand the concept of an *aveirah l-shmah*.[166] One approach understands the concept of *aveirah l-shmah* as a legal principle that arbitrates when it is permissible to perform an action that has components of sin and components of *mitzvah*. According to those who subscribe to this view, the term *aveirah l-shmah* is much like other Halakhic principles such as the laws permitting one to violate *Halakhah* in order to save a life. Most Halakhic authorities seem to accept this version of the term; it does not present *aveirah l-shmah* as a subversion of Jewish law—but as a principle working within the system of Jewish law.[167]

A second approach understands the concept of *aveirah l-shmah* as a referendum on the importance of intention relative to the importance of an action. Meaning *aveirah l-shmah* teaches that the most important component of our deeds is not the technical category of the action—either sin or commandment—but rather the intention while performing such an action. This approach certainly is also the most dangerous. As we will discuss shortly, if it is only proper intentions that distinguish the sinners from the righteous, one can easily devolve into antinomian behavior.

A final approach held by some is that *aveirah l-shmah* is a concept that is only to be used *ex post facto*—once a deed has already been done. According to this view *aveirah l-shmah* is never to be invoked as a positive norm dictating one to perform a sinful action. Rather, *aveirah l-shmah* is a principle that in retrospect, once an action has been done, adds Halakhic legitimacy to what occurred.

One's conceptual approach to *aveirah l-shmah* will bear upon their reading and translation of the term "*l-shmah*." Those that approach this concept as a legal principle, like the first approach, would favor reading the term *aveirah l-shmah* as "a sin done for the sake of a commandment." The ambiguous term *l-shmah* refers to another commandment that justifies transgressing a sin. Here an *aveirah l-shmah* is almost a two-step process—the initial sin and the later commandment the sin enables. Conversely, if *aveirah l-shmah* is really a conceptual affirmation of the power of intention—that even a sin with the proper intention can be holy—then it would make more sense to read the term *aveirah l-shmah* as a sin for the sake of God. In this reading, the term *aveirah l-shmah* is not a narrow legal principle justifying sin for a particular commandment but an affirmation that regardless of the sinful status of an action, when coupled with the proper intention, any action can be performed for the service of God.

Sin as a Technical Means for Good

The first approach, as mentioned, views *aveirah l-shmah* as a technical legal principle that allows in certain circumstances for the *Halakhah* to be broken for the sake of preserving another Halakhic value. As opposed to the other approaches, this conception of *aveirah l-shmah* is somewhat reductionist. The principle is not telling us about the inherent value of our intentions or the Godliness that may be implicit in acts of sin; rather it is a narrowly defined Halakhic principle that allows the law to be broken under a strict set of criteria.

One of the greatest contemporary Halakhists is Rabbi Hershel Schachter, a rabbinic leader in the Modern Orthodox world who has taught at Yeshiva University for over fifty years. Like the approach of many other Halakhists, Rabbi Schachter limits the applicability of *aveirah l-shmah* and presents the concept within a more minimalistic legal framework.[168] He points to a seemingly unrelated passage in the Talmud as a case study in the modern applicability of *aveirah l-shmah*. The Talmud (*Shabbat* 4a) presents a case whereby someone unwittingly places bread dough in an oven on Shabbat—unaware that this is prohibited. In such a case would someone else be permitted to remove the bread dough from the oven—a rabbinic prohibition—in order to help prevent the person who initially placed it there from violating the biblical prohibition of baking on Shabbat? The Talmud seemingly rejects this suggestion here by citing the opinion of Rav Sheshes, who rhetorically asks, "[d]o we ever tell someone to commit a sin in order to save someone else?!" The Talmud here clearly assumes that we would not allow someone to commit a sin in order to help someone else avoid a sin. Many of the medieval commentators point out that the conclusion of the Talmud in *Shabbat* seems to contradict another Talmudic passage (*Gittin* 41b), which allows someone to free a partial slave in order to complete a minyan. Normally, it is prohibited to free an indentured slave—so why in this situation does it seem that we allow a sin to be violated (freeing the slave) in order to avoid another sin (not having a proper quorum to pray with)? There are several answers presented to resolve this contradiction. Two are relevant to our discussion. The Tosafists explain

at the incident involving the minyan is different—since it is a command-
ient that involves not just an individual but a quorum.[169] For a communal
commandment, explain the Tosafists, we would allow an individualistic
sin to be committed in order to avoid a communal sin. Rabbi Shlomo ben
Aderet offers a different answer. He explains that we never allow one to
violate a prohibition to save someone else. We do allow, however, one to
commit a small sin to prevent oneself from committing a larger sin. The
incident involving the minyan, explains Rabbi Aderet, is different because
we are only violating a prohibition in order to save ourselves from sin.

According to the opinions of the Tosafists (that you can commit an
individualistic sin to avoid transgressing a communal obligation) and Rabbi
Aderet (that you can commit a sin to prevent yourself from committing a
greater sin), what is the Halakhic principle that allows for this negotiation?
Although it is not mentioned explicitly by either, Rabbi Schachter posits
that the principle of *aveirah l-shmah* is in play. According to Rabbi
Schachter, *aveirah l-shmah* is the operating mechanism that, according to
these opinions, allows one to commit a sin in certain circumstances to avoid
another. In this context *aveirah l-shmah* is a Halakhic principle that allows
for certain transgressions in order to avoid other sins. In Rabbi Schachter's
presentation, *aveirah l-shmah* is a legal principle that dictates when certain
sins can be legally committed in order to avoid others. This principle, however, differs from other principles such as saving another's life or the general principle that a positive commandment overrides a concurrent negative
commandment (עשה דוחה לא תעשה), since in those cases the sin in question
is deemed completely permitted. If one violates Shabbat in order to save a
life there is no requirement afterwards to repent for having violated Shabbat.
Contrastingly, in situations where *aveirah l-shmah* is invoked the existing
sin being committed is still operational and requires repentance.[170] Aside
from the sin's remaining in force and thereby requiring repentance, there is
another important distinction between *aveirah l-shmah* and other legal
principles that allow a prohibition to be abrogated. Rabbi Schachter
explains, based upon a premise developed by Rabbi Naftali Zvi Yehudah
Berlin, that in order to invoke *aveirah l-shmah* the proper intention while
committing the sin must be fully realized. Normally in cases of violating a
prohibition to save a life or overriding a negative commandment to perform a contingent positive commandment, there is no requirement for
having the proper intention. Regardless of one's intention, if a life is at stake
Shabbat can be violated. With *aveirah l-shmah*, however, the intention

is an inherent part of the legal allowance to commit the sin. The permissibility to commit a sin in order to avoid another, even in circumstances where this can be invoked, demands that the proper *l-shmah*—intention—be realized.[171]

In this approach *aveirah l-shmah* is not a commentary on the potential holiness of sin or an expression of any sort of antinomian sentiment. Instead, like other legal principles codified in *Shulkhan Arukh*, *aveirah l-shmah* is a precise legal mechanism that allows in certain circumstances for a sin to be committed in order to avoid other sins. Not everyone, however, agrees with this approach. Others have approached *aveirah l-shmah* much more broadly. They view *aveirah l-shmah* not as a legal principle but as a philosophical idea: an idea that was at the heart of one of the greatest controversies and heresies in all of Jewish history.

The False Messiah's Sin

Jewish history is littered with false messiahs. All throughout Jewish history there have been men—but so far no women—who have proclaimed themselves as the messiah ushering in redemption.[172] Arguably none have been as successful or as deleterious for the Jewish community as Shabbtai Zevi (1626–1676). The Shabbatean messianic movement, which began in 1665, swept through the Ottoman Empire and fomented controversy throughout the rabbinic establishment. It is hard to say definitively what made Shabbtai Zevi so successful. Gershom Scholem, the prolific scholar of mysticism, points to several factors.[173] Certainly the Jewish people, reeling from the recent 1648 Chmielnicki massacres and preoccupied with the mystical eschatology from the teachings of Lurianic Kabbalah, were looking for a savior. Shabbtai Zevi capitalized on the mystical fervor sweeping through Europe. Peddling his own brand of mysticism through his chief proselytizer, Nathan of Gaza, Shabbtai Zevi convinced laypeople and rabbinic leaders alike that his messianic revolution was authentic. The movement began to deteriorate in 1666 when Shabbtai Zevi converted to Islam, shocking his followers. For most, an apostatized messiah was simply inconceivable and the movement began to lose momentum. Others continued to have faith in him as a redeemer, attributing his conversion to some mysterious mystical quest. Even following his death, several factions within the Jewish community—some secretly, others openly—clung to their belief in the Shabbatean movement. No doubt, the movement has become the *locus classicus* for understanding the psychological determination of those looking for a messiah.[174]

One distinctive factor of particular relevance to our discussion is the Shabbatean movement's relationship to sin. Even prior to his apostasy, Shabbtai Zevi had a markedly antinomian persona. Throughout his life he performed rituals that openly flaunted his abrogation of Jewish law. While sinning, he was known to make a heretical blessing to God "who allows the forbidden" (המתיר אסורים), a repurposing of the traditional blessing to God who "frees the imprisoned." One year he celebrated all three of the yearly Jewish festivals Pesah, Shavuot, and Sukkot all in one week. Against Talmudic law, he pronounced the ineffable name of God and was known to eat the forbidden fats of an animal. Eventually, once his movement reached a euphoric peak, he abolished the fast days of the seventeenth of Tammuz and the ninth of Av and replaced them with days of celebration.

Within Shabbateanism *aveirah l-shmah* was a philosophy, not just a Halakhic principle. Rituals that contravened Jewish law were performed for the sake of some other, higher order commandment. Sin in the Shabbatean movement confirmed a messianic age that evolved from the allegedly temporal constraints of Jewish law. Torah itself, in Shabbatean thought, had evolved. Pre-messianic Torah and law were no longer necessary. The Shabbateans attempted to usher in a mystical antinomian age that required reorienting the Jewish people's relationship to their laws. As Scholem explains:

> Through a revolution of values, what was formerly sacred has become profane and what was formerly profane has become sacred. . . . Prior to the advent of the Redeemer the inward and the outward were in harmony, and this is why it was possible to effect great tikkunim by means of outwardly performing the commandments. Now that the redeemer has arrived, however, the two spheres are in opposition: the inward commanded, which alone can effect a tikkun, has become synonymous with the outward transgression. *Bittulah shel torah zehu kiyyumah*: the violation of the Torah is now its true fulfillment.[175]

In the supposed messianic age of Shabbateanism, sin was not the subversion of God's will—it was its expression.

Truth be told, even before the advent of Shabbateanism the messianic idea in Judaism had some antinomian undertones. Messiah is always identified as the offspring of King David, who himself was a descendant of Ruth the Moabite.[176] The entire Moabite family originated from an act of incest between Lot and his daughters, who had thought that their act was necessary to preserve humanity (Genesis 19:31–32). In fact the Talmud references the story of Lot and his daughters as a possible source for the very concept of *aveirah l-shmah*.[177] The messianic idea itself emerges from antinomian behavior. This connection was not lost on the Shabbatean movement. Scholem recounts Shabbatean apologists who pointed to the licentious origins of messiah as a justification for Shabbtai Zevi's antinomian behavior: "Lest no one, therefore rashly cast aspersions at the Lord's Anointed (i.e. Shabbtai Zevi)."[178]

Given the support in mystical texts for some of the Shabbatean movement's more extreme ideas, even mystics who opposed the Shabbatean movement found themselves subject to communal suspicion. In the radical world of mysticism it was hard to know the difference between mystical ideas that were radical but traditional and those that were heretical. One such figure, who had to publicly distance himself from the Shabbatean movement, was the renowned kabbalist Rabbi Moshe Hayyim Luzzato, known by his acronym Ramhal. Rabbi Luzzato composed an entire work, *Kinat Hashem Tzevaot*, explaining the differences between the Shabbatean usage of *aveirah l-shmah* and its proper place in traditional Jewish thought.[179] In this work Rabbi Luzzato makes several distinctions outlining the proper use of *aveirah l-shmah*, including the requirement of *hora'at sha'ah*, a temporary negation of the law, as well as some more mystical distinctions. It is not entirely clear whether these somewhat muddled distinctions helped Jews separate Rabbi Luzzato's mysticism from that of the Shabbatean movement. This problem—differentiating "traditional" mysticism from Shabbatean mysticism—would continue to plague many scholars, most notably among the Hasidim of Rabbi Israel Baal Shem Tov.

From its inception the Hasidic movement of Rabbi Israel Baal Shem Tov had to distance itself from Shabbateanism. In the mid-eighteenth century, when the Hasidic movement began, the Jewish community was still reeling from the Shabbatean movement and its later offshoot, the Frankists. The rabbinic establishment could hardly be faulted for its distrust of a new sectarian movement. Much of the early opposition to Hasidim, known as *mitnagdim*, cast the Hasidic movement as a new Shabbatean movement.[180] To be sure, some in the early Hasidic movement did take liberties with strict Halakhic practice. Many Hasidim prayed past the prescribed time in Jewish law. Others prayed with an ecstatic fervor foreign to traditional synagogues.[181] In response to the many antinomian actions within the

Hasidic community, Rabbi Hayyim of Volozhin, the prized student of the Gaon of Vilna, penned *Nefesh ha-Hayyim*, which articulated some of the primary concerns that the *mitnagdim* had with the Hasidic movement.[182] In *Nefesh ha-Hayyim*, Rabbi Hayyim emphasizes the importance of strict adherence to the details of Jewish law. Proper intention, Rabbi Hayyim cautions, cannot come at the expense of the proper execution of the commandments. However lofty one's intentions may be, he notes, what good is matzah eaten after the night of Passover?[183] In fact Rabbi Hayyim advanced the questionable theory that the concept of *aveirah l-shmah* is no longer applicable following the giving of the Torah at Sinai.[184] Before receiving the Torah there was more latitude when deciding to perform a sin or a commandment in the service of God. Following the giving of the Torah, he warned, the *Halakhah* is the only avenue to fulfilling the will of God.

Early *mitnagdim* and some later scholars attempted to paint the Hasidic movement as a monolith with regard to their approach to *aveirah l-shmah*. It is easier to dismiss a movement or cast aspersions on their approach when all such movements can be heaped together. As Yehoshua Mondshine, the noted Chabad scholar and librarian at the National Library of Israel, humorously noted, "Sometimes it seems that, in the opinion of some scholars, the followers of hasidism spent most of their time studying Sabbateanism, and the remainder of their time they devoted to obscuring and camouflaging this pursuit."[185] Instead, Mondshine emphasized that *aveirah l-shmah* was used in a variety of ways throughout Hasidic literature. "I hope," he writes in his important article on *aveirah l-shmah* in Hasidic thought, "that I have succeeded in demonstrating the instability, indeed the fluidity, of categories in Hasidism, which by its nature resists the imposition of constant and firm definitions."[186]

Fluidity of categories, to use Mondshine's phrase, was not restricted to Hasidic thinkers. As we have seen, there were several different approaches to the concept of *aveirah l-shmah* in Jewish intellectual history. The notion of fluidity, however, resonates throughout. If religion is to dictate all of the contours of our lives, there are situations where ideals will inevitably need to be negotiated. If *Halakhah* provides firm categories for the rituals of our lives, *aveirah l-shmah* is a mechanism that allows the chaos and fluidity of our individual lives to fit those molds. Certainly there are varying views on the scope of such negotiations, but their existence is simply a fact of life. *Aveirah l-shmah* ensures that even the crevices where our ideals cannot reach are still filled with holiness.

6

DOES GOD REPENT?

Dearest Father,

You asked me recently why I maintain that I am afraid of you…

…I too believe you are entirely blameless in the matter of our arrangement. But I am equally entirely blameless. If I could get you to acknowledge this, then what would be possible is—not, I think, a new life, we are both much too old for that—but still, a kind of peace; no cessation, but still, a diminution of your unceasing reproaches.

—Franz Kafka, *Letter to His Father*

Somebody's Son

Few people have heard of Richard Pindell, but many people have heard some version of his famous story "Somebody's Son." Of course, most people don't know the story by its formal title, but if they heard the story it would sound familiar. Likely it was a story they heard at a campfire or a moving speech at a religious retreat. The story begins with a boy named David who runs away from home. David, we learn, had a big fight with his father and decided to continue his life on his own—until he changes his mind. David begins to regret his decision and writes a note home to his mother in the hopes that she can convince his Dad to let him back home. This is David's letter from the original story:

Dear Mom,

If dad will permit it, I would like to come home. I know there's little chance he will. I'm not going to kid myself. I remember he said once, if I ever ran off, I might as well keep on going.

All I can say is that I felt leaving home was something I had to do. Before even considering college, I wanted to find out more about life and about me and the best way for us (life and me) to live with each other. Please tell Dad—and I guess this'll make him sore all over again—I'm still not certain that college is the answer for me. I think I'd like to work for a time and think it over.

You won't be able to reach me by mail, because I'm not sure where I'll be next. But in a few days I hope to be passing by our place. If there's a chance Dad will have me back, please ask him to tie a white cloth to the apple tree in the south pasture—you know the one, the Grimes Golden beside the tracks. I'll be going on the train. If there's no cloth on the tree I'll just quietly, and without any hard feelings toward Dad—I mean that—keep on going.

Love,
David[187]

David finds someone to mail the letter and boards a train home. He is anxious of course, not knowing whether his father will welcome him back home. The train ride is a distance of a few days from his parents' home and throughout the ride David is unsure if he will ever be invited back to the place where he grew up. Hundreds of miles of track separate David from the answer of his father. As the train approaches his home, David is simply too overwhelmed to look—will the white cloth be on the tree as a sign of his acceptance back home? Or will he just have to keep riding the train and find a new life for himself without his father's love? Knowing his answer is only a few moments away, David becomes too frightened even to look. What if his father doesn't want him back? What if instead of a white ribbon on a branch, "he would find, staring back at him, just another field, just another somebody else's strange place?" David can't bring himself to look. Instead the story concludes:

> Desperately, he nudged the passenger beside him. "Mister, will you do me a favor? Around this bend on the right, you'll see an apple tree. I wonder if you'll tell me if you see a white cloth tied to one of its branches?"
>
> As they passed the field, the boy stared straight ahead. "Is it there?" he asked with an uncontrollable quaver.
>
> "Son," the man said in a voice slow with wonder, "I see a white cloth tied on almost every twig."[188]

Richard Pindell, a Binghamton University professor who taught writing and Civil War literature, has a knack for producing universalistic stories.

He makes it easy for the reader to see themselves in David. Pindell himself acknowledged that "Somebody's Son" is "far and away my most popular story." Even if you have never run away from home or written a plea to a parent, Pindell frames the story in such a way that the reader can identify with David's plight. Who hasn't confronted a fissure with a spouse, ruptured a relationship with a parent, or become angry with a child? David's story is the story of someone trying to bridge a gap and traverse a relationship that has become estranged. It is no surprise that this story has become exceptionally popular in religious circles. As it is most often told, David's relationship with his father is a metaphor for the human relationship with God. "Somebody's Son" is read as the story of a person on the path of sin who is looking for a sign that their relationship with God has not been permanently broken. All people want is a small sign—a white cloth wrapped on a tree to know that the relationship can still be salvaged. A patient and loving God wraps every twig with white ribbons. God wants every one of us back.

Hurling Words Heavenward

Sin is the mechanism that deteriorates our relationship with God. But is it possible that it can work the other way around as well? Can God sin and, by extension, repent? At first glance this of course seems blasphemous. A central tenet of Jewish thought is God's perfection. God's perfection should preclude any notion ascribing sin and repentance to the Almighty. Curiously though, the Talmud seems to suggest just that:

> Rabbi Shimon ben Pazi notes a contradiction: "'And God made the two great lights'; as it reads, 'The large light, and the small light.' The moon said to the Holy One, Blessed Be He, 'Master of the Universe, How can two kings share one crown?' He said to her, 'Go and diminish yourself!' She said to him: 'Master of the universe, because I said a logical thing before you, I should diminish myself?'" . . .
>
> The Holy One said, "I will bring an atonement on Me for I have diminished the moon."
>
> And so that is what is meant when Rabbi Shimon ben Lakish said, "What is the difference in how the New Moon offering is written, 'A he-goat offering on the new moon, FOR THE LORD?' Because the Holy One is saying, 'Let this he-goat be an atonement FOR ME, for the diminishment of the moon.'" (*Hullin* 60b)

Only one time in the Torah is a sacrificial offering described as being "for the Lord." Based on that description, the Talmud takes a hermeneutical leap and considers that the sacrificial offering for the new moon is actually "for the Lord"—it is atoning for God's sin, if you will, of diminishing the size of the moon. Not surprisingly, many Talmudic commentators tempered the theo-logical polysemy of this passage. Tosafot, for instance, explain that it is not God who needs atonement but the Jewish people. God is only responsible for establishing a consistent time to offer this sacrifice (i.e., on *Rosh Hodesh* when there is a new moon).[189] Others insist that the term the Talmud uses for atonement—*kapparah* [כפרה]—does not mean atonement in this context but rather appeasement. According to this reading God does not seek atone-ment. How could He? God is perfect. Rather, this sacrificial offering is a measure of appeasement to the diminished moon.

This is not the only instance in rabbinic literature where God is described imperfectly, but it is likely "the boldest expression."[190] Professor Dov Weiss, who teaches religion at the University of Illinois at Urbana-Champaign, wrote a book about rabbinic protests against God entitled *Pious Irreverence: Confronting God in Rabbinic Judaism.* It is a remark-able academic work with a jarring thesis illustrating "how the rabbinic humanization of God provided the sages with a mechanism to anchor their confrontations."[191] Throughout the work Weiss cites rabbinic pas-sages that portray rabbis protesting God or putting God on trial. Weiss demonstrates that in some instances protesting God is not only consid-ered theologically legitimate but is a form of prayer.[192] In one instance the *Midrash Psalms* (90:2) asks, "Are not their prayers forms of protest?"[193] The Jerusalem Talmud (*Berakhot* 4:4) compares the act of approaching prayer to a soldier preparing for battle.[194]

There is a great divide between the Jewish and Christian approaches to protesting to God. In Christian literature the concept of protesting to God is noticeably absent or, at the very least, deliberately muted. Weiss presents a few explanations for "the fact that, unlike the rabbinic tradi-tion, the Christian tradition has generally speaking, not revived the bibli-cal model that celebrates expressions of theological dissent."[195] Likely the Christian approach was a product of Augustine's doctrine of original sin, which emphasized man's responsibility for the world's imperfection. God in Augustine's view was entirely blameless for the world's imperfection, making any protests to the contrary misdirected. Protesting and theolog-ical argumentation are markedly Jewish exercises. While such acts may be seen as dogmatic blasphemy, as Weiss beautifully expresses, protesting God is really a product of a rich experiential relationship with God. He writes:

> When a person's life is infused with a consciousness of a providential and personal God, very real feelings of frustration and dismay are bound to surface. Indeed, disappointment is a typical experience in all loving relationships, and this certainly should be the case in the human-God encounter. Beyond being unnatural or even painful, holding back feelings of anger might even be detrimental to an honest and open relationship. To paraphrase Genesis Rabbah, "Love without rebuke is not love." (Genesis Rabbah 54:3)[196]

It is no wonder that protesting to God features so prominently in Hasidic literature. In a world where a vivid experiential relationship with God is sought, protesting to God is seen as affirmation of such a relationship—not its negation. Great Hasidic masters such as Rabbi Levi Yitzhak of Berditchev and Rabbi Klonymous Kalman Shapira distinguished themselves as traditional leaders who were unafraid to challenge God.[197] The latter, much of whose writing was produced inside the Warsaw Ghetto, openly challenges God to realize that the Jewish people cannot bear such excessive suffering.[198]

Forgiveness is Divine

One of the more interesting features of Jewish protests towards God is the notion that God is bound to keep Jewish law. In general theological protests have an anthropomorphic quality, but the assumption that God is obligated in Jewish law provided rabbinic literature "a tangible mechanism to ground and justify their protests."[199] So in one instance the biblical obligation of restitution of damages is invoked to obligate God to rebuild Jerusalem.[200] Another example has the Jewish people reminding God of the prohibition of seeking vengeance and beseeching God to withdraw his wrath on His people.[201] The notion that God observes all of the command-ments did not just appear in the context of protest. God wears *tefillin*.[202] God keeps Shabbat.[203] Basing his thinking on this foundation, Rabbi Zadok of Lublin asks, does God do *teshuvah*?

The Talmud ascribes some notion of sin to God, as demonstrated through God's offering an atonement sacrifice on His own behalf. We also find the notion of regret ascribed to God. Genesis 6:6 describes God's reaction to the moral deterioration of man as follows:

וַיִּנָּחֶם ה' , כִּי-עָשָׂה אֶת-הָאָדָם בָּאָרֶץ; וַיִּתְעַצֵּב, אֶל-לִבּוֹ.

And the Lord regretted that He had made man on the earth, and he became grieved in His heart.

Seemingly, the term *va-yinachem* [וינחם] ascribes some sense of regret to God. Similarly, the Talmud in *Sukkah* plainly states that God has four regrets. How do the notions of regret and repentance apply to a perfect God?[204]

Forgiving the Divine

God may be perfect, but creation is not. Suffering and failure are inescapable parts of experiencing this world. Rabbi Joseph B. Soloveitchik (1903–93) explains that human limitation is the cause of God's need for atonement. In his seminal work *Halakhic Man*, he writes:

> The Jewish people bring a sacrifice to atone, as it were, for God's not having completed the work of creation. The Creator of the world diminished the image and stature of creation in order to leave something for man, the work of His hands, to do, in order to adorn man with the crown of creator and maker.[205]

The diminished size of the moon represents the enduring imperfections found in creation. Ironically, the starkest example of creation's imperfection is, of course, us. And here, too, we find none other than Moshe insisting that God assume some of the blame for man's failures. Following the Jewish people's sin with the golden calf, the Talmud records Moshe's audacious insistence to God that He forgive His nation:

> And Rabbi Elazar said: Moshe spoke impertinently toward God on High, as it is stated "[a]nd Moshe prayed to the Lord" (Numbers 11:2), Do not read to [*el*] the Lord, onto [*al*] the Lord. . . .

> Rabbi Hiyya bar Abba said that Rabbi Yohanan said: This is comparable to a person who had a son; he bathed him and anointed him with oil, fed him and gave him drink, and hung a purse of money around his neck. Then, he brought his son to the entrance of a brothel. What could the son do to avoid sinning? . . .

> This teaches that Moshe grabbed the Holy One, Blessed be He, as a person who grabs his friend by his garment would, and he said before Him: Master

of the Universe, I will not leave You be until You forgive and pardon them. (*Berakhot* 32a)[206]

God allowed for the possibility of sinning. In some instances it may even feel like we have no other choice. What could the son do to avoid sinning? Creating man with a separate sense of self and the capacity for free will, while necessary, obscured God's presence in the world. Here we ascribe the notion of regret to God. In the aforementioned passage of Talmud, in fact, God is depicted as regretting His creation of the evil inclination. Metaphorically, is God asking Himself—did I go too far? Are sin and failure simply too accessible? Can man still reach out from the obscurity of the world and find a hidden God? God, so to speak, has remorse for the struggle His creations must endure.[207]

Inviting God Back

Who moved? When any relationship deteriorates, there is inevitably blame cast from both parties over who initiated the rupture. Normally, in our relationship with God we think of a person as moving away from His presence. A person likely thinks that human sin distances people from God. But perhaps the movement is not unilateral. God, we protest, also moved. God allowed us to sin with such ease. God created an imperfect world with the capacity for failure. Like the moon, human light is diminished and casts only a faint luminescence. God laments, "Is there more I could have done to help the son avoid sinning?"

If this is divine remorse, then divine repentance is where God draws closer to man. Or as Rabbi Zadok explains, God generates within man thoughts of repentance that would have otherwise been lost. When someone becomes so distant from spirituality that even thoughts of remorse seem unattainable, God can still reach out and whisper to return. God's repentance allows man to return when return seems impossible. Through His prophets, God gives people an assurance: "Return unto Me and I will return unto you" (Malakhi 3:7). It is not just man who can become distant—so can God. And just as every person can return, God can also return.[208]

Let's return to our story. Normally when we read a story about a son estranged from his father, the sensible analogue would be mankind as the son becoming estranged from God the father. The child has erred and has been cast away by the parent. Nothing, however, is quite as human as reimagining an analogy.[209] Maybe when rereading Richard Pindell's "Somebody's Son," the castaway David is not a symbol for man's rebellion but rather God's. The story can be reread of as a tale of God's abandoning His people rather than His people's abandoning Him. God metaphorically writes back to mankind and wonders whether He still has a home among His creations.

I think about this reading of "Somebody's Son" every Yom Kippur. As I read through the litany of sins from the previous year while solemnly beating my chest, I wonder (dare I say protest), "Why, God, has sinning become so easy?" Why does failure become so inevitable? Our reflections on the previous year are supposed to center around our transgressions, but sometimes my mind can wonder and consider God's distance. Sure, doors were closed during the past year—but were all of them shut by me? Surely some people in shul today received diagnoses this past year that made them feel bereft of God's presence. Surely God could have made it easier for the son to avoid sin. But every Yom Kippur I look around and consider that it might not be just man who is doing *teshuvah*—surely it is also God. Once a year, prayer becomes more instinctual. Once a year, His presence seems more attainable. And once a year, we imagine God is asking us that we let Him back into His world. And as God symbolically passes by the shul on Yom Kippur, He petitions His people, "If you want me back in your life— give me a sign." And each year on Yom Kippur we all wear white so when God peers into our lives, wondering if the relationship can still be salvaged, we remind Him and ourselves that He is invited back. The whole shul is clothed in white.

SECTION II

CASE STUDIES IN SIN AND FAILURE

7

ONCE A JEW ALWAYS A JEW? WHAT LEAVING JUDAISM TELLS US ABOUT JUDAISM

I have been driven many times upon my knees by the overwhelming conviction that I had nowhere else to go.

—**Abraham Lincoln**

During these days of reflection, he said, he had been asking himself what makes us keep being Jews when it's such a struggle, "And I found the answer in six words," he said. "Six words in the Talmud, written by Rashi: 'He will not let us go.'" It isn't a matter of our choosing whether to quit God, the old rabbi explained; it is God who chooses not to quit us.

—**Stephen J. Dubner, "Choosing My Religion"**

A Monk Walks Into Israeli Supreme Court

On November 19, 1962 a Roman Catholic monk appeared before Israel's highest court. Wearing the traditional brown tunic and sandals, the man who stood before the court could not have looked less Jewish. But based on Israel's Right of Return, the 1950 legislation that granted every Jew the right to live in Israel, Brother Daniel insisted that he should be treated as a

Jew. Before becoming a Roman Catholic monk, he explained, he was born a Jew. Brother Daniel was once Oswald Rufeisen, a Polish Jew who was introduced to Catholicism while escaping Nazi persecution. His plea for immigration rights provoked Israel's highest court to carefully consider the parameters of Jewish identity.

A report the next morning in *The New York Times* emphasized the importance of Brother Daniel's case: "His action is expected to lead for the first time to a formal and binding legal definition of what is a Jew within the meaning of the Law of Return, a question that has always agitated the nation."[210] The Law of Return raised difficult questions from the outset. The legislation that guaranteed "every Jew has the right to come to Israel as an immigrant"[211] never made the definition of a Jew entirely clear. Was a Jew to be defined based on their national identification? Or, perhaps, based on Jewish law? And as any question to be decided by Jewish law raises, whose interpretation of Jewish law would be favored?

To clarify the ambiguities within the Law of Return, David Ben-Gurion asked Jewish scholars and leaders throughout the world to consider how Jews should be defined in the context of this legislation. His letter received responses from the entire denominational spectrum of Jewish leadership. The responses were later collected into the fascinating volume, *Jewish Identity: Modern Responsa and Opinions*, a documentary history compiled by Baruch Litvin and edited by Sidney B. Hoenig.[212] Ben-Gurion's question of "Who is a Jew" solicited responses that are a veritable "Who's Who" of Jewish leadership. Despite the prestige of the questioner and the responses, however, Ben-Gurion's questions did not really address Brother Daniel. Ben-Gurion was concerned about the issue of matrilineal versus patrilineal Jewish descent in establishing Jewish identity. His concern was regarding the definition of who was born a Jew, but he did not clarify whether those who are born Jews can lose their Jewish status. The novelty of Brother Daniel's question was not about which parents create Jewish identity but whether Jewish identity can be lost.

Apostasy: An Age-Old Issue

The question Brother Daniel posed was certainly new for the Israeli Supreme Court, but the phenomena of apostasy—leaving religion—has been an issue for over a millennium. The Talmud is replete with references to those who abandon their Jewish identity. Referred to as *meshumadim*, from the Hebrew term *meshumad*, meaning to destroy,[213] the Talmud placed several sanctions on such Jews, such as invalidating their ritual slaughter and prohibiting wine they have handled.[214] But the Talmudic definition of a *meshumad* differed in some ways to our modern notions of apostasy. The Talmud evaluated the *meshumad* based on their actions—such as violating Shabbat, worshipping idols, or neglecting commandments—and intentions, either as an act of rebellion or moral weakness, but the Talmud did not consider the status of those who formally converted to another religion. Rabbi Louis Jacobs makes this point in his intriguing study on Christianity in Jewish law:

> In Talmudic times the question regarding the status of a Jew converted to a religion other than Judaism could not have arisen. The Jew who worshipped the pagan gods did not become 'converted' to paganism, abandoning his faith for another. . . . The whole problem of Halakhic attitudes towards other religions could have no meaning until the emergence of the 'daughter' religions, Christianity and Islam. That is why all the Halakhic discussions on the question date from the middle ages.[215]

In the middle ages, the question of apostasy took on a new dimension as Rabbis needed to grapple with the implications of baptismal ceremonies.[216] While there were different Halakhic sanctions imposed on apostates during the middle ages, the most telling signs of the Jewish communities' deep concern for apostasy were in two medieval reactions: namely, conversion rites for former apostates who wanted to return to the Jewish community and mourning rites for living Jews who had converted. Regarding the former, many Halakhists insisted that apostates who returned to the Jewish community even after renouncing their conversion should undergo the formal steps of conversion to Judaism. During the time of the Crusades, when forced conversion became all too common, this ceremony enacted formal Halakhic borders for reentry into the Jewish community.[217] Strictly on Halakhic grounds, of course, no such ceremony should have been necessary, as a baptism for the overwhelming majority of rabbinic scholars was a Halakhically meaningless act that did not alter the recipient's Jewish identity. Nonetheless, beginning in the twelfth century many returning former apostates were denied reentry into the Jewish community until they formally "re-converted." This requirement, which is codified in the *Shulkhan Arukh*,[218] has a long and varied history in rabbinic literature but most certainly underscores the severity with which rabbinic authorities approached apostasy.

A second, even more questionable reaction towards apostates was the custom of some to sit *shiva* if a family member converted to another religion. This custom has even less actual grounding than the former in Halakhic texts. The *shiva* custom for apostates originated from a simple misreading. Rabbeinu Gershom, one of the founding leaders of Ashkenazic Jewry, is recounted in many Halakhic texts as having sat *shiva* after his son, who apostatized.[219] A closer reading of the story makes it clear that Rabbeinu Gershom did not actually sit *shiva* in his son's lifetime; he rather observed added mourning rites upon his son's death. With his son's having died an apostate, his loss was compounded as it was not only a father who lost a son but our Father in Heaven that lost someone who died without returning to the Jewish community. The misreading of this story did, however, lead some Jews, especially those in Europe, to believe that families should actually sit *shiva* if a family member apostatized.[220] It is less clear how often families actually observed such mourning ceremonies, but it is apparent that the notion of such mourning rites was well known in Europe. Rabbi Moshe Sofer was adamant that mourning for a living apostate undermines the very real possibility of a return to the community. "Certainly there should be no mourning so long as the apostate is alive," he writes, "…but for the parents to cry and lament is certainly appropriate as it may evoke God's mercy to awaken the heart of the apostate to return before he dies."[221]

Once a Jew, Always a Jew? Debating the Status of Apostates in Jewish Law

The symbolism of the aforementioned customs aside, most correctly assume (as Jewish *bubbies* have maintained for generations), "once a Jew, always a Jew." This was certainly the assumption of Brother Daniel when he entered Israeli Supreme court. But can we be so sure that this adage is indeed true? How do we know that a Jew who converts to another religion is still indeed Jewish?

Rabbi Shlomo Yitzhaki, the great commentator Rashi, was posed this very question. In his response Rashi bases the immutability of one's Jewish identity on a Talmudic passage that states, "although he has sinned he is still a Jew."[222] This passage, according to Rashi, is the basis on which apostate marriages are given the Halakhic import of a Jewish marriage, thereby requiring a proper divorce. Some, while agreeing with Rashi's prooftext, did disqualify apostates from certain rabbinic rituals, notably *yibum* and *halitzah*; based on the more stringent requirements for levirate marriage, namely that that the parties involved must be considered like "brothers."[223] Some opinions argued an apostate could not be considered a brother, but in the case of marriage and in evaluating his underlying Jewish identity they did concur that "although he has sinned he is still a Jew."[224]

The context of the Talmudic passage "although he has sinned he is still a Jew" does raise other difficulties. This phrase appears regarding a little-known biblical personality named Akhan. In the Book of Joshua following the Jewish people's crossing of the Jordan, Joshua declared that God prohibited any Jew to plunder from the spoils of their conquests. In the subsequent battle against the people of Ai, the Jewish people suffered a crushing defeat. Joshua, devastated from the defeat, cried out to God to learn the reason for their loss in battle. God explained that the loss was in retribution for someone within the camp who had violated God's earlier instruction not to take any spoils of war. "Israel has sinned," God explained, "they have also violated my covenant that I have commanded them; they have also taken from consecrated property; they have also stolen; they have also denied; they have also placed it in their vessels." God was not pleased. After casting a divinely inspired lottery, Joshua revealed the culprit: Akhan.

The Talmud focuses on God's response to Joshua, "Israel has sinned," stressing that even though Akhan sinned, he is still described as a part of Israel:

> "Israel has sinned" (Joshua 7:11). R. Abba Bar Zavda said although they have sinned, they are still Israel. R. Abba said this is reminiscent of the adage "A myrtle that stands amongst willows is still called a myrtle and people as well still refer to it as a myrtle." [The Talmud continues to expound the end of the previous verse] "And they also have broken My Covenant which I commanded them, and they also have taken property from the ban, and they also have stolen, and they also have denied, and they also have put into their vessels." R. Illa said in the name of R. Yehudah bar Masapa: This teaches that Akhan transgressed the Five Books of the Torah, for in the verse "also" is written five times.[225]

From the story of Akhan Rashi concluded that future apostates also remain Jewish despite their transgressions. Rashi's textual leap from this Talmudic text, however, was not without its doubters. Jacob Katz in his seminal article on apostasy[226] notes the questionable use of this passage as a source for Rashi's ruling on apostasy. "In its original Talmudic context," Katz notes, "this sentence appears in an aggadic setting only, and not in relation to apostasy."[227] Indeed, Akhan is never accused of converting to another religion. In fact the plain reading of the passages in Joshua only ascribe the more mild offense of stealing from the spoils of war—it is only Rabbi Illa's interpretation that finds Akhan guilty of violating the entire Torah.

Around five hundred years after Rashi's original decision, the marriage of a Marrano couple renewed questions about Rashi's prooftext and the conclusions he reached. In the sixteenth-century Rabbi Samuel de Medina was asked whether the marriage of a Marrano couple who still lived as non-Jews should be considered legitimate according to *Halakhah*. In his response de Medina questions the consensus that had developed for Rashi's approach:

> The entire source that we learn that a Jew still retains his holy identity is derived from the story of Akhan—but in the case of Akhan himself we don't find any sin aside from his transgression of using plundered goods. But with respect to all other commandments, Akhan was kosher! So we can only derive from this story that which is similar to Akhan, namely, someone who only commits one sin.

De Medina continues to dismiss the Talmud's attribution of Akhan's violating the entire Torah to the minority opinion of Rabbi Illa. According to de Medina the only conclusion to be extrapolated is that a Jew who violated an isolated sin is still Jewish. But, suggests de Medina, a Jew who becomes an apostate or violates the entire Torah forfeits their Jewish identity.[228]

The suggestion of de Medina is certainly startling but has some appeal to modern sensibilities. If Jewish identity can be forfeited, it would stand to reason that it also needs to be earned. An immutable religious identity for many sounds too close to a racial theory of Judaism. The possibility of losing one's Jewish identity also emphasizes contemporary notions of free will and choice—our religious identity needs to be personally developed and maintained.

So which is it? De Medina asks some incisive questions on Rashi, but the near unanimous consensus among Halakhists sides with Rashi. While everyone agrees with Rashi's conclusion—once a Jew, always a Jew—almost no one explicitly responds to the issues raised by de Medina. What response, if any, is there to de Medina's objections?

From an early age until his death at the age of ninety-one, Rabbi Moshe Feinstein was considered one of the leading twentieth-century scholars on

Jewish law. He decided *Halakhah* during an exciting time—technology was flourishing and Jews were acclimating to the United States. It was also a contentious time to decide *Halakhah*. The United States, where religious freedom was afforded to all, proved a fertile ground for the flourishing of multiple denominations within Judaism. As Orthodox Judaism struggled to find footing in the New World, Conservative Judaism was quickly embraced as the perfect blend between the innovation of Reform Judaism and the old-world traditions of Orthodoxy. Rabbi Feinstein was sent many questions from members within the Orthodox community regarding the Halakhic legitimacy of Conservative and Reform Jewish practice. His answers drew clear boundaries surrounding the Orthodox community, separating it from the practice of other denominations. Egalitarian prayer, non-Orthodox divorce, and conversion were not in his opinion legitimate practices.

Rabbi Feinstein's decisions, of course, were not motivated by animus or politics but by his nonpartisan approach to Jewish law. His opinions earned him accolades and ire from those on the religious right and left of him. But Rabbi Feinstein, whose Halakhic responsa spans eight volumes, continued to pen incisive Halakhic opinions for nearly his entire life. A *New York Times* profile written during his lifetime begins with the old joke that upon completing rabbinic training, young rabbis receive their ordination and the telephone number of Rabbi Feinstein.[229] Rabbi Feinstein's authority, like most great Halakhic voices through the ages, did not derive from any position or title. "You can't wake up one morning and decide you are an expert on answers," explained Rabbi Feinstein. "If people see that one answer is good and another answer is good, gradually you will be accepted." The Halakhic authority of Rabbi Feinstein emerged by acclamation and reputation. His answers, no matter how difficult or painful, were good.

Though Rabbi Feinstein authored many of the seminal decisions that solidified the Jewish denominational divide, he was also adamant regarding the immutability of our essential Jewish identity. Less than a handful of rabbinic thinkers comprehensively responded to the questions raised by de Medina—Rabbi Feinstein is one notable example. The man who shaped Orthodoxy in America was an equally pivotal figure in ensuring the immutable identity of the Jewish people.[230]

Rabbi Feinstein presents the following theory as to why apostate Jews retain their Jewish identity. Rashi, he explains, never meant to suggest that the story of Akhan was *the* prooftext guaranteeing Jewish identity even for an apostate. The Talmudic phrase "although he has sinned he is still a Jew" is not the source establishing that an apostate Jew remains a Jew—it is just a succint and neat expression of that concept. What Halakhic concept, then, does guarentee the immutability of one's Jewish identity? Rabbi Feinstein proposes a rather simple explanation:

> The reason why the Talmud assumes that an apostate is considered a Jew for all intents and purposes is because it is simply impossible for a Jew to transform into a non-Jew. There is a specific Torah innovation that a non-Jew is able to become a Jew through the formal Halakhic process of conversion, but nowhere in the Torah—not in Scripture and not in any tradition—is there a halakhic concept of a Jew that can transform into a non-Jew. And therefore [an apostate] remains a Jew with a holy Jewish identity for all commandments...[231]

The laws of conversion, aside from detailing the process of entrance into Jewry, also explain why an apostate remains a Jew. If the Torah needs a formal Halakhic process to guide the creation of a Jewish identity, then logic would dictate that a similarly formal process would be needed to dissolve one's Jewish identity as well. From the fact that no such formal Halakhic process exists to announce apostatsy, it stands to reason that even an apostate is recognized as a Jew under Jewish law.

This logic actually informed many apostate Christians looking to reverse the religious affirmation of baptism. Edwin Kagin, one of the leaders of the American Atheist movement, developed a formal ritual for Christians to reverse their baptisms. Wielding a blowdryer, Kagin would symbolically blowdry the liquid remnants of the baptism out of the supplicants' hair.[232] Of course, this was likely intended as pure theatrics, but the underlying motive underscores the logic of Rabbi Feinstein. *Halakhah* is a formal system in which ritual and law govern action and identity. There is no way to blowdry away the process of conversion, so regardless of the beliefs and action of an aposticised Jew—the Jew remains Jewish.[233]

The Apostate's Message

Brother Daniel's legal counsel argued that to deny Brother Daniel his Right of Return to Israel—because of his apostasy—would transform Israel into a theocratic nation. However, his appeal was ultimately rejected by the Supreme Court on those very grounds: Israel is not a theocratic nation.

Under traditional religious rule, the Supreme Court conceded, Brother Daniel was still to be considered a Jew, but it is not religious law that binds Israeli citizens. Brother Daniel was denied the Right of Return because the secular understanding of the word *Jew* is different from its religious connotation. The majority opinion explained:

> The prevalent view in Jewish law is, in my opinion, that an apostate is regarded in law as a Jew in all respects, expect perhaps for a few marginal rules that are of no importance for the question of principle. The term Jew in the Law of Return has a different meaning from that term in the rabbinical courts' jurisdiction law. The latter has a religious sense in the meaning accorded to it by Jewish law, while the former has a secular sense in the meaning of the ordinary usage of men...[234]

It turned out that the distinction between Jewish law and secular law, a distinction for which Brother Daniel's counsel advocated, was precisely what disqualified him. This was not lost on the judges: "The case before us proves this. Had we applied the categories of religious law to the applicant he would have been considered a 'Jew.'"[235]

Brother Daniel, the court concluded, was a Jew—but only according to traditional Jewish law. According to Israeli law, an apostate Jew is no longer Jewish. Legal interpretation, it turned out, was not as flexible as religious identity.

The court's opinion, aside from its crucial implications for legal precedent in Israel, raises important considerations for the boundaries of identity in general. The case recognized that identity, aside from the strict boundaries found in religious law, can be lost. The case also recognized that identity is not always simply a product of personal choice, but the community with which you are identifying plays an important role in shaping the borders of identity.[236] According to the Israeli Supreme Court, an apostate does not define the legal implications of the word *Jew* when the entire community plainly understands otherwise.

A few months after the Brother Daniel decision, Rabbi Aharon Lichtenstein (1933–2015), *Rosh Yeshiva* at Yeshiva University and Yeshivat Har Etzion, wrote a lengthy treatise reflecting on the incident.[237] Rabbi Lichtenstein presents a fascinating analogy to understand the nature of an apostate's Jewish identity. Apostates, he explains, can be likened to the Land of Israel. The holiness of Israel derives from the formal settlement of the Jewish people. But prior to the formal settlement of Israel, were those lands to be considered completely mundane—no different in Jewish sanctity than Quebec or Newfoundland? Of course not. Although the formal settlement of the land of Israel is necessary to endow the land with its holiness, even absent such a ritual the land still remains unique—at the very least it retains the capacity for holiness. The ritual of settlement endows the land of Israel with holiness, but there is an essential designation of that land as Israel that is immutable—even absent any ritual act to endow holiness.

The same is true for the apostate. Rabbi Lichtenstein explains:

> I think a similar distinction should be established with reference to an apostate. If we ask, in purely descriptive terms, whether anyone born of Jewish parents is a Jew, the answer must be—yes. As an epithet, it remains applicable to any individual who was ever endowed with Jewish status— even to a *meshumad*. Hence, he is obligated to pursue a Torah life and, should he decide to return, he would perhaps require no new conversion. However, if we ask whether a *meshumad* has anything of Jewish personality and character and whether, therefore, he continues to be endowed with the personal status of a Jew, the answer is a ringing no. He remains a Jew without Jewishness. What he retains is simply the descriptive epithet—*shem yisrel*. Of *kedushat* Israel, however, of sacredness of the Jewish personality, that which essentially constitutes being a Jew—he is bereft.

The apostate, like the Land of Israel before Jewish settlement, preserves Jewishness *in potentia*. A Jew can never become like Canada—even the settlement of the entire Jewish people there would not endow it with the holiness of Israel. But the apostate is also not the settled land of Israel. He is a blank page bereft of a narrative. Only through settlement into the collective history and commandedness of peoplehood can the apostate's holy Jewish identity be restored.

Much has been learned from the plight of Brother Daniel, but what can we learn from Akhan, the prototype of apostasy? Akhan's story, according to Rabbi Feinstein at least, may not be the actual legal proof text for the immutability of Jewish identity, but it is still the place where the Talmud felt most appropriate to canonize this message. Why Akhan, though? Why did this seemingly insignificant sinner become the narrative anchor for the adage "although he has sinned he is still a Jew"?

Normally, Talmudic hermeneutics avoid attributing sin unnecessarily to biblical figures. Aside from one exception, the Talmud (*Sanhedrin* 106b) explains, you should not negatively interpret verses about anyone except for

Balaam. Curiously, however, Akhan seems to be a major exception to this rule invoking a veritable Talmudic pile-on. It wasn't just the spoils of war, interprets the Talmud; he also violated the entire Torah. What message did the Talmud hope to impart by establishing his story as the model for the immutability of Jewish identity?

Rabbi Zadok of Lublin has a counterintuitive approach to the Talmud's presentation of Akhan.[238] A plain reading of the story of Akhan does not yield the dastardly deeds that the Talmud later ascribes to him. The Talmud, however, was not interpreting his narrative negatively but in fact was implying a message of consolation within the concept of apostasy. The Talmud heaped upon Akhan seemingly unnecessary sins not as a sign of negativity for him but as a symbol of optimism for the Jewish people. Once God referred to Akhan as "Yisrael" even following his sin, the Talmud wanted to emphasize the lengths to which the immutability of Jewish identity is applicable. Each sin the Talmud ascribed to Akhan effectively extended the boundaries of the possibility for Jewish redemption. The further from God the Talmud described Akhan, the closer it allowed future generations to feel—regardless of their sins. If Akhan, given the litany of sins attributed to him, could still be described by God as one of "Israel," there was a measure of optimism for future sinners as well. The Talmud was not casting out Akhan but rather extending the strength and boundaries of Jewish identity. Akhan was not just the prototype for apostasy; he was also the prototype for the resilience of Jewish identity.

Some scholars attribute the second paragraph of the prayer *Aleinu* to Akhan.[239] Beginning "*Al Ken Nekavah*"—"Therefore we hope"—the paragraph describes the anticipation and longing for a future redemption. The first three letters of that prayer, *Al Ken Nekavah*, spell Akhan. Apostasy is destructive, but it is also a reminder of our individual resilience. So long as our Jewish identity can never be eradicated, there is always cause to anticipate a future redemption. True, as the decision in the Brother Daniel case reminded, "experience teaches us that apostates are destined to be cut off completely from the nation's family tree."[240] But that likely outcome does not prevent optimistic anticipation so long as it is not realized. The apostate, aside from representing the worst of Jewish decisions, is also a reminder for the best of Jewish hope. If there did indeed exist a boundary from which we could never return, beyond that point any longing would be futile. But the apostate reminds us that wherever we may find ourselves, there is also a way back. No matter how far we drift, there is always reason, however small, to anticipate a return.

8

WHEN LEADERS FAIL

All men have stars, but they are not the same things for different people. For some, who are travelers, the stars are guides. For others they are no more than little lights in the sky. For others, who are scholars, they are problems . . .

— **Antoine de Saint-Exupéry,** *The Little Prince*

Religious Oppression and the Grand Inquisition

One of the most profound discussions of religion in literary history is presented as a story inside of a story. In Dostoevsky's *The Brothers Karamazov* a poetic story known as "The Grand Inquisitor" is retold that imagines the return of Jesus to earth during the fifteenth-century Spanish Inquisition. The story, which is told by the religious skeptic and pessimist Ivan to his brother Alyosha, an aspiring priest, left a lasting impression on religious discourse. Elie Wiesel once told his class that if he could take only one piece of literature on a desert island it would be this story. (He quickly corrected himself, adding that this would be the case so long as a Talmud and *siddur* were already present on the island as well).[241] Essentially, the story presents Jesus' imagined return to the streets of Seville in Spain, where he is initially adored and followed by the local Christian community. Shortly afterwards, however, Jesus is locked up by the leadership of the Inquisition. Of course, this is a puzzling development. Why would members of the Inquisition, a movement that was established to combat Christian heresy, imprison their savior? As Jesus lies in prison he is visited by the Grand Inquisitor, the chief Church leader of the Inquisition. The Grand Inquisitor explains in a stunning revelation why the Church officials decided to detain Jesus and sentence him to death. He tells Jesus:

> Perhaps it is Thy will to hear it from my lips. Listen, then. We are not working with Thee, but with him—that is our mystery.

The Church, the Grand Inquisitor explains to Jesus, is not working for the sake of God but has sided with the devil. Mankind would not benefit from the freedom Jesus offered. Rather, mankind would have more to gain from the ignorant bliss of a dictatorial Church leadership in league with Satan.

Usually, this story within a story is used as a lens to discuss the religious philosophy of freedom and free will. The Grand Inquisitor also provides another moral. It is a poetic depiction of the capacity of a messenger to betray the values of the message. A Church in league with the devil to protect mankind is the ultimate betrayal of religious responsibility. Christian leaders should ostensibly have allegiance to Jesus. Instead, they decided that they understood what mankind needs better. The leaders betrayed their founding values and more importantly, the trust of their followers. It is a cautionary tale of failed religious leadership.

Unfortunately, unsavory religious leadership is not just the purview of nineteenth-century novelists. Over the years, many religious leaders—rabbis, priests, imams—have breached the trust of their congregants. Sometimes, like the Grand Inquisitor, it is because they think they know better. Religious authority can intoxicate the judgment of leaders, especially when they see themselves as the sole arbiters of authenticity. Other times partnership with the devil comes in more subtle ways. Religious leaders are as subject to human temptations and error as any other religious practitioner. The stakes, however, of religious failure are much higher for religious leaders. In the wake of religious leadership it is not just the soul of the leader that is at stake—their followers can suffer even greater losses. Betrayed religious trust is hard to ever heal. What is a religious community to do when they discover that their leader was not "working with Thee, but with him"? What happens when leaders fail?

Learning from Broken Vessels

Jewish leaders who fail are as old as the Bible. When enumerating the different sin offerings, each offering is prefaced with the qualifier "if." *If* a Kohen sins, *if* the Jewish people sin. Except one: The leader's sacrifice.[242] When presenting the possibility of a leader's bringing a sin offering, the Torah writes "[w]hen a leader sins,"—not "if" a leader sins. To some degree failure is an inevitable component of leadership.[243] Aspirational leaders will always fall short of ideals. There will almost always be stumbling as the vanguard steers its constituents to higher ground. Nearly every major biblical figure committed some serious sin or had some serious failure. Avraham was criticized for lying. Moshe hit the rock. David saw Batsheva.

Still, there has been a reticence in rabbinic thought to ascribe sins or imperfections to biblical characters. Part of the traditional rabbinic conception of biblical leaders is their seemingly unreachable greatness. Certainly, educators of young children normally present stories that emphasize the near infallibility of biblical characters. Writing to a group of Jewish educators, Rabbi Jacob J. Schacter posed the following questions regarding ascribing failures to biblical characters:

> Is it now appropriate to ascribe whatever "faults, errors and weaknesses" we want to the patriarchs? Is there a line to be drawn beyond which such ascriptions are inappropriate? Where do we draw the line? ...Clearly we assert, and to my mind must genuinely believe, that they are just not like "you and me;" indeed, they are much, much greater, an entirely different dimension of being. In the words of Gary Kamiya, "To feel the pedestal is to call the very idea of the pedestal into question."[244]

Over the years, educators have given different answers to these questions. Dr. Zev Eleff in his article "Psychohistory and the Imaginary Couch: Diagnosing Historical Biblical Figures" recounts some of the more sensational polemics associated with some of the questionable character analyses of biblical characters within the Orthodox world.[245] He rightfully concludes that such character scrutiny "cut at the very core of Orthodox values and its historical memory." Aside from Orthodox values, such inquiry may also tug at our conceptions of leadership. Do we fashion our conception of religious leadership from the same psychological materials, replete with all of its imperfections and deficiencies, from which we develop our own self-conceptions? Or do religious leaders perhaps emerge from a more refined place? One Talmudic approach sets a high bar.

Rabbis should be like angels. Based on the verse in Malakhi (2:7) that states, "For the priest's lips should keep knowledge, and they should seek Torah at his mouth; for he is a messenger [malakh] of the Lord of hosts," the Talmud states, "If the teacher is similar to an angel [malakh] of the Lord, seek Torah from his mouth, and if not, then do not seek Torah from his mouth."[246] The standard for studying Torah from a Rabbi, then, is that his conduct should be comparable to that of an angel. Conversely, a rabbi who is not comparable to an angel should not be teaching. This Talmudic ruling is codified in Jewish law.[247]

Why angels? It is somewhat unusual that the standard for a proper rabbinic role is couched in the term angel [*malakh*]. Judaism does not normally regard angelic status as something that should be emulated. Sometimes man is considered even more elevated than an angel.[248] Perhaps in this context the term *malakh* is not used just to evoke the purity and righteousness of "angels" but, more importantly, their loyalty to their mission. The term *malakh* derives from the same Hebrew verb meaning to send on a mission.[249] The angel is the ultimate messenger. Many opinions, notably Maimonides, contend that an angel does not even have the capacity to alter its mission.[250] The messenger remains synonymous with the message. Unlike the Grand Inquisitor, angels cannot betray the faith of their constituents. No matter what a rabbi's personal questions or objections may be, a true teacher has fealty to the message. Such is the model of rabbinic leadership.

Historically, many non-angelic rabbis have emerged in the Jewish community. There have been a host of lines drawn to assess whether the teaching of such rabbinic leaders can still remain within the boundaries of the traditional Jewish community. Some consideration is given to the type of infractions committed by the rabbi and, notably, many consider making distinctions in the medium of the message—namely are the teachings of the disgraced rabbi written or oral? The aforementioned verse specifically notes that an angelic personality is needed to "seek Torah from his mouth." Perhaps, some suggest, a written relationship is still sustainable.[251] The greatest challenge, however, to the angelic standards of rabbinic leadership was a Mishnaic figure named Elisha ben Avuyah. He was a rebellious rabbi who embodied the prototypical sinful leader in rabbinic literature. He was unambiguously non-angelic, to the point where the Talmud asks how his student, Rabbi Meir, could even learn from him following his spiritual downfall. The Talmud insists that Rabbi Meir was the exception, given his ability to focus only on the proper parts of Elisha ben Avuyah's teachings and discard the rest.[252] For all other intents and purposes Elisha ben Avuyah was excised from the boundaries of the rabbinic community. In fact, he is no longer referred to by his name in Talmudic literature. He is simply called *Aher*—the Other.

Except the Other or Accept the Other?

There is little uniformity in the tale of how Elisha ben Avuyah became *Aher*, the Other. Several different accounts of the genesis of his heresy exist.

Some of the episodes contradict each other; many can be read as complementary. Yet however they are read, the story of *Aher* has captured both scholarly and popular imaginations. Perhaps most famously in the fictionalized account in Milton Steinberg's *As a Driven Leaf*, the story of *Aher* has become the central Talmudic case study in failed rabbinic personalities.[253] Given the vast amount of scholarship dedicated to the life of *Aher*, one scholar described offering his own interpretation as "daring to enter the *pardes* of Talmudic scholarship"—the very undertaking, as we shall see, that doomed *Aher*.[254] Still, into *pardes* we must veer. And hopefully, unlike *Aher* we will emerge unscathed.

Elisha ben Avuyah lived in second-century Jerusalem around the time of the destruction of the second Temple. Both the Babylonian and the Jerusalem Talmud use a story from the middle of his life as a narrative point of departure.[255] They offer differing accounts of what precedes and what follows this incident but establish the same middle point—the entrance into *pardes*. Four rabbis, we are told, enter *pardes* [פרדס], literally translated as a garden. This, of course, was not any garden. It is either an allusion to a mystical vision or to mystical study.[256] Once the quartet enter, each rabbi reacts differently. Ben Azzai glimpses and dies. Ben Zoma glimpses and gets injured. *Aher* gazes and uproots the sprouts. Rabbi Akiva exits safely. Interestingly, only Rabbi Akiva is identified by his name in this passage. The other three figures have already lost their names. Elisha became *Aher*.[257]

What does it mean that *Aher* "uprooted the sprouts"? The Jerusalem Talmud presents a few narrative explanations. In one passage it refers to *Aher's* murdering young students of Torah. Another explanation offered is that *Aher* steered young students away from Torah study. In the Babylonian Talmud *Aher's* uprooting is read more literally. During a rendezvous with a prostitute, in order to prove he was not the famed rabbinic figure, he uprooted radish saplings on Shabbat. Based on his open violation of Shabbat, the prostitute surmised, "You must indeed be another (*aher*)."[258]

Similarly, the Babylonian and Jerusalem Talmud differ in their accounts of what precedes the story of *pardes*. In the Jerusalem Talmud the seeds of *Aher's* heresy are planted either through early questions he had with theodicy or, alternatively, they already existed in the womb—a product of his mother's inhaling the spiritually poisonous fumes from a house of idolatry.[259] Jeffrey Rubinstein explains that both of these explanations play important theological roles; the Talmud is trying to account for how such a serious Torah scholar could become so mired in sin. He writes:

The sustained interest in the provenance of Elisha's sin and the multiple explanations provided are attempts to account for such a figure. The focus on the father (and/or mother) as sources of Elisha's unfortunate fate is an effective strategy. Attributing the cause of Elisha's sin to circumstances prior to his birth and out of his control makes it easier to accept that a sage could go astray. His sin was not only fated, but the Torah he learned was tainted *ab initio* and could not protect him from error. Combine these factors with the eternally difficult question of theodicy and one has a plausible account of the making of a sinning sage.[260]

Each of these accounts are attempts to reconcile the coexistence of sin and Torah in one individual. If *Aher*'s sin is predetermined, maybe the normal trajectory for someone immersed in Torah is divinely warped as well.

Aher does little better in the Babylonian Talmud's presentation of his history. That narrative attributes the roots of *Aher*'s heresy to a divine vision he had while in *pardes*.[261] *Aher* sees the angel Metatron sitting and writing the merits of the Jewish people. Normally such an activity would be reserved only for God, but unbeknownst to *Aher*, Metatron was given divine permission to partake in that activity. Assuming that God no longer had exclusive control of heaven, *Aher* becomes a heretic. Unlike the version in the Jerusalem Talmud, the Babylonian Talmud does not include elements of theodicy or parental predetermination. Here *Aher*'s heresy is the result of a misunderstanding of the role of the angel Metatron in his divine vision. Still, a glaring emphasis is missing, namely choice. Both versions of *Aher*'s heresy dull the role of choice and free will in the narrative of his descent.[262] The Talmudic texts seem unwilling to consider that a scholar of such renown could simply choose heresy and resolve never to repent. Instead, the arc of *Aher*'s narrative is already curved towards sin.

Nevertheless, following *Aher*'s heresy he remains in touch with his student Rabbi Meir. In one story found in the Jerusalem Talmud, *Aher* rides on a horse on Shabbat, a prohibited act, as he speaks to Rabbi Meir. Together they discuss the book of Job. Rabbi Meir cites Job 42:12, "The Lord blessed the latter days of Job's life more than the beginning." Rabbi Meir understands the verse to mean that God doubled Job's money. *Aher*, citing Rabbi Akiva, counters with a more profound explanation:

Alas for things lost and not found. Akiva your master did not expound it like that. Rather, 'The Lord blessed the latter days of Job's life more than the beginning'—on account of the mitzvoth and good deeds that he had done from the beginning.

Several other exegetical exchanges are recorded, each of which serves a dual purpose, as Rubinstein notes. First, all vignettes establish *Aher* as a superior and creative Torah scholar whose scholarship remained intact even after his heresy. Second, Rabbi Meir and *Aher*'s discussion of Job intentionally parallel *Aher*'s own odyssey. Both Job and *Aher* were wealthy: Job, materially; *Aher*, spiritually. Each eventually becomes impoverished from his respective wealth.[263]

In the version in the Babylonian Talmud a different form of exegetical dialogue appears as well.[264] Rabbi Meir drags *Aher* to the study hall and asks a child to recite the verse he is learning that day. This is a somewhat common form of divination that appears throughout the Talmud. Following the cessation of prophecy, a way of conjuring divine guidance was through listening to the implications of a random verse cited by a child.[265] Rabbi Meir, clearly hoping for a promising answer, visits thirteen houses of study. Each time the child responds with a foreboding verse. The final child in the thirteenth house cites the most troubling passage. The Talmud writes:

> At the last one, he said to him: Recite your verse to me. He recited to him: "[a]nd to the wicked [*ve-larasha*] God says, what is it for you to declare My statutes" (Psalms 50:16). That child had a stutter, so it sounded as though he were saying to him: *Ve-le'elisha* (i.e. and to Elisha) God says.

Aside from the ominous exegetical signs appearing before *Aher*, both the Babylonian and Jerusalem Talmud feature an even more hostile testament to *Aher*'s condemnation: a heavenly voice. At some point in each Talmudic narrative *Aher* relates that he heard a *bat kol*, a heavenly voice, declare, "Return rebellious children (Jeremiah 3:22)—except *Aher*." His fate, it would seem, had already been sealed. *Aher*'s exit left no invitation to return.

Now would be an important time to emphasize that I have not presented the *Aher* narrative in its entirety, nor have I presented all of the nuanced differences in text and structure within the different retellings. There are already scholars far greater than I, most notably Rubinstein, who have presented a clear structural breakdown and analysis of these texts. I have only given abbreviated highlights of some of the key moments from

Aher's life distilled in rabbinic texts. Instead I would like to narrow my focus to consider *Aher* as the prototype for the failed rabbinic leader. What can the story of *Aher* tell us about failed leaders?

Aher is convinced that he is hopeless. A cursory reading would suggest that he has good reason to believe so. No less than a voice from heaven proclaims him irredeemable. Each child in the study hall quotes a verse pointing towards his bleak fate. Everyone has hope except him. But what if *Aher* only hears what he wants to hear? Neither heavenly voices nor exegetical divination provide definitive judgement. Both in fact were interpretive frameworks employed primarily following the cessation of prophecy. Once God's explicit voice ceased, these were ways to reconstruct His message through interpretive devices. Normally, at least in the context of Jewish law, such divinations are to be ignored. Jay Rover alludes to this point as well:

> [Aher] is far too easily discouraged by the declaration of his doom. Instead of calling the heavenly bluff by repenting, Elisha becomes Aher, an apostate incapable of entertaining the possibility of doing so. True, the evil decree was confirmed by a *bat kol*, but the Bavli elsewhere affirms that *ein mashgihim be'vat kol* ("We do not regard a *bat kol* as authoritative").[266]

Aside from Rovner's correct contention that heavenly voices are normally ignored, their meaning is very much a product of the recipient's interpretation. Heavenly voices are a reflection of the inner construct and interpretive lens of the listener. *Aher* doesn't become hopeless because he heard a heavenly voice; his hopelessness is the filter through which he hears all heavenly messages. Rovner assumes the voice and the bibliomancy are legitimate, but he also acknowledges that *Aher*'s reaction is a product of his inner world. Discussing the narrative strategy of the Talmudic redactor, he writes:

> Not only has he (i.e. the Talmudic redactor) recreated Elisha as a sympathetic character whose apostasy resulted from an innocent mistake, but he has located the problem in part in Elisha's personality: certain character issues contributed to the latter's unfortunate decision to accept the *bat kol*'s decree and embark on a life of sin thereby sealing his fate.[267]

Heaven does not reject *Aher*; Elisha ben Avuyah rejects *Aher*. He could not reconcile his Torah with the direction of his life. He therefore begins to interpret all Torah and divinity as pointing him in the direction away from God. Rubinstein addresses this point as well:

> Elisha's interpretation and self-exemplification amount to a pessimistic
> fatalism; what was bad from the beginning turns out bad in the end. So,
> there is no "return" for him, no way to remedy the loss of faith, of merit and
> of opportunity to repent.[268]

At the core of *Aher*'s failure is theological cynicism and pessimistic fatal-
ism. Everything he sees points him in the wrong direction. His loss of faith
in God is intertwined with the loss of faith in himself. *Aher*—the Other—is
in many ways what he condemns himself to be.

Optimistic Leadership

In the damp prison cell, the Grand Inquisitor explains to Jesus why they
have obscured his work and replaced it with the Church's authoritative
religious structure. The Grand Inquisitor did not have faith in the people's
ability to make the right choices. His words:

> But what about the rest? Why should the rest of mankind, the weak ones,
> suffer because they are unable to stand what the strong ones can? Why is
> it the fault of a weak soul if he cannot live up to such terrifying gifts? Can
> it really be true that You came only for the chosen few? If that is so, it is a
> mystery that we cannot understand; and if it is a mystery, we have the right
> to preach to man that what matters is not freedom of choice or love, but a
> mystery that he must worship blindly, even at the expense of his conscience.
> And that is exactly what we have done. We have corrected Your work and
> have now founded it on miracle, mystery, and authority. And men rejoice
> at being led like cattle again, with the terrible gift of freedom that brought
> them so much suffering removed from them.

Much like the story of *Aher*, pessimism underlies the perspective of the
Grand Inquisitor. *Aher* suffered from his own self-contempt, the Grand
Inquisitor from cynical contempt for man's capacity for choice and change.
Both religious leaders allow their fatalistic negativity to coopt the opportu-
nity to alter a perceived religious destiny.

If *Aher* is the quintessential failed religious leader, his foil is Rabbi
Akiva, who entered *pardes* and emerged complete. *Aher*, to paraphrase
Churchill, saw the difficulty in every opportunity while Rabbi Akiva saw
the opportunity in every difficulty. Throughout *Aher*'s dialogue with Rabbi
Meir, Akiva's exegetical perspective suggests indefatigable opportunity.

Rabbi Akiva's own outlook on life was optimistic. *Aher* began a scholar and ended a heretic, while Akiva began his life antagonistic of rabbinic authority and ended his life a scholar.[269] Akiva, even as the second Temple was aflame, managed to find reason for positivity. While others were crying destruction, Akiva found reason for laughter. In this oft-cited Talmudic story, Akiva's colleagues respond to him, "Akiva, you have comforted us, Akiva you have comforted us."[270] *Aher* the unrelenting pessimist saw closed doors even when there was still hope of an entrance. Akiva found reason for comfort even when all entrances seemed obstructed.

Tractate *Yoma* (39b) retells the story of the death of Shimon Ha-Tzadik, one of the most celebrated High Priests in Jewish history. In the last year of his life Shimon Ha-Tzadik gathered all his students and told them he was going to die. How did he know? He explained to them that each year on the holiest day of the year, Yom Kippur, in the holiest place in the world, the Holy of Holies, he had a vision. When Shimon was alone inside the Holy of Holies, he met an old man who was dressed in white and wrapped in all white garments. This man would enter with Shimon and exit with him. This year, however, he saw someone else. Shimon saw a man dressed all in black. The man entered with Shimon but did not exit with him. And as Shimon predicted, he died a few weeks after Yom Kippur. Of course, the glaring question is who was the man he envisioned appearing in the Holy of Holies? I once heard a moving suggestion that encapsulates much of our discussion of leaders—both successful and failed.[271] The man whom Shimon saw was the *Saba Kaddisha* [סבא קדישא] of the Jewish people—the manifestation of how Shimon Ha-Tzadik viewed the Jewish people. As long as Shimon's vision was of the congregation dressed in white—optimistic, ambitious, and open to opportunity—he knew he still had a future as a leader of these people. However, once his representation of the Jewish people was dressed in all black—pessimistic, cynical, and negative—he knew his time as a leader was expiring.

A leader's success or failure is very often a reflection of that person's own self-image and image of their followers. Aspirational leaders see the best in themselves and insist on the same for their constituents. Cynical leaders project the same negativity and hopelessness they see in themselves in those they serve as well. To estimate a leader's success, find out how they look at themselves and their followers.

9

AN ALCOHOLIC WALKS INTO A BAR: PUTTING YOURSELF IN SIN'S PATH

"I will have no man in my boat," said Starbuck, "who is not afraid of a whale."
By this, he seemed to mean, not only that the most reliable and useful courage
was that which arises from the fair estimation of the encountered peril, but that
an utterly fearless man is a far more dangerous comrade than a coward.

—**Herman Melville,** *Moby Dick*

Who Should Bartend?

Alcoholics are not great bartenders. Sure, they know the product—but far too intimately. Whether a *recovered* alcoholic would make a good bartender is a much more hotly contested question. A 2009 *New York Times* profile highlighted the challenges for recovered alcoholics who serve as bartenders.[272] The article presents two approaches for bartenders struggling with sobriety. The first is championed by the story of Del Pedro, a recovered alcoholic with fifteen years of sobriety. Del Pedro doesn't drink at all socially but allows himself once a week carefully to taste new drinks he has concocted. He admits his profession does not make sobriety easy and, according to the standards of Alcoholics Anonymous, he is not even technically sober. Mr. Pedro compares himself to a vegan chef who has to eat pork but quickly adds that the comparison isn't perfect—"People don't lose everything because they eat too much pork." At the other end of the spectrum is Liz Scott, a former chef for Brooke Astor who, following a near-fatal car accident, has been sober for ten years. Her approach, which she relayed in a lecture at the Culinary Institute, is drastically different. For Ms. Scott abstinence from alcohol must be absolute. She uses substitutes for recipes that require alcohol, much as you would prepare a meal for someone who keeps kosher or who has an allergy. The approaches of Mr. Pedro and Ms. Scott, as well as everything in between, certainly have merit, but they raise important questions about how people should relate to the areas of weakness in their lives. What is the authentic sign of vanquishing a vice—complete avoidance or the ability to abstain even in its presence?

The famed *Big Book*, which has guided the practices and policy of Alcoholics Anonymous for nearly eighty years, takes a moderate approach to this issue:

> In our belief any scheme of combating alcoholism which proposes to shield the sick man from temptation is doomed to failure. If the alcoholic tries to shield himself he may succeed for a time, but he usually winds up with a bigger explosion than ever. We have tried these methods. These attempts to do the impossible have always failed.
>
> So our rule is not to avoid a place where there is drinking, if we have a legitimate reason for being there. That includes bars, nightclubs, dances, receptions, weddings, even plain ordinary whoopee parties. To a person who has had experience with an alcoholic this may seem like tempting Providence, but it isn't . . . But be sure you are on solid spiritual ground before you start and that your motive in going is thoroughly good.

It is not entirely clear what constitutes a "legitimate reason." Should an alcoholic walk into a bar just to test his fortitude? The answer to this question is central to overcoming all weaknesses, including religious. Much like the differing approaches alcoholics take for their sobriety, struggling with sin presents a similar set of dilemmas. What is the correct approach to surmounting our spiritual vices? The answer, much like the question of the alcoholic, has spurred spirited debate among rabbinic scholars.

Same Time, Same Place

When is someone ever properly rehabilitated from sin? The Talmud (*Yoma* 86) cites the opinion of Rav Yehudah who says that a person is not considered completely rehabilitated from sin until two opportunities to sin again present themselves and sin is avoided each time. What qualifies as an opportunity to sin? Rav Yehudah follows up his statement with a startling qualification: "The same woman, the same time, the same place." It seems Rav Yehudah insists that in order to be considered truly rehabilitated, the alcoholic must revisit the proverbial bar. Maimonides adopts the plain reading of this passage as well.[273] According to Maimonides complete repentance requires a sinner to be placed in the same exact situation as the original sin and leave spiritually unscathed.

Some, however, rightfully pointed out that such a literal interpretation of this passage could be dangerous. The Hasidei Ashkenaz had many radical ideas regarding repentance.[274] One distinctive feature of their thought was the doctrine of *Teshuvah Ha-Ba'ah* [תשובה הבאה], meaning repentance that denies succumbing to sin even when given the opportunity. This form of repentance, which is based on the aforementioned passage in *Yoma*, figures prominently into the school of thought of the Hasidei Ashkenaz. While this form of repentance is lauded, they caution that it cannot be arranged voluntarily, meaning alcoholics would be decidedly prohibited from voluntary entering a bar to prove their resolve. Engineering opportunities to resist temptation was simply considered too risky, however valuable *Teshuvah Ha-Ba'ah* may be.[275] Given the danger of entering such situations, Hasidei Ashkenaz noted that *Teshuva Ha-Ba'ah* was not frequently realized.[276]

Interestingly regarding the system of penance employed by the Hasidei Ashkenaz, some scholars speculate whether the notion of *Teshuvah Ha-Ba'ah* has some Christian parallels. Much like Hasidei Ashkenaz, Christian scholars living in the same area in Europe also cautioned priests from arousing their temptations even for the sake of repentance. Fishman notes, "A work composed by a Christian cleric who lived closer to the locale of Hasidei Ashkenaz contains another condemnatory allusion to the attempt to promote spiritual progress by arousing and withstanding temptations of the flesh."[277] It is hard to say definitively which work, if any, was influencing which. Of course, in any system prizing religious purity extremes of self-discipline are bound to be explored. As Rubin mentions in his study on repentance in the world of Hasidei Ashkenaz, "Wherever the duty of resisting temptation to sin was placed in the forefront of religious practice, as it was among monks and priests, there was bound to occur certain radical elements who carried the practice to extremes."[278]

Rabbi Nahman and Rabbi Zadok Struggle with Struggle

The Hasidic leaders Rabbi Nahman of Bratslav (1772–1810) and Rabbi Zadok of Lublin (1823–1900) both stand out as iconoclasts even within the revolutionary world of Hasidut. Both were associated with persecuted Hasidic sects and their respective works confront some of the most controversial aspects of Hasidic theology, such as redemptive sin, sexuality, and Maimonidean controversy. Although they lived a generation apart, Rabbi Zadok, who became Hasidic later in life, was clearly influenced by Rabbi Nahman's works. Rabbi Zadok even annotated Rabbi Nahman's *Sefer ha-Midot*, a book of rabbinic aphorisms. The area of Hasidic thought where Rabbi Nahman's influence is most apparent in Rabbi Zadok's work is their approach to religious resilience even in the face of despair.[279] However, as we shall see, their respective approaches to the religious value of religious struggle also highlight an area where Rabbi Zadok clearly departed from the influence of Rabbi Nahman.

One of the most pervasive themes in Bratslav Hasidut is the exhortation never to give up hope and never to despair. In what has now become a slogan among contemporary Bratslav Hasidim, Rabbi Nahman famously declared, "There is absolutely no despair in the world whatsoever."[280] Though the actual passage citing this phrase in Rabbi Nahman's work *Likutei Moharan* is quite brief, it clearly played a defining role in general Bratslav theology.[281] The passage reads:

והעיקר לחזק עצמו בכל מה שאפשר [כי אין שום יאוש בעולם כלל. (ואמר אז בזה הלשון:
קיין יאוש איז גאר ניט פאר האנדין), ומשך מאד אלו התבות קיין יאוש וכו' ואמרם בכח גדול
ובעמקות נפלא ונורא מאד כדי להורות ולרמז לכל אחד ואחד לדורות שלא יתיאש בשום אופן
בעולם אפילו אם עבר עליו מה] ואיך שהוא אפילו אם נפל למקום שנפל רחמנא ליצלן מאחר
שמחזק עצמו במה שהוא עדיין יש לו תקוה לשוב ולחזור אליו יתברך.[282]

And the core idea is to strengthen oneself however possible; for there is absolutely no despair in the world whatsoever. And this he explained in the following language *"keyn ye'ush iz guer nit fahr hondin,"* and he prolonged the (pronunciation of the) words *"keyn ye'ush..."* and he said them with great strength and wondrous depth and awesomeness in order to indicate and allude to each and every one, for all generations, that he should not despair whatever the case may be, no matter what has transpired to him and his current state. Even if he has fallen to the place where he has fallen, God forbid, once he can strengthen himself to whatever degree, there is still hope for him to return and to have the Blessed One returned to him.[283]

The phraseology in Rabbi Zadok's work is nearly identical. He writes:

אין ליהודי להתייאש משום דבר, בין בעניני הגוף כמו שאמרו (ברכות י' סוף ע''א) אפילו
חרב חדה על צוארו אל ימנע מהרחמים, בין בעניני הנפש אפילו נשתקע למקום שנשתקע
וחטא בדבר שאמרו ז''ל (זוה''ק ח''א רי''ט ב) שאין תשובה מועלת חס ושלום, או שתשובתו
קשה, או שרואה עצמו משתקע והולך בעניני עולם הזה, אל יתייאש בעצמו לומר שלא יוכל
לפרוש עוד, כי אין יאוש כלל אצל איש יהודי, והשם יתברך יכול לעזור בכל ענין.

A Jew should never despair for any reason. Whether in matter of physical
well-being, of which it is said, "Even if a sharpened sword is on your neck
to not withhold yourself from seeking mercy," (*Berakhot* 10a) or in matter
of spiritual well-being—even if you have entrenched to the place where you
have been entrenched and you have sinned in a matter of which it is said
(*Zohar* 1:219:2) that repentance will not help, God forbid, or that repentance
is exceedingly difficult, or you see that you have fallen and become absorbed
in mundane matters, regardless, never despair on yourself and say that you
will not be able to separate (from sin) any longer. Because there is no despair
at all for a Jewish man and God can help him in any circumstance.[284]

Nahman's ability to address the most downtrodden and forlorn Jews
influenced Rabbi Zadok's ideas and terminology. The term "there is absolutely no despair in the world" trickled into Rabbi Zadok's works; more
generally, Reb Zadok adopted Bratslav's radical Hasidic optimism even
when confronting religious desolation. In fact Shilo Pachter, in his invaluable dissertation regarding the prohibition of masturbation, singles out
Rabbi Nahman and Rabbi Zadok as the embodiments for what he calls,
"Encouragement and Comfort in the Hasidic View."[285]

Even on a personal level, both Rabbi Nahman and Rabbi Zadok identified with the religious value inherent in failure. As a child Rabbi Nahman
already struggled with the pains of religious frustration and spiritual
absence, as Rabbi Nathan, Rabbi Nahman's most prominent disciple,
describes in his biography of his teacher:

He would often speak to God in heartfelt supplication and pleas . . . but
nevertheless he felt he wasn't being noticed or heard at all. On the contrary,
it seemed to him that he was pushed away from the service of God in all
kinds of ways, as though he were utterly unwanted. Days and years passed
by, and still he was far from Him; he had not attained any sense of nearness
at all. . . . At times he would become depressed, he would say that despite his

begging and pleading to draw near to God's service, no attention was being
paid to him at all.[286]

The spiritual angst and heartrending emotion pervading Rabbi Nahman's
writing is a hallmark of Bratslav thought. Green notes this as a difficulty in
studying and systematically analyzing Rabbi Nahman's work.

> When Nahman says that "everyman is filled with suffering," Nathan
> reminds us that Nahman himself was pained greater than that of any other
> man. When Nahman speaks of the great distance from God that the man
> of faith may feel at certain times, we cannot but recall those passages in
> Nathan's biographies which speak of Nahman's own awareness of the gulf
> between himself and God. While Nahman never speaks in the first person
> in the *Liqqutim* themselves, it is quite clear that a great many passages in
> them cannot be understood except as oblique references to his own spiritual
> situation. In this way he is unique among Hasidic authors. The homilies of
> most Hasidic masters are largely impersonal in character; indeed, there is
> sometimes little in either style or content to distinguish the teachings of one
> zaddiq from those of another. Nahman's teachings, on the other hand, are
> always recognizable by their highly personal mythology . . . [287]

The struggles and oddities of Rabbi Nahman's life are intertwined with his
works and theology, as is evident in countless examples.[288] It was a crucial
part of Rabbi Nahman's theology that one's personal life circumstances
must be actively incorporated and synthesized into the greater body of
one's scholarly works. A common refrain in Rabbi Nahman's work is the
power of failure and struggle to enrich and empower an individual.[289]

In fact, an entire chapter in Rabbi Nathan's biography on Rabbi Nahman
is dedicated to Rabbi Nahman's spiritual struggles.[290] These stories are quite
atypical for a Hasidic work, which usually tend to focus on the miracle working and piety of the Hasidic leader. The legacy Rabbi Nahman hoped to
impart was not one of inborn piety but rather of spiritual torment and struggle that ultimately nurtured a deeper and more mature religious life.

Rabbi Zadok, though far less turbulent than Rabbi Nahman,
also incorporated his life's struggles into his work, albeit much more
obliquely. Two struggles loom large over the course of his life: his
divorce and subsequent wandering through Europe, and his never
having had children. Rabbi Zadok never addresses his divorce in his
writings, but he alludes to childlessness many times. His collection of

sermons, *Pri Tzadik*, is an allusion to his own perception of his children
(referred to in Rabbinic literature as the *pri*, the fruits of an individual)
being represented by the Torah thoughts he imparted to his students.[291]
Additionally, Rabbi Zadok dedicated an entire work entitled *Poked
Akarim*,[292] *The Remembrance of the Barren* to the theological implications of the inability to conceive.

The only source of autobiographical information we have from
Rabbi Zadok himself is in his work *Divrei Halomot*, *The Message of
Dreams*, which documents his dreams. The dreams are mostly theological or Talmudic in nature but a few have autobiographical insights. In the
third dream, dated 1843, Rabbi Zadok describes what he calls "the roots
of my soul".[293] This text is the most authoritative presentation of Rabbi
Zadok's self-image. Its interpretation, however, cannot be definitively
determined. The thrust of the dream is the powerful religious energy
present in sins and the potential to channel such energy into greatness,
ultimately resulting in the redemption. Why this relates to "the root" of
Rabbi Zadok's soul is less clear.[294] What emerges from this dream is the
central role that the Hasidic idea of "descent in order to elevate" played
in Rabbi Zadok's life. This idea appears in many Hasidic works dating
far earlier than Rabbi Zadok; however, its passionate articulation as "the
root" of his soul is certainly distinct.[295]

Given their respective emphasis on the religious value of struggle it
is not surprising that both Rabbi Nahman and Rabbi Zadok address the
question of whether a person is permitted deliberately to seek out spiritually compromising situations. If religious struggle is enlightening, why
not seek it out? Rabbi Nahman and Rabbi Zadok, however much they
agreed in other areas, sharply disagreed about searching for opportunities
to sin in order to test religious fortitude.

In Rabbi Nahman's biography there is passage which states Rabbi
Nahman not only welcomed temptation, he prayed for it. Discussing his
teacher's battles with sin, Rabbi Nathan writes:

> The Rebbe said: "I actually begged and prayed that God should send me
> temptations. I was very confident that I would not rebel against God, as
> long as I did not lose my mind—for how can a person sin and disobey God
> unless he is literally insane. With just a little sense, all temptations can be
> overcome."[296]

Rabbi Nahman sought opportunities to prove his self-restraint. He seems bound to realize the Talmudic description of "same place, same woman" literally. As described by Rabbi Nathan, Rabbi Nahman appears cavalier about the prospect of succumbing to sin:

> The Rebbe said: If the Rabbis had not explicitly said it is forbidden to say "An arrow in Satan's eye" (*Kiddushin* 30a), I would say it. I simply cannot understand the stories we are told about the sages of the Talmud who found sexual desire a very hard and burdensome thing to deal with. For me, it is nothing. Nothing at all . . . . For me there is no difference between a man and a woman.[297]

Aside from the aforementioned Talmudic passage, there is another precedent for such requests, as seen with King David, who sought to cement his status as worthy of being included as one of the forefathers by requesting a test from God.[298] As students of King David's life know, he did not pass his test with Batsheva. Nonetheless, Rabbi Nahman may have extracted from the story of the baffled King that temptation, however dangerous, can still be requested. After all, though struggles with sin may cause a minor fall, they can also create a major lift.

Rabbi Zadok, on the other hand, is emphatic that placing oneself into situations of potential temptation is prohibited. In his long treatise on repentance Rabbi Zadok mentions that he was in possession of a work known as *Rav Yaiva*, which did permit a person to test his own fortitude by returning to the proverbial "scene of the crime." He writes:

> . . . A while back I was in possession of the work *Rav Yaiva*[299] and I saw there in his commentary on Psalms on the verse "He flatters himself in his own eyes (until his iniquity is to be found hateful)" (Psalms 36:2), that he cites in the name of the Baal Shem Tov in the name of the Heavenly Yeshiva that it is permitted to bring oneself, the person who is involved in repentance, to such a situation. Later on I saw written in the work *Kli Yakar*[300] (the beginning of *Parshat Hukat*) writes similarly and explains in the name of others the Talmudic passage "in the place where the penitent stand there even the wholly righteous cannot stand." Meaning that [the righteous] are forbidden to seclude themselves (with a woman) and bring upon themselves spiritual trials, as opposed to the penitent (who are permitted to do so) . . . and regarding this matter it requires a tremendous amount of study to determine if it is true and it should not be spoken of at all . . . and if such

> an activity was permitted (to bring oneself to a spiritual trial) perhaps it is only in regards to those instances where the person is not explicitly violating any prohibitions. Similar to the story cited regarding Kind David (Jerusalem Talmud *Sanhedrin* 2:3)[301]. . . . In truth, even in this regard it is not clear to me for the evil inclination desires and conquers and is not satisfied unless it has apprehended that which is prohibited . . . and [David] did not do this in order to purify his repentance and trials, rather just in order to awaken his righteous inclination over his evil inclination and break his desires.[302]

Rabbi Zadok is adamant that the process of repentance need not involve actually entering into spiritually compromising situations. The place where penitents stand may be more spiritually meaningful than those who have never fallen, but they still cannot actually enter places where their faith will be tested.[303]

Rabbi Nahman and Rabbi Zadok both stood in unique places. They extended the blanket of Hasidic thought to provide comfort and encouragement to people that others may have neglected. Still, however large and warm that blanket may be, Rabbi Zadok cautioned that it should not be used to allow limitless validation. Those who struggle with temptation, according to Rabbi Zadok, need to be honest about their limitations. Rather than reentering the locations where sin occurred, let the Knower of Concealments testify on your behalf.

The Limitations of Learning from Failure

Dr. Sim Sitkin knows how to fail. A professor of management at Duke, he wrote a long article on how organizations should strategically incorporate failure into their corporate culture.[304] Not all failures encourage learning. In order to learn from failure you need to fail strategically. In an approach he calls "the strategy of small losses" he points to five ingredients "that contribute to the intelligence of failure":

> (1) They result from thoughtfully planned actions that (2) have uncertain outcomes and (3) are of modest scale, (4) are executed and responded to with alacrity, and (5) take place in domains that are familiar enough to permit effective learning.[305]

Instead of viewing failure as an organizational liability, he asks his readers to consider "that failure may actually be a safety and survival-enhancing asset in organizations."[306] Still, he cautions:

Failure should not be pursued for its own sake. It is a means to an end, not the end itself. If the goal is learning, then unanticipated failure is the unavoidable byproduct associated with the risks inherent in addressing challenging problems.

You need the right kind of failure to produce effective learning.

The limitations on learning from failure may shed light on a puzzling passage of Talmud about the value of learning from failure. In tractate *Gittin* (43b) the Talmud records the oft-cited phrase, "A person cannot understand words of Torah until they (i.e., the words of Torah) have caused him to stumble" [אין אדם עומד על דברי תורה אלא אם כן נכשל בהן]. On the surface this phrase is simple enough—in order to successfully develop Torah knowledge, failure will inevitably be a part of the process. The context of this passage, however, is puzzling.[307] The Talmud is in the midst of a discussion about betrothing a woman who is half slave and half free. One opinion erroneously suggests that such a marriage should be invalid since it is comparable to trying to betroth just half of a woman, which is decidedly void. In explaining the flawed analogy, the Talmud says:

> Are the cases comparable? There, where he betroths half a woman, he leaves a portion of the woman out of his acquisition. That is why the betrothal does not take effect. However, here, she was a half-maidservant half-free woman when he betrothed her, and he did not leave a portion of the woman out of his acquisition, so the betrothal should take effect.

After correcting the mistaken analogy, the Talmud presents the passage that a person does not understand words of Torah before first falling.

In one respect this passage does connect to the broader legal discussion of the Talmud since the mistaken analogy is an example of stumbling on words of Torah. Still, the context is strange. This is the only time in the entire Talmud where this passage is evoked to justify a mistaken assumption. There must be thousands of instances in the Talmud where an initial suggestion is rejected in the process of coming to a conclusion. The dialectic process of rejection and refinement is a hallmark of Talmudic discourse. So why, of all places, does the Talmud decide to teach us about the value of failure in the process of learning here—in the seemingly unrelated and obscure discussion of half betrothals?[308]

Perhaps there's a reason why this passage appears here. The Talmud was discussing the comparison between betrothing a woman who is only half-free and betrothing only half a woman. The distinction between the cases is that in the half-slave case, the act of betrothal was complete despite the fact that only half of the woman was eligible for marriage. But he did a complete acquisition. In the latter case of betrothing just half of a woman, there still remains another half that could be betrothed. His act of acquiring was only performed halfway. Herein lays the connection to failure. There is much to learn from failure. But in order to learn from failure, first every effort must be made to avoid it. You can't leave anything in your act of acquiring. Failure, as Dr. Sitkin emphasized, cannot be sought. Educational failures emerge from concerted and sincere efforts to succeed that naturally fall short. Pursuing failure in order to learn will just leave a mess. Life will provide plenty of opportunities to learn from failure—but don't go looking for them. You can be sure that they will find you. And when they do, there will be a lot to learn.

10

RABBI'S SON SYNDROME: WHY RELIGIOUS COMMITMENT CAN LEAD TO RELIGIOUS FAILURE

I ask nothing of you in the way of a declared position on religion. Your mother may have demanded more of you here,—entreated more; I cannot. I ask but this: that you will give earnest, serious consideration to the fact that we exist on this planet for a shockingly brief fraction of Eternity; that it behooves every man to diligently seek an answer to the great question,—Why am I here? And then, as best he can, to live up to the ideal enjoined by his answer. And if this carries you far, and if it leads you to embrace any of the great creeds of Christendom, this will be to your mother an unspeakable joy, and perhaps not less so to me; but it is a question which cannot be settled by the mere filial desire to please.

—John Swain to his son William J. Bennet,
The Book of Man: Readings on the Path to Manhood

The Challenge of Children of Rabbis

In a cramped office overcome with rabbinic tomes and papers in need of filing sits a daughter with her father. Her name is Tamar and she is showing her father an artistic rendering of their relationship. On her laptop she shows her father a crude animated rendering of a girl walking in her father's shadow. No matter where the girl walks in relation to her father, his shadow is cast over her. And Tamar's father does indeed cast a long shadow. Tamar Aviner is the daughter of Rabbi Shlomo Aviner, a *Rosh Yeshiva* of a prominent yeshiva, rabbi of a noted community, and one of the acknowledged visionaries of the Religious Zionist movement in Israel. This scene, part of the moving 2011 Israeli documentary "The Rabbi's Daughter," powerfully depicts some of the struggle of growing up as a child in the home of a rabbinic parent. The documentary, which presents three different stories of daughters of prominent Israeli rabbis, highlights the somewhat counterintuitive relationship that those who grow up in rabbinic homes often have with religion.

Whether you are a son or a daughter of a rabbi or any other clergy member, it is somewhat intriguing that growing up in a devout religious home can often create a deleterious relationship with religion. A rabbinic home, one would assume, should be the best environment in which to grow up in order to ensure lasting religious commitment into adulthood. And to be sure, some of the most prominent rabbinic leaders in history have been a part of rabbinic dynasties. The Sofer family, the Soloveitchiks, and the Kotlers are but a tiny sampling of examples in the rich history of rabbinic dynasties. Nonetheless, children of rabbis and clergy in general do have a particular struggle with religion. Understanding this phenomenon—the religious struggle of children of clergy—can help provide a framework to consider why religion itself leads some away from religion.[309]

In a 1988 article entitled "Children of Rabbis," psychologist and professor Irving Levitz investigated "the impact of the rabbinate on the developing self-identity of rabbinic children."[310] The study, which was conducted through a series of in-depth interviews with thirty children of rabbis across the denominational spectrum, uncovered some important themes in the religious struggle of children of Jewish clergy. While the subjects in the study were from American families, some of their testimony could have just as easily been featured in the Israeli documentary. One woman in Levitz's study expressed the following:

> I always struggled to maintain an identity of my own. I was always introduced by name, then followed by "the Rabbi's daughter." It was as if I couldn't be whole without having the attachment to my father's profession noted . . . . My brothers had it worse . . . . I used to cringe at overhearing congregants comment on the "Little Rabbis." Even though I really believe that many of these remarks were well intended, the reality was that my brothers and I felt as if we were stripped of the dignity of being who we were first and foremost."[311]

For many children growing up in rabbinic homes, the otherwise difficult struggle to develop a personal identity is compounded by the cumbersome expectations foisted upon them. Citing an earlier study from 1980, Levitz emphasizes the connection between religious struggle and religious expectations:

> ...[T]he higher standards and greater expectations placed upon children of clergy create for them inordinate difficulties in growing up. Consequently, children of clergy experience feelings of isolation and inner conflict emanating from the strong desire to maintain the family image while being accepted by peers as individuals with an identity apart from their ancillary role.[312]

Religious life by definition demands higher religious standards. Growing up in a rabbinic home, however, puts children squarely in the center headquarters where those standards are shaped and regulated for the community.

The loneliness and isolation created by the religious expectations within the rabbinic home are, of course, nothing new. David Assaf, in his incisive work *Untold Tales of the Hasidim*, examines some of the more infamous tales of children of rabbis who eventually left religion altogether.[313] Most of his analysis centers on the varying versions surrounding the religious departure of Moshe, son of Rabbi Shneur Zalman of Liadi, the first Chabad Rabbi. Before delving into the precise details surrounding Moshe's alleged apostasy, Assaf cites a moving memoir of Yehudah Leib Levin, whose grandfather was Rabbi Moshe of Kobrin, a harbinger of the Slonim Hasidic dynasty. Yehudah recounts how his parents' anguish exacerbated the difficulty of his departure:

> My parents anguish and their sighs depressed me. Alas, would that my parents had been cruel, would that they had excoriated and humiliated me, or had lifted a hand to punish my rebelliousness, for then I would have already departed and found my path in life. But my merciful, kind parents, who loved me more than themselves, melted and tortured me with their tears and their distress, and though my heart was torn by pity I was unable to still or to calm them.[314]

The cultural openness ushered in by the Enlightenment made such parental pain all too common. As the walls around the Jewish ghetto eroded, families and communities were left unsure how to stem the tides of assimilation. For children of rabbis the pain of departure includes an added element whereby the very efficacy of their parents' rabbinic powers could be called into question. If the communal rabbi cannot inspire his own children, how can he expect the community to be any different? Such questions, however, disregard the prevalence of rabbinic children who chose another path. Far from being an indictment on the parents, the history of children of rabbis who struggle with religion, as we will soon see, may be as old as the rabbinate itself.

A Rabbinic Dynasty Considers Why Rabbinic Dynasty May Be Challenging

One of the most successful rabbinic dynasties in history is undoubtedly the Sofer family. Begun by Rabbi Moshe Sofer (1762–1839), also referred to as the Hatam Sofer, his descendants continue to serve in rabbinic leadership positions in the Jewish community. All of Rabbi Moshe Sofer's sons became rabbis. Following Rabbi Sofer's death, his eldest son Avraham Shmuel, also known as the Ktav Sofer, assumed his father's position as head of the Pressburg Yeshiva. Curiously, this famed father-son rabbinic success story both (in separate essays) ascribe the first incident of struggling rabbinic children to the first rabbinic leader of the Jewish people: Moshe.[315]

"These are the offspring of Aaron and Moshe on that day God spoke to Moshe at Mount Sinai" (Bamidbar 3:1). Oddly, however, the Torah proceeds to recount only the children of Aaron. Rabbi Shlomo Yitzhaki, noticing the discrepancy in his famed commentary Rashi, explains that although only Aaron's sons are mentioned they are still considered the offspring of Moshe as a lesson that whoever teaches a child Torah, it is as if the child is that person's offspring. Still, why leave out Moshe' children altogether? In an astonishing indictment on Moshe's parental focus, both Sofer father[316] and son[317] contend that Moshe's communal obligations obstructed his parental obligations. Moshe's sons are absent from the recitation of his offspring because they did not appreciate or benefit from Moshe as a parent. In fact, adds Rabbi Moshe Sofer, the verse specifically recalls God's revelation to Moshe at Mount Sinai to reinforce that it was the experience of revelation—and the subsequent communal responsibility it demanded—that interrupted Moshe's focus on his biological children.[318]

The Sofer family were certainly no strangers to the demands of communal responsibility and the potential strains it places on the family. Their successful negotiation of these demands likely presented a newfound appreciation for the ease with which some parents may succumb to finding the proper balance between communal and familial responsibility. For those for whom finding the proper balance has proven elusive, there is consolation in knowing that Moshe, our first rabbinic leader, dealt with the same struggle.

A Talmudic Take on Rabbinic Children

The Talmud was not oblivious to the struggle of children of rabbinic parents as they come to terms with their religious affliction and expression. In fact, the Talmud (*Nedarim* 81a) asks outright, "Why do the children of rabbis so rarely become rabbis themselves?" In response to this question the Talmud presents five approaches:

> Rav Yosef says it is so that people do not say Torah is an inheritance. Rav Sheishet the son of Rav Idi says so that they do not become arrogant among the community. Mar Zutra says so that they do not become too dictatorial against the community. Rav Ashi says it is because they call people asses. Ravina explained because they do not make the requisite blessing on the Torah.

Of all of the explanations, Ravina's seems to be the most puzzling. What does the blessing of the Torah have to do with the religious outcome of one's children? And are we really to assume that great rabbinic scholars all skipped the biblically mandated blessing on the Torah that is normally made each morning? Surely, the connection between the blessing on the Torah and the struggles of rabbinic children needs to be more carefully considered.

Rabbi Yehudah Loew (1512–1609), known as the Maharal, explains why the blessing on the Torah is so critical for the success of the children of rabbis.[319] Love of Torah can be divisive. Torah learning is inherently a pursuit for the religious ideals of life. The love for the ideals contained in Torah can easily distract from one's love of God or even love for other people. Many families have surely been party to the potential discord buried within the quest for religious advancement. Personal ideals easily pave the way for expectations for others. Individual religious achievement is sometimes built upon the dissatisfaction or disapprobation of others' religious laxity. In order for personal religious achievement to translate into interpersonal success we need to recite the blessing on the Torah. The blessing of the Torah is not a typical blessing that one makes, for instance, on food or even other commandments, but it is also a prayer of sorts that our love for scholarship does not obscure our love for people.

The text of the blessing of the Torah, when read carefully, contains a reminder that our personal pursuits of religious perfection do not come at the expense of our appreciation of others. The blessing reads:

> Blessed are you, Lord our God, King of the Universe, who has made us holy through our commandments and has commanded us to engage in study of the words of Torah. Please, Lord our God, make the words of Your Torah sweet in our mouths and in the mouths of Your people, the house of Israel, so that we, our descendants (and their descendants), and the descendants of Your people, the house of Israel, may all know Your name and study Your Torah for its own sake. Blessed are You, Lord, who teaches Torah to His people Israel.

We do not simply recite a blessing on the commandment to study Torah, but we pray that it is received by those who study and those we teach with sweetness. It is not just a blessing on our scholarship but a prayer for scholars and students. Our Torah, we plea, should not divide—it should unite, for this generation and the next.

The Blessed Reminder of the Kohanic Blessing

This theme emerges not just in the blessing of the Torah but can also be seen in the text of Torah chosen as the staple text on which we recite the blessing. Standardized in each *siddur*, following the blessing of the Torah is the text of the blessing of the *Kohanim* (Numbers ch. 6). Why was this text chosen as the standard-bearer for the first Torah text we study each day? This question is further underscored when we consider that the other texts chosen to be studied immediately after the blessing on the Torah each relate to the importance of Torah. Why, then, did they not select verses that relate specifically to Torah study? What message does the blessing of the *Kohanim* contain related to our daily affirmation of our obligation to study Torah?[320]

For many Jews who are themselves not *Kohanim*, the blessing of the *Kohanim* evokes memories of listening quietly to the Kohanic chants while under a *tallit* or with faces buried inside of a prayer book. Surely, the blessing of the *Kohen* seems like an odd choice to juxtapose next to the blessing of the Torah. But the true nature of the blessing of *Kohanim* is lost on many. The Kohanic blessing is not just an obligation for the *Kohen* to bless, but it is also in many ways an obligation on the people to feel blessed.[321] Before the *Kohanim* recite their blessing they say a blessing of their own "to bless the people of Israel with love." No other blessing ends with this particular formulation. We do not recite the blessing on the *lulav* to "take it with love" or a blessing on matzah "to eat it with love." Only the blessing of the *Kohen* ends specifically with an acknowledgment of love because inherent in the obligation of the blessing is that the recipient, the people of Israel, feel beloved. In fact, a *Kohen* who is not in good standing within the community or is involved in communal disputes is not allowed to bless the people. Rabbi Leible Eiger (1817–88), himself a scion of a famed rabbinic family, summarized the essence of the blessing of the *Kohanim* as "a reminder to root within our hearts the love of the Jewish people that each person should seek the good in his fellow man."[322] Specifically, he writes, "If there is, God forbid, some burden pressing on a particular individual, then we should anticipate and long for expansiveness to be bestowed on such a person." The blessing of *Kohanim* is an acknowledgement that the Jewish people are blessed and beloved.[323]

This in turn may be why the blessing of the *Kohanim* is situated so prominently following our blessing of the Torah. As we begin each day recognizing the centrality of our obligation to pursue our attainment of Torah, we also pause to recognize the possible dangers inherent within a singular focus on Torah study. The ideals of Torah study cannot be achieved at the expense of the appreciation of the people. Our study of Torah, like the blessing of the *Kohanim,* should leave those in our lives feeling more beloved and more blessed. The blessing of the *Kohanim* and the blessing of the Torah preceding it dually ensure that our Torah study is not just the fulfillment of a commandment but an endeavor that is sweet for all those around us: sweet for us and our children.

"For the rabbi's child," concludes Levitz, "self-esteem is enhanced with the experience of feeling valued as an integral part of the family group in its designated work with the congregation." It is a sad fact of religious life that our personal growth can often come at the expense of others' self-worth and self-esteem. The Torah and Talmud were both acutely aware of this danger. The ideals and expectations of religious life can be divisive wedges within families and communities. Each morning, when saying the blessing of the Torah followed by the blessing of the *Kohanim,* we pause and tacitly acknowledge that concern. But if our blessings are successful, we can rest assured that our religious commitments remain "sweet in our mouths and in the mouths of Your people."

11

JONAH AND THE VARIETIES OF RELIGIOUS MOTIVATION: RELIGIOUS FRUSTRATION AS A FACTOR IN RELIGIOUS MOTIVATION

The consolations of Religion, my beloved, can alone support you; and these you have a right to enjoy. Fly to the bosom of your God and be comforted.

—Letter of Alexander Hamilton to Elizabeth Hamilton, July 4th 1804

RUST COHLE. What do you think the average IQ of this group is, huh?

MARTY HART. Can you see Texas up there on your high horse? What do you know about these people?

RUST COHLE. Just observation and deduction. I see a propensity for obesity, poverty, a yen for fairy tales, folks putting what few bucks they do have into little wicker baskets being passed around. I think it's safe to say that nobody here is gonna be splitting the atom, Marty.

— True Detective, Season 1, "The Locked Room"

An Educator's Frustration

The journey towards more fervent religious life so often begins with personal turmoil. Some people turn to religion because they are lonely, some are looking to cope with feelings of mortality, and others may turn to religion in the hopes that it will serve as a respite from a broken family. As a religious educator, it is hard to ignore the gnawing feeling that the object of these people's search is not authentic spirituality but a very—almost secularly driven—emotional catharsis from the everyday pain of life. Of course, as an educator I have a duty to remain egalitarian as to the religious motivations of those who seek counsel, but can I be faulted for noticing that so many people who are seeking religious commitment would seem to be better suited in finding simple, healthy social interactions? Does the teenager looking to make sense of her or his parents' impending divorce really need theological purpose or would she or he be better suited with the guidance of a mental health professional and a friend?

I don't think I am the first educator to develop fatigue from watching many who begin with intense motivation and then slowly watch said motivation (d)evolve into either disappointment or disuse. The prime suspect in my eyes of such abortive entries into religious life has often been the nature and substance of the motivation that brought people there in the first place. Perhaps, I wondered, if people came to religion for the "right reasons," if such can even be said to exist, the resulting religious experience would be more fruitful.

Of course I recognize that everyone is welcome to seek meaning where they see fit, but my frustration was couched not so much in the breadth of what motivates religiosity as by incredulity towards the religious commitment that emerges from such fleeting emotional pain. A person can surely find God after a devastating diagnosis, but what enduring sense of duty could such motivation produce? Can religious motivation devoid of theological urgency still foster lasting religious commitment? It is an uncomfortable question to ask, for who has the authority to question others' religious search? But it was a question I nonetheless found myself asking, however quietly.

I don't know if I ever found a definitive answer to my difficulties, but my frustrations were assuaged somehow. In December of 2014 I was invited to deliver a series of classes at a weekend program for teenagers. Many of the participants would have the personal backgrounds that typically irked me in my endeavors at religious education. But those classes changed my view on the varieties of religious motivation and experience. My classes focused on a personality, who I learned dealt with a set of frustrations and difficulties similar to the ones with which I had been grappling. His name was Jonah.[324]

Jonah's Frustration

Jonah was approached by God to convince the people of Nineveh to repent and return to Him. Instead of listening, Jonah chose to run. Why did Jonah, a prophet, decide to run?

Like many biblical characters, Jonah's underlying religious ethos is alluded to in his name. He was Jonah the son of Amittai, which derives from the Hebrew word *emet*—meaning truth. Jonah was a man of truth. He was not interested in religious comfort or convenience. He was not concerned with escaping the terror of death and finitude. Jonah was motivated by truth. Jonah's religiosity was founded on theological fact and doctrinal integrity.

After fleeing, Jonah finds himself on a boat in a tempestuous storm. His fellow sailors begin to panic. "And the mariners were afraid, and cried every man unto his god." Throughout the story the operative description of the sailors is fear. The religious motivation of the seamen is based on the impending crisis of their own mortality. Jonah, however, takes a nap. He is not interested in being a prophet on this boat. The task of reminding them of repentance so as to escape death's grasp is the very job from which he'd absconded by running away from Nineveh. Jonah understands that the people on that boat are not seeking religious truth but rather religious comfort.

After being thrown overboard in the midst of the storm, Jonah is saved from drowning by miraculously being swallowed by a fish. Inside the fish Jonah prays and recommits himself to God, who in return ensures he is safely returned to dry land. Jonah, now seemingly reformed, agrees to return to Nineveh—which he does. The Nineveh community, hearing Jonah's exhortations to repent, promptly responds with a communal commitment to return from evil, which God just as promptly accepts.

Jonah, however, is still in pain. His outreach work still leaves him unfulfilled. He finally discloses to God why he ran (Jonah 4:2):

וַיִּתְפַּלֵּל אֶל ה' וַיֹּאמַר, אָנָּה ה' הֲלוֹא זֶה דְבָרִי עַד הֱיוֹתִי עַל אַדְמָתִי—עַל כֵּן קִדַּמְתִּי, לִבְרֹחַ
תַּרְשִׁישָׁה: כִּי יָדַעְתִּי, כִּי אַתָּה אֵל חַנּוּן וְרַחוּם, אֶרֶךְ אַפַּיִם וְרַב חֶסֶד, וְנִחָם עַל הָרָעָה.

He prayed to God and said: Please, God, was this not my contention when
I was still on my own soil? Because of this I fled towards Tarshish; for I
knew that You are a gracious and merciful God, slow to anger, abundant in
kindness, and who relents of evil.

While Jonah clearly intends to offer an explanation as to why he ran, his
justification at first glance still remains unclear. A close reader, however,
will notice that Jonah invokes the opening of the familiar refrain of Moshe
(or God, depending on whom you ask) known as the Thirteen Attributes,
which are repeated throughout the High Holiday season—albeit with one
exception. The standard sequence of God's attributes that most readers are
surely familiar with ends not with the term *niham al ha-raah* but rather with
the term *emet*—truth. The word *niham* derives from the word *nehamah*,
comfort. Jonah in his aggravated description of God substitutes comfort
for truth. Jonah the son of Amittai finally discloses his frustration with outreach to God. "You want to know why I ran away? Because for most people
God, religion, spirituality—it's not about truth—it's about comfort."

Why does the fear of death and mortality seem to have no bearing on
Jonah's religious outlook? Perhaps it was his childhood. I Kings, chapter
17 presents the story of the widow Zarephath, whose son dies only to be
revived by the Prophet Elijah. That son, according the Midrash, is Jonah.[325]
Death for Jonah, then, is not an abstract fear lurking in his future but a
reality he has already experienced. Having already lived through the terror
of death, Jonah seeks another motivation to ground his religious commitment: truth.

Jonah's concern has been articulated by many critics of religion. David
Hume, in his *History of Natural Religion*, considers the concerns that motivated the advent of religious commitment. Hume, who was quite skepti-
cal of religion, assumes that religion began not in the search for truth but
rather in a search for comfort:

But what passion shall we here have recourse to, for explaining an effect
of such mighty consequence [i.e., religion]? Not speculative curiosity
surely, or the pure love of truth. That motive is too refined for such gross
apprehensions; and would lead men into enquiries concerning the frame of
nature, a subject too large and comprehensive for their narrow capacities.
No passions, therefore, can be supposed to work upon such barbarians, but
the ordinary affections of human life; the anxious concern for happiness, the
dread of future misery, the terror of death, the thirst of revenge, the appetite

for food and other necessaries. Agitated by hopes and fears of this nature, especially the latter, men scrutinize, with a trembling curiosity, the course of future causes, and examine the various and contrary events of human life. And in this disordered scene, with eyes still more disordered and astonished, they see the first obscure traces of divinity.[326]

His pessimistic view of the underlying motivation for religion is shared by many philosophers. Ernst Becker, in his Pulitzer Prize winning book *The Denial of Death*, flatly declares that "religion solves the problem of death." No doubt, this view is best encapsulated in Karl Marx's often cited declaration that "religion is the opiate of the masses."[327] An opiate does not bring its users truth, of course; it is a specious solution for the harsh pain of a harsh world.

Long ago, Maimonides was also concerned with this issue. In his *Laws of Repentance* (10:2), Rambam makes an important distinction regarding the proper motivation for religious commitment:

Whoever serves God out of love, occupies himself with the study of the Law and the fulfillment of commandments and walks in the paths of wisdom, impelled by no external motive whatsoever, moved neither by fear of calamity nor by the desire to obtain material benefits—such a man does what is true because it is true...

The ideal form of religious commitment, according to Maimonides, is founded upon truth as opposed to the solace religion proves in the face of calamity. Of course, he readily concedes that most will never achieve such purity of motivation—but it stands as an ideal nonetheless.

In 1967 Gordon Allport wrote "Personal Religious Orientation and Prejudice," an important essay that invoked a similar dichotomy in religious motivation to that of Maimonides. According to Allport, religious motivation can be characterized based on two binary poles—intrinsic versus extrinsic motivation. He succinctly defines this scale as follows:

Perhaps the briefest way to characterize the two poles of subjective religion is to say that the extrinsically motivated person uses his religion, whereas the intrinsically motivated lives his religion. As we shall see later, most people, if they profess religion at all, fall upon a continuum between these two poles. Seldom, if ever, does one encounter a "pure" case.[328]

Using Maimonidean terminology, those motivated by truth could therefore be considered intrinsically motivated while those motivated by fear of calamity or, for that matter, by social, emotional, or any other form of temporal comfort could be typified as extrinsically motivated. Thus, what plagues Jonah is his insistence on pure intrinsic motivation.

The story of Jonah can be read as the narrative of a frustrated outreach professional. As a prophet Jonah has proclaimed God's impending wrath to wayward communities and time and again he sees them repent out of fear. When confronted with his own mortality, man finds comfort in the community and eternal promises offered by religion. Jonah, however, grows tired of serving as the temporal haven for man's fear of crisis and transience. If religion is only a blanket to provide warmth from the cold, harsh realities of life, do concerns of theological truth and creed even matter?

God's Comfort

What is God's response to Jonah's religious torment? The story of Jonah ends abruptly. God provides a tree for the ailing Jonah to find shade. After momentarily providing Jonah comfort, God summarily destroys the tree. Jonah is crestfallen. With the sun beating down on Jonah, he pleads for death. God, in the closing statement of the story, rebukes Jonah for becoming so attached to the comfort of the tree while still failing to develop any empathy for the religious struggle of the people of Nineveh.

Comfort, God reminds Jonah, is a need inherent in the human condition. The comfort provided by a tree no more obscures the role of God than the comfort that religion provides. The means through which we find solace need not obscure the ultimate source from which all comfort derives.

Christian Wiman, a noted American poet, knows that his religious motivations are looked at with suspicion. After living as an atheist for much of his teens, he rediscovered God following a bout with cancer. As he acknowledges in his brilliant collection *My Bright Abyss: Meditations of a Modern Believer*, "That conversions often happen after or during intense life experiences, especially traumatic experiences, is sometimes used as evidence against them."[329] As he surely was accused of himself, "The sufferer isn't in his right mind. The mind tottering at the abyss of despair or death, shudders back toward any simplicity, any coherency it can grasp, and the man calls out to God."[330] Wiman, however, does not accept this skeptic narrative of religious motivation: "To admit that there may be some psychological need informing your return to faith does not preclude or diminish the spiritual imperative any more than acknowledging the chemical aspects of sexual attraction lessens the mystery of enduring human love."[331]

Religious motivation, however fleeting, however fearful, can still beget dignified religious commitment. Many people seek out religion just as Jonah thousands of years ago desperately sought shade. Few, if any, are purely and intrinsically motivated by theological truth—but the story of Jonah teaches that their stories are still endowed with religious depth and significance. Perhaps this is why the story of Jonah is read on Yom Kippur. People come to synagogue for all sorts of reasons on Yom Kippur; many come only on this day. Reading the story of Jonah is an apt reminder that it doesn't matter what brought you to synagogue, be it comfort, truth, or otherwise.

Religious integrity is not determined by the door through which you enter or even the length of your stay. Our momentary religious experiences are meaningful regardless of their motivations or durations. So whatever brings you to prayer on Yom Kippur, know that your presence has meaning. We're glad you're here.

SECTION III

RESPONSES TO SIN AND FAILURE

12

I KIND OF FORGIVE YOU: HALF APOLOGIES AND HALF REPENTANCE

Don't turn your head.
Keep looking at the bandaged place.
That's where the Light enters you.

—**Saki Santorelli,** *Heal Thyself*

Corporate Confessionals

Sometimes when you try to fix something you only make it worse. Few things highlight this principle better than a botched apology. A poorly formulated act of apology compounds the guilt. Not only did you fail, your attempt at restitution failed as well. And the art of apologies is no longer the exclusive domain of broken friendships or personal relationships—increasingly they are being carefully crafted and strategized in the corporate and government sector. Particularly in the corporate sector, a rich body of academic literature has been developed analyzing the ingredients of a successful apology.[332] There may be no single formula for a well-executed *mea culpa*, but there are certainly commonalties in those that fail.

"If any of my comments or actions have indeed been unwelcome, or if I have conducted myself in any way that has caused any individual discomfort or embarrassment," said former Senator Bob Packwood in 1992 in response to allegations of sexual impropriety, "for that I am sincerely sorry."[333] This formulation of contrition was doomed by the first word he spoke: if. He was roundly condemned for his attempt at contrition, which some commentators explained gave the impression that "only in the event that someone should choose to take offense, why then he is sorry."[334] Another common refrain found in empty apologies is the vapid expression, "mistakes were made." This phrase, especially popular among politicians, was once mockingly described as "the past exonerative."[335] Whether it is a carefully placed *if* or the flat "mistakes were made," both formulations accomplish the same thing: namely, avoiding responsibility. This is in stark contrast to apologies that have emphasized personal culpability and ownership of the mistake. One frequently cited example of a responsible display of remorse is the letter Reed Hasting, CEO of Netflix, sent to his subscribers following a very public misstep of the company. "I messed up," it begins. He acknowledges that many of his actions may have "lacked respect and humility." He closes his letter with an affirmation of the importance of apologies: "Actions speak louder than words. But words help people to understand actions."

The connection between corporate crisis management and the religious rituals of repentance is not entirely lost on professionals in the communications sector. Dr. Keith Michael Hearit, a professor at Western Michigan University, wrote the book *Crisis Management by Apology*, which examines the ways corporations and institutions express remorse in times of organizational crisis. His book quite deliberately appropriates language and religious ritual and considers them in a corporate setting. In fact, each chapter in the book begins with a citation from Scriptures. Hearit, citing Kenneth Burke's *The Rhetoric of Religion*, sees the act of corporate apology as a "ritualistic form of communication." Even the term scapegoat, used to avoid responsibility, derives from the Yom Kippur ritual.[336] Apologies are not just speeches but carefully choreographed rituals that purge organizational guilt and restore social legitimacy. Indeed, nearly all literature on crisis management points to two separate objectives of strategic crisis communications. Firstly, following an organizational lapse such as a leadership scandal or financial fraud, the corporation or institution needs to address the immediate cause of the failure. A second, higher-order step is also necessary. It is not enough to focus narrowly on the current crisis—a broader form of organizational learning is also necessary. The latter step does not just consider the preceding incident but considers the future and opportunities that have been created through the crisis. No wonder, as many have pointed out, that the symbol for *crisis* in Mandarin is also dangerous opportunity.[337]

Just as crisis management uses religious language, as demonstrated by Hearit, the act of repentance in a religious context can learn from corporate crisis management. Religious repentance can sometimes be considered somewhat transactional. A sin requires an act of repentance. But just as with corporate crisis, it is not enough to have a minimalistic focus on the preceding sin; repentance requires a more holistic approach that considers restoring the sinner's reputation for religious integrity as well as optimizing the opportunities for improvement that emerge in times of personal crisis.[338] Sin, like a corporate scandal or malfeasance, needs to be rectified on more than one level. No thinker more clearly articulated the dual nature of sin and repentance than Rabbi Joseph Ber Soloveitchik (1903–93).

Restitution and Restoration

There are two distinct terms used to describe the cleansing process of Yom Kippur. "On this day," the verse in Leviticus (16:30) states, "I will atone [יכפר] for you to purify [לטהר] you." These two terms—*kapparah* [כפרה], meaning atonement and *taharah* [טהרה], which means purification—appear throughout the Yom Kippur service. Based on these two terms, Rabbi Soloveitchik developed a creative perspective on the distinct components of sin and repentance. According to Soloveitchik, sin has two components. Firstly, sin obligates. Much like the imagery of sin as debt discussed earlier, the act of sinning incurs a debt of sorts that obligates repayment.[339] Second, sin also defiles. Sin creates an existential impurity that distances man from God. The two words of repentance each respectively correspond to the two effects of sin. *Kapparah*, a word which derives from the formal legal act of withdrawing a property claim, rectifies the obligation that sin incurs. Normally an act of sin requires a punishment; *kapparah* absolves the obligation of punishment. In this regard the sin and repentance process is quite transactional. The sinner has debt; *kapparah* removes the sinner's obligation to repay that debt. *Taharah*, however, provides purification. This act addresses the impurity caused by sin. On Yom Kippur we hope to rectify both residual effects of sin— יכפר עליכם לטהר אתכם.

Typically the process of repentance is divided into four stages: ceasing the act of sinning, remorse, resolve not to repeat the wrongdoing in the future, and verbal confession. This is the process Maimonides presents in his *Laws of Repentance* (2:2). Rabbi Soloveitchik contends that this process suffices only for achieving *kapparah*, the obligation of sin and absolution from punishment. Purity, however, requires a much more drastic transformation. For *taharah* Rabbi Soloveitchik points to Maimonides's description in the *Laws of Witnesses* (12:5–8) which prescribes a much more drastic atonement process. In order for a reformed gambler to become eligible to testify in court, Maimonides insists that the gambler not only cease from gambling, but he also must destroy any remnants of his past, be they his dice or cards. Why is this added level of repentance necessary? Shouldn't the process detailed in *The Laws of Repentance* suffice to allow the reformed gambler to be accepted as a witness in court hearings? Here again Rabbi Soloveitchik returns to his distinction on the dual effects of sin and the commensurate forms of repentance. In order to achieve purity, a more serious form of repentance is necessary. *Kapparah* may absolve punishment, but "[m]etaphysical sin on the other hand, becomes part of man's existential experience and the deeper the sin, the deeper the experience of repentance which follows."[340]

Like a corporate crisis, sin requires a multifaceted approach. Some have suggested that the dual approach of sin and repentance should be considered in the secular legal system. Stephen P. Garvey, a professor at Cornell Law School, suggests that the secular model of punishment should embrace aspects of the religious model of atonement. Crimes contain elements of harm and moral wrongs, but our criminal justice system, he laments, "makes amends for the harm the wrongdoer does, but not for the wrong he has done."[341] Garvey advocates adopting a secular model of atonement in which criminals are afforded the opportunity to seek secular atonement—not from God but from the community. In a subsequent article in a Fordham Law journal, Samuel Levine presents Garvey's model of atonement in a Jewish context.[342] There, Levine applies Rabbi Soloveitchik's dual approach to sin and repentance. The irony of Garvey's innovative suggestion being rooted in traditional Jewish textual interpretation is not lost on Levine. As he concludes:

> Ultimately, it is perhaps ironic that, in providing a new theory of punishment
> for American legal thought to consider in a future millennium, Garvey has
> in fact looked back to theories of atonement and teshuva that have spanned
> millennia of the past. The path to teshuva may indeed provide insight in
> formulating a new perspective on the notions of punishment underlying
> American law.[343]

Half Repentance

Can someone only half repent? In Rabbi Soloveitchik's dual typology of sin and repentance, he seems to take it for granted that *kapparah* can exist without *taharah*, but *taharah* cannot exist without *kapparah*. In other words, one can fulfill the more basic elements of repentance and achieve *kapparah* while still falling short of the existential transformation required for *taharah*. Ostensibly this makes sense. It is perfectly conceivable that a sinner may have sufficient remorse to be absolved from punishment yet still lack the more transformational change in identity needed to attain true purity. Interestingly, some uncommon cases may also allow for someone to achieve *taharah* while still missing what is necessary for *kapparah*. For instance, a child who commits theft as a minor may still begin adulthood with the freshness of *taharah*, but returning the stolen item is still required for a proper *kapparah*.[344] Similarly, a convert who sinned before converting may still be considered a new person in terms of the purity of their newfound religious identity yet retain the obligations to rectify their prior sins for the process of *kapparah* to be completed.[345] Sure, such cases may not be common, but they have important implications for our conception of repentance. Repentance, much like our earlier discussion of sin, is not binary. The process of atonement is not a zero-sum game that is either won or forfeited. In fact, in his treatise on repentance the medieval scholar Moshe ben Joseph di Trani (1505–85) explicitly distinguishes the legal prerequisites for repentance from legal requirements found for other commandments. Whereas *tzitzit*, as he points out, requires strings on all four corners of a garment and is meaningless if there are only three— repentance is different. There may be several steps in the legal process of repentance, but even without completion of each step there is still religious value.[346] Sin comes in many shades and repentance purifies with different hues. Indeed, as the text of our silent prayer suggests, we ask God for forgiveness and then ask God to return us to Him. They may not always occur simultaneously, but we pray to realize both in our lives.

Half Apologies

One of the most essential components of repentance is verbal confession.[347] When the object of a sin is another person, the offender is required to ask the person offended for forgiveness. Consequently, there is always that one guy who walks around before Yom Kippur asking everyone he bumps into for forgiveness. Perhaps even more common than the haphazard apology is the half-accepted apology. "Sure, I forgive you." Begrudged, insincere acceptances of apologies happen all the time. Are they worth anything? More precisely, if someone responds to a request for forgiveness with an insincere acceptance, is the petitioner absolved from the requirements to ask for further forgiveness? This question was posed by Rabbi Yosef Engel (1858-1920). In his glosses to Talmud *Kiddushin* (49b) Rabbi Engel points out that the Talmudic legal principle that unspoken feelings do not have any legal significance (דברים שבלב אינם דברים) should apply to instances where forgiveness is insincerely offered. Since unspoken feelings do not have legal significance in Jewish law, forgiveness granted even disingenuously is still efficacious.

Some have questioned the effectiveness of an insincere apology. Rabbi Avraham Genichovsky (1937–2013), a brilliant Talmudic scholar little known outside of the cloistered Israeli Yeshiva world, added a cryptic remark about the ruling of Rabbi Engel. In a small pamphlet collecting Rabbi Genichovsky's Talmudic thoughts, he writes regarding Rabbi Engel's novel suggestion, "And I have what to respond, but I don't want to."[348] Arguing on the ruling of Rabbi Engel, he explains, could be dangerous. Once a ruling has already been issued validating insincere apologies, "I don't want to ask any further questions for perhaps the Heavenly Court has ruled so as well and it will turn out that (by challenging the ruling) I will cause others to forfeit their absolution." Rabbi Genichovsky never makes it clear what exactly is his objection to the ruling of Rabbi Engel. It is likely based on a notable exception to the rule that unspoken feelings are not legally binding. In some circumstances unspoken feelings *are* deemed legally significant. For instance, as Rabbi Hayyim Ozer Grodzinski, the famed Chief Rabbi of Vilna (1863-1940) points out, someone who intends to convert but harbors reservations about their commitment to Judaism—such reservations, even unspoken, may hinder the conversion from taking effect. Essentially, when the entire legal matter is contingent on an internal commitment then even internal hesitations have legal ramifications. Applying this logic to the case of insincere forgiveness, assuming that forgiveness is primarily a matter of securing an emotional commitment, then unspoken feelings in the case of forgiveness would also be legally significant. So it turns out half forgiveness may not provide much forgiveness at all.

All may not be lost. Even considering the objections alluded to by Rabbi Genichovsky, a ruling of Maimonides may still be applicable to salvage the effectiveness of insincere forgiveness. Maimonides (*Laws of Divorce* 2:20) writes that a divorce document secured through the coercion of a Jewish court is valid so long as the husband verbally commits that he wants the divorce. Even though a divorce document requires consent and the husband's acquiescence is secured through coercion, it is still valid since, Maimonides writes:

> Someone whose evil inclination seizes him to annul the performance of a commandment or to violate a transgression and they are beaten until they fulfill their obligation or distance themselves from the prohibition—this is not considered coercion. Rather, this person is coercing himself with his wicked thoughts.

According to Maimonides a Jew is assumed to have an inner desire to act in accordance with Jewish law.[349] It is really his improper thoughts that are coercing him to do otherwise. So if verbal consent is secured, even with coercion, the presumed inner desire to live as a Jew is sufficient to consider the divorce document legally binding. This ruling could likely be applied to the situation where someone offers forgiveness half-heartedly. Presumably, in this situation as well we could rely on the assumption that a person's inner will is to do the right thing and forgive the other party. Though internally a person may not want to offer forgiveness, a verbal agreement coupled with the inner desire to live as a proper Jew should be enough to make a half-forgiveness whole.[350]

Creating Space for Repentance

The first step in crisis management is recognizing that there is a crisis. Oftentimes companies and institutions are so narrowly focused on their day-to-day operations that early warning signs of crisis are missed. One management professor, John W. Collins, lists myopia and tunnel vision as two of the seven deadly sins of management.[351] If companies are too focused on daily responsibility they will never develop the agility and vision to anticipate larger crises and opportunities for growth. Tunnel vision does not just plague organizations, it can also affect interpersonal relationships. Friends, couples, or family can get so caught up in their own individual routines that they do not leave enough space to recognize the other. Normally, when we think about "space" in the context of relationships it is accompanied with a shudder. "I need space" is often the death knell of a relationship. But space of a different sort may be the only way to restore a relationship. In order for two people to connect they each need to make sure their separate lives are not too cluttered to allow one another to connect. Pema Chödrön, an acclaimed author on meditation, expresses the importance of space this way:

> Really communicating to the heart and being there for someone else—our child, spouse, parent, client, patient, or the homeless woman on the street— means not shutting down on ourselves. This means allowing ourselves to feel what we feel and not pushing it away. It means accepting every aspect of ourselves, even the parts we don't like. To do this requires openness, which in Buddhism is sometimes called emptiness—not fixating or holding on to anything. Only in an open, nonjudgmental space can we acknowledge what we are feeling. Only in an open space where we're not all caught up in our own version of reality can we see and hear and feel who others really are, which allows us to be with them and communicate with them properly.[352]

Forgiveness requires creating space for another. In fact, the word *mehilah* [מחילה], usually translated as *forgiveness*, may derive from the word *halal* [חלל] meaning *space*.[353] The act of forgiving is the act of creating space. When we forgive we create space for another in our lives. And when we forgive we create space in ourselves by no longer clinging to our wounds and offenses. Whether it is half or whole, the sacred ritual of forgiveness creates space in ourselves and others so we can be absolved and purified.

13

TO WHOM IT MAY CONCERN: RABBINIC CORRESPONDENCE ON SIN AND FAILURE

If you want to build a ship, don't drum up the men to gather wood, divide the work and give orders. Instead, teach them to yearn for the vast and endless sea.
—**Antoine de Saint-Exupéry**

Meeting Rabbis through Letters

Lately, it seems we are meeting rabbis in all the wrong places. Too many rabbis are introduced to the general public through prohibitive rulings, disgraceful headlines, and controversial platitudes. Much of this, of course, is due to the arcane and desultory nature of rabbinic writing, which would otherwise be the appropriate place to discover rabbinic wisdom and personalities. Even seasoned yeshiva students who are "rabbinic natives" often never confront the personalities behind the dense tomes of rabbinic writing they spend their time studying. A neglected area of rabbinic literature that can address our all-too-impersonal encounters with rabbinic writing lies within the nascent body of rabbinic correspondence now available to the public. As opposed to dense Talmudic commentary, transcendent theology, or obsequious hagiography, rabbinic correspondence highlights an otherwise unavailable aspect of rabbinic wisdom: the personal. While most other forms of rabbinic writing are intended for the larger public, thereby carrying a more detached tone, rabbinic correspondence can show the intimate and oftentimes playful side of rabbinic thought.

The joy of studying rabbinic correspondence has not quite yet taken hold within the Jewish community, though correspondence in general has received newfound attention in the secular world. Thanks to wonderful work of Shaun Usher in his book *Letters of Note: An Eclectic Collection of Correspondence Deserving of a Wider Audience*, a fabulous collection of private correspondence with figures such as Albert Einstein, E.B. White, and Elvis Presley is available to the general reading public. In the book's introduction Usher aptly advocates for attention to correspondence. He writes, "I can think of no better way to learn about the past than through the often candid correspondence of those who lived it."[354] While this is certainly true, I believe the imperative to study rabbinic correspondence relates just as much to a better understanding of our collective Jewish future as it does to a proper understanding of our past.

Gordon A. Craig, the eminent historian of Germany, noted in his 1991 article "The Pleasures of Reading Diplomatic Correspondence"[355] that the best rebuttal to those who overlook the study of correspondence is to present them with examples of letters that "give the sensitive reader deep aesthetic and intellectual pleasure." Rabbinic correspondence is no different. While even the most sensitive translation certainly detracts from the intricate aesthetic of rabbinic writing, reading rabbinic correspondence gives a rare pleasure unequaled in other rabbinic forums. The candor of rabbinic correspondence is particularly evident in their approach to sin and failure. When discussing sin and failure, rabbinic correspondence highlights a rare blend of theological nuance that may have been less fitting in more public writings as well as personal empathy which, without the individual correspondent only the literature of correspondence affords, is rarely seen.

The Peculiar Place of Penance among the Pious

Why were rabbis corresponding about sin in the first place? Concepts of penance and confession are most often associated with Catholicism. What then is the place of rabbinic correspondence on sin?

The story of sin in rabbinic correspondence has a startling beginning— one that some have argued is not even authentically Jewish. Beginning in Germany during the twelfth and thirteenth century, a movement known as the Hasidei Ashkenaz emerged that radically changed the Jewish approach to sin and failure. The Hasidei Ashkenaz were a group of mystic pietists that advocated a strict adherence to a broadly conceived notion of God's Will. As characterized by Haym Soloveitchik: "To recover, to lay bare this Will in its fullness, to mold their lives in its accord and to guide others through its sinuous paths was the self-appointed task of *Haside' Ashkenaz*."[356]

The expanded notion of God's Will advocated by the Hasidei Ashkenaz made for some very strange prescripts that, until the advent of the movement, are not easily found in previous rabbinic writing, if at all. The work of Rabbi Yehudah of Regensburg (known as Rabbi Yehudah Ha-Hasid), *Sefer Hasidim*, is the most enduring text of the movement and contains many peculiar dictums that are absent in rabbinic writings outside of the movement. The most notoriously unusual aspect of the Hasidei Ashkenaz was their approach to sin.

Rabbi Eleazer of Worms, a student of Rabbi Yehudah Ha-Hasid, wrote a work called *Sefer ha-Rokeah*, which details the approach of the pietistic movement to sin and repentance. The work advocates for what is called *teshuvat ha-mishkal*, which gives detailed directions for the penances required for each major sin. Ranging from sexual immorality to dishonesty and from regret to fasting to even self-mortification, there is a wide range of both sins and recommended penances found inside of the work.

Just as the Hasidei Ashkenaz expanded the notion of the Will of God, they ritualized and expanded the penance needed to atone for violating His Will. As Soloveitchik explains:

> R. El'azar Ha-Roke'ah was both a Tosafist and a German Pietist, and, as a Pietist, he believed, together with his teacher/colleague R. Yehudah he-Hasid, that the canonical corpus did not give full expression to the Divine will in its plentitude. R. Yehudah felt this to be so in many areas; R. El'azar felt it strongly in at least one—that of penance. [357]

Of course, the parallels between the penance among the Hasidei Ashkenaz to the concepts of penance in Catholic thought have not gone unnoticed by scholars. Scholars have long debated whether the emphasis on fasting and self-mortification found *Sefer ha-Rokeah* are merely a collection of disparate and elusive traditions that existed within rabbinic writing or a product of Christian influence on Jewish atonement practices. Talya Fishman, in her study on the origins of the practices of penance in Hasidei Ashkenaz,[358] acknowledges that there is some precedent in Jewish thought for the type of penance they discuss but concludes that it is unlikely that the penance of the Hasidei Ashkenaz is without Christian influence. She writes:

> I am suggesting that while ancient traditions of Eretz Yisrael were indeed alive and well in Hasidut Ashkenaz, some might have been only recently resurrected. In their Sisyphean attempts to reject and deny what may well have been irresistible cultural influences, Jews of the medieval Rhineland foregrounded themes and practices which had in previous centuries played only bit roles in the historical and religious texture of Jewish life. . . . In the course of their overarching pursuit of the absolute, Hasidei Ashkenaz unconsciously appropriated the demanding penitential practices, which had gained new visibility in the medieval Rhineland, of their Christian neighbors.[359]

The possibility of Christian influence is certainly telling. The majority of later rabbinic correspondence made a marked effort to depart from this approach to penance. Nonetheless, for centuries such behavior—influenced by Christians or not—had a major impact on the rabbinic approach to sin. In fact, of all the diversified interests in the orbit of Hasidei Ashkenaz, this area of their thought likely left the largest imprint on later rabbinic writing. As Fishman introduces in her aforementioned study:

> The greatest impact of Hasidut Ashkenaz on Jewish culture at large has arguably been in the realm of penitential theory and practice; the ascetic behaviors and acts of self-mortification documented in the writings of twelfth- and thirteenth-century Rhineland pietists left their mark not only on non-pietist Ashkenazi culture but also on the Jewish subculture of France, Provence, Spain and Safed.[360]

Hundreds of years following the death of Rabbi Eleazer Ha-Rokeah, his program of penance continued to be positively invoked. Jews would write to their rabbi, describing their sins and asking for the proper penitential regimen to achieve atonement. Typical examples of this sort of correspondence can be found littered throughout rabbinic responsa. For instance, Rabbi Yaakov b. Yehudah Weil, the fifteenth-century German rabbi, was asked for the proper course of penance for someone who swore falsely. Invoking the regimen of the Rokeah, he recommends that the man, named Phoebus of Munich, should fast for forty days accompanied with a biweekly flogging and fasting (following the initial forty day fast).[361] In an earlier responsum[362] to an adulteress, Rabbi Weil concedes that the regimen of the Rokeah may be too intense to tell a penitent sinner all at once. Rabbi Weil refers to the program of the Rokeah as an obligation but suggests that the requirements, including rolling around in the snow and sleeping on the floor, can be delayed until a proper confession is extracted.[363]

A Second Hasidic Revolution: Sensitivity towards Sinners

The influence of the Hasidei Ashkenaz on the road to repentance did not last forever. Beginning in the eighteenth century the rabbinic approach to sinners began to soften.

A major turning point in the rabbinic approach to sin began with a different Hasidic revolution, the Hasidim of the Rabbi Israel Baal Shem Tov, of no relation to the Hasidei Ashkenaz. Like most any historical movement, scholars have struggled to define what made the movement of the Baal Shem Tov innovative—and in fact whether it can be considered a movement at all. Such precise historical definition, however, is not necessary for our purposes. Instead we will rely on the simple characterization of their movement by Michael Rosen, who describes the revolution of the Baal Shem Tov as a "God-intoxicated people—who felt a sense of God's energy in everything."[364]

Hasidim of the Baal Shem Tov championed the relationship that even the common man can have with God. As such, the movement wrote a great deal about the importance of the relationship formed with God through repentance and how such a relationship is accessible to all. Repentance is given far too voluminous a treatment in Hasidic writing to give a detailed analysis of each approach but an overall outline of the central themes can still be considered.

Each strand of Hasidut has its own personality. An old adage in the Hasidic world states that the work *Noam Elimelekh* by Rabbi Elimelekh of Lizhensk is for the righteous; the works of Rabbi Shneur Zalman of Liadi, the founder of the Chabad branch of Hasidut, are for people who are struggling between righteousness and sin; and the works of Rabbi Nahman of Bratslav are for the sinners. Some have added that the works of Izbica Hasidut are for Jews who embody each of these characteristics[365] (or maybe for Jews who aren't sure which category they belong to). Each Hasidic sect manifests its own idiosyncratic approach to sin and sinners, reflecting the distinct intuition of each sect's founding rebbe.

The Hasidic world of Rabbi Elimelekh of Lizhensk was dominated by the *Tzadik*. Normally, the average Jew has trouble connecting to the world of piety. How are piety and righteousness, normally so inaccessible and detached from the masses, supposed to be accessible to a simple Jew? In the world of Rabbi Elimelekh, piety is made accessible to everyday folks by connecting to the *Tzadik*—a righteous leader. The center of the Hasidic community in this model is the *Tzadik*. And the *Tzadik*, as Rabbi Louis Jacobs describes, had two jobs: "He brings man near to God and he brings down God's grace from heaven to earth."[366] As the channel for spirituality, the *Tzadik* also played a central role in dealing with sin and repentance. He advocated for those struggling with sin to visit the righteous, "for the Evil urge is powerless in the presence of the zaddikim."[367] The antidote for sin, as developed by Rabbi Elimelekh, was connecting to a *Tzadik*.

Rabbi Shneur Zalman of Liadi, on the other hand, has a different emphasis. His magnum opus *Tanya*, of which the first section is called "The Book of the Average Men" (*Sefer Shel Beynonim*), is replete with thoughts for those struggling with internal conflict between attaining righteousness and thoughts of sin. His audience was not those who considered themselves righteous but rather those who found themselves somewhere in the middle. The third chapter of *Tanya* is known as *Iggeret ha-Teshuvah*, and it serves as the core presentation of his philosophy of repentance. As opposed to Rabbi Elimelekh's emphasis on the *Tzadik*, *Iggeret ha-Teshuvah* focuses on God. Sin, he explains, can affect the very presence of God in this world, so to speak. The act of repentance returns God's presence to this world. Hence the word *teshuvah* is an amalgamation of the word "*shuv*", to return and the letter *hei* (ה), representing God's presence. *Teshuvah* returns God's immanence to this world. On its more base level, the focus of *teshuvah* is on the repentant. In the highest form of *teshuvah*, however, known as *Teshuvah Tata'a*, the focus of repentance is on God Himself.[368]

An old joke told in yeshiva circles asks, "Why do we only have a special introduction to prayers on Yom Kippur that requests permission to pray with the unrighteous [*le-hatir la-hitpallel im ha-avaryanim*] and not on Rosh Hashanah?" Because, the joke goes, on Rosh Hashanah they are all in Uman. Aside from eliciting a chuckle from those familiar with the Bratslav custom to visit the grave of Rabbi Nahman in Uman on Rosh Hashanah, this joke does highlight the stereotype that Rabbi Nahman provided a path in Hasidut for the unrighteous. The joke, of course, is not the real basis for the change in liturgy, but the stereotype has some merit. Rabbi Nahman of Bratslav was candid about his own struggles. His biography, written by his famed student Rabbi Nathan, spends an entire chapter detailing his spiritual volatility. Likely his own personal spiritual battles informed his theological writings. Rabbi Nahman, when it came to sin and distance from God, did not dismiss the questions of the heretics—he validated them. In his complex mystical structure, Rabbi Nahman provided grounding for those who feel like the world is bereft of God's presence. Heretics and those struggling with faithlessness were not grappling with mere illusion but they in fact had stumbled upon the divine absence that remained after God's creation. As Magid describes, Rabbi Nahman's approach empathized with the atheistic sense of God's absence. Instead of dismissing those who felt abandoned by God, Rabbi Nahman "began, however, with the assumption that the heretical question must be taken seriously if it is to be overcome."[369]

We've shared Hasidic paths for the righteous, the middle ground, and the unrighteous. What about those who are a little bit of each? Such confused souls may find comfort in the world of Izbica. As previously discussed, Izbica Hasidut incorporated elements of determinism into their theological worldview.[370] Even within the deterministic structure of Izbica Hasidut man is cautioned not to assume that his actions are in fact divinely sanctioned. Instead, a continual process of self-evaluation known as *berur* [בירור] is necessary in order to be assured of God's endorsement of an individual's actions.[371] Navigating this tension between continuous self-doubt in a world of determinism is certainly confusing, but Izbica Hasidut in many ways is intended for the confused. Izbica Hasidut provides a complex mystical decision-making system that allows certain individuals to reach total harmony between their individual prerogatives and the transcendent divine will. As Brill describes, "When the consecration of daily life in the heart reaches a state of clarified consciousness (*berur*), it is possible to perform one's actions, even sin and desire, in harmony with inner Divine will."[372] Within the world of Izbica even the confused can find clarity and even clarity can seem confusing.

Hasidic literature is rich with creative paths and hidden doorways for sinners to rediscover their relationship with God. A central tenet of Hasidic thought is the Zoharic passage that "there is nothing besides Him" [לית אתר פנאי מיניה]. Whether you consider yourself among the righteous, on middle ground, unrighteous, or downright confused there is a path in Hasidic thought to stand beside Him.

The Practical Empathy in Halakhic Responsa

Advice to the repentant was not restricted to the Hasidic world. Particularly in responsa literature, non-Hasidic rabbinic writing is replete with correspondence from those seeking a path towards repentance. In general, rabbinic responsa do not have the same overt mystical and theological tone found in Hasidic sources, but their approach to repentance is nonetheless quite creative.

Rabbi Yehezkel Landau (1713–93), often referred to as the *Nodeh B-Yehudah*, the title of his responsa, was first and foremost a Halakhist. His responsa remain a classic contribution to the genre that still continue to be quoted today. One responsum in particular is frequently cited regarding the penance needed for a repentant sinner.[373] In 1770 a future rabbi, who is unnamed for obvious reasons, sent Rabbi Landau an astonishing question. The anonymous questioner had an affair with a married woman for three years. Now, in a twist that could have come from a modern day talk show, he is married to this woman's daughter. His question is twofold: is he obligated to tell his father-in-law about the affair and how should he perform *teshuvah* for his prolonged affair? The latter question is of particular relevance to our discussion. In response to his inquiry about *teshuvah* Rabbi Landau gives a detailed response about his view on the penance process. In general, Rabbi Landau explains, he does not answer such questions "since I am not accustomed to responding to questions that I cannot find a source for in the Talmud and Halakhic authorities." Rabbi Landau is quite clear that he does not look favorably at the more detailed penance plans that were popularized by many associated with the Hasidei Ashkenaz. While he does express reverence for the work of Rabbi Eleazar of Worms, later books that detail penance "are by and large built upon logic from their stomachs without any foundation—each work just relying on the words of the other."[374] Fasting and acts of asceticism are not an essential part of repentance. Instead, he reminds, "The essence of *teshuvah* is leaving the sin, confession with a broken heart, and wholehearted regret."[375] Given the gravity of the sin, Rabbi Landau does not let his correspondent off easily. He still details an onerous menu of fasting, Torah study, asceticism, prayer, and charity to atone for the affair. Nonetheless, he continually emphasizes that it is important to distinguish between the essential components of *teshuvah* and the ritual that is ancillary. In essence, *teshuvah* is not about fasting and penance. Real repentance is a brokenhearted confession with a wholehearted commitment not to repeat the sin.

Rabbi Moshe Sofer (1762–1839) lived in the generation following Rabbi Landau. Together they were the towering Halakhic figures that shaped Jewish life during the Enlightenment.[376] In a response requesting his views on penance he reinforces much of Rabbi Landau's position—the essence of *teshuvah* is not fasting but rather confession, regret, and a commitment to abandon the practice of sin.[377] Rabbi Sofer, however, adds an innovative ritual to the process of *teshuvah*: a personal day of reflection. Yom Kippur is traditionally the day on which the Jewish people collectively focus on repentance. Rabbi Sofer suggests that for those who struggled with a particular sin, an additional personal day of reflection be added to reflect on that particular mistake:

> And it appears to me, that it is proper and correct for someone performing *teshuvah*, after fulfilling all of the standard practices for *teshuvah*, he should establish one day in the year—either the day in which he initially succumbed to sin or the day in which he resolved to return to God. On that day it should be for him each year a day of fasting and repentance with tears and grief as well as confession and regret. This is along the lines of the verse "and my iniquities are always before me" (see Psalms 51:5). This is no less reasonable that someone who had a miracle performed for him which saved him from bodily harm for which it is proper to establish a day to remember the miracle (see *Berakhot* 54a). All the more so, should he do such for a spiritual danger when his soul was saved.

It is unclear if this ritual was ever practically observed. While Rabbi Sofer mentions an earlier source suggesting a similar idea, it is still a remarkable innovation. This practice is a reminder of the personal component of the repentance process. On Yom Kippur we return collectively, but we may all need to create our own personal Yom Kippur in addition.

Buried at the end of the sixth volume of *Igrot Moshe*, the Halachic magnum opus of Rabbi Moshe Feinstein, are four responsa to questions posed by people dealing with serious sin. As opposed to most of Rabbi Feinstein's reponsa, which concern practical questions of *Halakhah*, these letters deal with the process of repentance and advice to the repentant. As with the previous examples, it is worth pausing to consider that people struggling with behaviors so outside of the bounds of normative Halakhic practice still felt compelled and comfortable enough to address the leading Halakhic figure in their time. All of the questions are dated between 1975 and 1977 and in order of publication deal with homosexuality, masturbation, a marital affair, and extramarital sex. Contrary to most of Rabbi Feinstein's other responses, all of these are published without the name of the questioner. Clearly, they are grouped together because they deal with a similar theme—how to repent for serious sins. Rabbi Feinstein's approach could be characterized as practical empathy; he both commiserates with the pain of the questioner while also affirming the traditional Halakhic standards.

In response to the person who asked for penance for homosexual behavior, Rabbi Feinstein explains that even though he is overwhelmed with more practical Halakhic responsibilities he feels compelled to answer given the extra latitude provided in Halakhic literature to help those seeking repentance.[378] "I did not find a Halakhic question in your letter," Rabbi Feinstein writes. Yet he responds "to provide encouragement not to become depressed and become mired in something which requires strengthening from the strategies of the evil inclination." A repeated theme, which appears in this letter as well, is that in-depth Torah study is the best antidote to succumbing to base desires. Rabbi Feinstein references Maimonides's conclusion in the *Laws of Prohibited Intercourse* (22:21), which state that thoughts of sexuality only overcome those whose minds are absent of wisdom. The best strategy to avoid sin is to become preoccupied with loftier matters.

The third letter responded to a woman who engaged in an inappropriate relationship with her boss while serving as his secretary. She turned to Rabbi Feinstein several years after the incident for advice on how to repent properly. His response ends with a tender note of optimistic encouragement:

> Furthermore, you need to understand that God forbid you should not be depressed. Rather, you should rejoice that you have merited repentance and a marriage to a scholar. And on Yom Kippur God will grant you complete forgiveness.

Rabbis Landau, Sofer, and Feinstein all tempered the more ominous and onerous process of repentance developed by Hasidei Ashkenaz. Perhaps even more so than the encouragement found in the works of the Hasidim of the Baal Shem Tov, it was especially necessary for Halakhic literature to reclaim a more streamlined and text-based process of repentance. Without dismissing the stature of Rabbi Eleazer of Worms, these Halakhic leaders were able to define a more practical and attainable path to penance by removing many of the extra-Talmudic pietistic practices advocated by Hasidei Ashkenaz. The road towards repentance should not just be for the pious but accessible enough for any petitioner to traverse.

The Radical Empathy in Rabbinic Correspondence

It is not just about *what* advice rabbis gave to sinners, but it is also important to consider *where* they imparted that advice. As this discussion noted initially, there is something unique about rabbinic correspondence. Sure, rabbinic responsa is probably the most well-known form of rabbinic correspondence, but there is another category known as *igrot* [אגרות], personal correspondence, which even more plainly captures the practical advice rabbinic personalities offered to people who struggled with religious crisis or failure.[379] Responsa are primarily concerned with Halakhic questions; *igrot* are mostly concerned with personal and communal issues.[380] Both of these forms of correspondence differ in one important way from normal rabbinic commentaries—there is a specific recipient. The fact that correspondence is addressing a specific individual infuses rabbinic writing with a deeply personal tone. As opposed to classic rabbinic commentaries, rabbinic correspondence exists on the nexus where abstract theology meets practical communal and personal policy.

The entire genre of rabbinic correspondence throughout history deserves its own study, but that is clearly outside of the scope of our discussion. Instead we will limit our focus to two rabbis whose personal correspondence dealt a lot with religious crisis and failure: namely, Rabbi Yaakov Yisrael Kanievsky (1899–1985) and Rabbi Yitzhak Hutner (1906–80). While both of these rabbis published on a wide range of topics, neither published formal Halakhic responsa. The only correspondences we have from each are their *igrot*, their personal letters. And as we will see, their personal letters developed a radical empathy towards religious failure and crisis.

Rabbi Yaakov Yisrael Kanievsky, also known as the Steipler, was renowned for his simple piety.[381] His brother-in-law, the famed Rabbi Yeshayah Karelitz, known as the Hazon Ish, was said to have chosen Rabbi Kanievsky as a suiter for his sister based on his perceptible piety and natural awe for God. Nonetheless, for reasons that are not entirely clear Rabbi Kanievsky became an address for people struggling with all sorts of psychological issues and religious lapses. Dr. Yaakov Greenwald, a noted psychoanalyst in the American *Haredi* community, exchanged letters for many years with Rabbi Kanievsky regarding yeshiva students who were struggling with depression and religious despair.[382] Rabbi Kanievsky's letters are also mentioned by Drs. David Greenberg and Eliezer Witztum in their book *Sanity and Sanctity*, a discussion of mental health among the ultra-Orthodox in Jerusalem. They cite the following letter from Kanievsky in response to a yeshiva student who had lost the will to live:

> If he is capable of holding a job as a Talmud teacher, then giving him such responsibility would increase his interest, encourage him to study in depth, and in this way his feelings would be developed towards everything. If he is exceptionally gifted, he should be advised to edit a religious text. . . . The awakening of his emotions in this one area will lead to general improvement. If he is an outstanding student, then he should start studying with a fellow student the texts of dietary laws requisite for becoming a rabbi, so that while studying he will have an ambition to become a rabbi. If this happens, then his other feelings will follow suit.[383]

A recurring panacea is the importance of staying busy and productive. In a series of collected letters to those struggling with masturbation, Rabbi Kanievsky constantly emphasizes not to waste time or despair.[384] "And the very essential principle is," he reminds, "do not despair, God forbid, for you must constantly have hope that God will help you."[385] While recognizing the vicissitudes of religious life, Rabbi Kanievsky asserts that "the primary time for the service of God is during times of decline."[386]

In a particularly moving letter, Rabbi Kanievsky seems to portend the trending slogan #ItGetsBetter. To a student described as "feeling emotional pain without finding satisfaction in anything," he writes:

> Many times people such as this come to me and I treat them a lot by strengthening for them the notion that this is only a passing phenomenon. And I tell them that I know many people like this who, after time, a year or two, return little by little, and are like any other person. And with this knowledge, when they believe me that this time will pass, it generally lessens the tension. I also remind them that in truth everyone in their community suffers. Some from poverty, some with debt, some have been disgraced, some have difficulty with children. And sometimes, this too brings some modicum of comfort.[387]

The collection of Rabbi Kanievsky's letters are called *Kreina d-Igrassa*, which is based on a Talmudic passage in *Sanhedrin*. Following the incident where Zimri, the leader of the tribe of Shimon, has relations with the Midianite princess Cozbi, Moshe is unsure of the Halakhic punishment for Zimri. Pinhas reminds Moshe that the law says he should be killed by zealots. Moshe, urging Pinhas to fulfill this law, responds to Pinhas, "Let the one who reads the letter be the agent (to fulfill its contents)." And indeed, the substance of Rabbi Kanievsky's letters is meant to be fulfilled by its readers. The issues that they address, particularly regarding mental health and religious difficulty, occur far too often in the Jewish community. Rabbi Kanievsky's answers really are simple yet essential religious truths. Productivity, patience, and optimism return again and again as the remedies for religious upheaval. Whoever reads these letters is transformed from a reader to an agent for their execution.

Rabbi Yitzhak Hutner, the leader of Yeshivat Chaim Berlin, spent his youth learning near Kovno in Lithuania at Yeshivat Knesset Yisrael, known as the Slabodka Yeshiva, under the tutelage of Rabbi Nosson Tzvi Finkel, affectionately known as the *Alter* (elder). One morning while all of the other students had already paired up for *havruta* (paired) learning, the *Alter* found Rabbi Hutner learning by himself. The *Alter*, concerned that Rabbi Hutner did not have a study partner, asked, "Where is your *havruta*?" Rabbi Hutner explained that he was learning with his *yetzer ha-rah*—his evil inclination. "Instead, why don't you learn with your *yetzer tov*—your good inclination?" asked the *Alter*. Rabbi Hutner, who was known for his wit, replied, "I can always count on my *yetzer ha-rah* to show up on time for morning studies. The *yetzer tov* is not as reliable."

This story captures both Rabbi Hutner's clever wit and much of his approach to religious failure. For Rabbi Hutner, it was preferable to have his evil inclination as a study partner rather than his more angelic nature. The latter was bland; challenging the former produced the friction that could propel someone to greatness.

Throughout his letters Rabbi Hutner returns to a single theme: greatness that emerges from challenge. Rabbi Hutner explains that you can only detect the strength of a person's grasp when you try to remove the object from the person's hand.[388] He writes: "It is entirely possible to learn with diligence in yeshiva and nonetheless, based on that, you still cannot evince the person's relationship with Torah."[389] A relationship is only proven after it is challenged. For this reason Rabbi Hutner often reminds his students that his ideas may resonate only after they have departed from his presence. Cleverly marshaling the verse in Psalms (34:12), "Go my children, listen to me," Rabbi Hutner explains that a remote relationship often establishes the imperative for attentiveness.[390] Intimacy is forged through absence.

It is not just absence from the walls of yeshiva that is given significance—spiritual voids are also invested with the presence of spiritual meaning. In an oft-cited letter (No. 94), Rabbi Hutner offers a brilliant analogy to someone whose secular accomplishments feel like a hypocritical duality in an otherwise spiritual existence. Rabbi Hutner assures the questioner that nothing could be further from the truth:

> Someone who rents a room in one house to live a residential life and another room in a hotel to live a transient life is certainly someone who lives a double life. But someone who has a home with more than one room has a broad life, not a double life.

Rabbi Hutner advocated for a broad life—with expansive unity—and he modeled it. He also understood that in the pursuit of breadth, some students may fall short. It was in the possibilities and realities of failure, in fact, that Rabbi Hutner's letters shine most brilliantly. We may not know which tests are which, but certainly through the course of life, people will confront failures that were simply inevitable.[391] The true test, according to Rabbi Hutner, is not one's ability to avoid sin and failure but developing an appropriate reaction and evaluation of the occurrence of sin.

Such assessment should not happen, writes Rabbi Hutner, during times of self-doubt and insecurity. Just as Jewish law prohibits judgment during the nighttime, our self-assessment should not occur during times of personal darkness.[392] Failure, when properly assessed and integrated, can be a fertile ground for personal and spiritual development.

Rabbi Hutner's consoling approach to sin and failure is likely the most enduring perspective contained in the collection of his letters. Yeshiva and seminary students who may have never heard of Rabbi Hutner or seriously studied his writings have likely been shown or read portions of his 128th letter—his fundamental treatise on sin and failure. The letter, which begins by lamenting the hagiographic nature of rabbinic biographies, reminds a student that greatness does not emerge from the serenity of our good inclinations but from our struggles with our baser tendencies. The verse in Proverbs (24:16), "The righteous fall seven times and stand up," has been perennially misunderstood. It is not despite the fall that the righteous stand up—it is because of the fall that the righteous are able to stand confidently. Greatness does not emerge despite failure; it is a product of failure.

If the medium is in fact the message, the message of these missives is the integration of theological profundities in the clothes of personal correspondence: the personal and subjective are seamlessly woven together with the eternal and enduring. Throughout the collection of Rabbi Hutner's letters, none of the recipients' names are listed. Listing the intended destinations of these letters would certainly have increased their historical value, but their absence likely increases the feeling of contemporary relevance they convey. The names are missing because the modern reader is intended to be their enduring addressee.

The Consolation of Correspondence

Rabbinic correspondence on sin and failure emphasizes that all of history is marked with struggles and failure. Matt Potter, a contemporary author like Shaun Usher, collects fascinating correspondences. He, however, collects a very specific kind of correspondence: resignation letters. In his book *The Last Goodbye: A History of the World in Resignation Letters*, Potter explains why he anthologized this form of history:

> History is written by the winners. It's the survivors—the faithful servant, the insiders, the ones who stick around, who can adapt to almost any condition—who get to write the official histories . . . . The quitter's tale offers a far more compelling, and often a more honest take.[393]

Like the quitter's tale, the sinner's tale has also been neglected. Rabbinic correspondence, however, gives a rare lens into this rich history. Each generation and each individual's struggles are unique, but the history of sin and failure as documented in rabbinic correspondence can help reorient the way we look at ours. The prolific author and psychologist Irvin Yalom writes, "Even though you're alone in your boat, it's always comforting to see the lights of the other boats bobbing nearby."[394] Centuries of rabbinic correspondence on sin and failure provide such a glimpse and, hopefully, such solace.

ENDNOTES

1   For a full account of the banning, read the author's subsequent *Anatomy of a Ban* (Jerusalem: Private Printing Publishers, 2003). See also Yoel Finkelman, *Strictly Kosher Reading* (Brighton, MA: Academic Studies Press, 2011), 106–107n36 as well as Immanuel Etkes, "Al Itzuv Demutam shel ha-'Gdoilim' bi-Safrut shel ha-Shevahim ha-Haredit-Litait," in *The Gdoilim*, ed. Benjamin Brown and Nissim Leon (Jerusalem: Magnes Press, 2017), 58–66.

2   Rabbi Shimon Schwab, "Jewish History," in *Selected Writings* (Lakewood: C.I.S. Publishers, 1988), 232–235.

3   See Robyn Fivush, Jennifer G. Bohanek, and Marshall Duke. "The Intergenerational Self: Subjective Perspective and Family History," in *Self Continuity: Individual and Collective Perspectives*, ed. Fabio Sani (New York: Psychology Press, 2008), 131–143.

4   Bruce Feiler, "The Stories that Bind Us," *New York Times*, March 15, 2013.

5   See Gen. 5:1. For a moving presentation of this analogy, see Rabbi Jonathan Sacks, *A Letter in the Scroll* (New York: Free Press, 2004), 39–41.

6   See Rabbi Yitzhak Hutner's *Pahad Yitzhak: Igrot U-Ketavim* (New York: Gur Aryeh, 1987), Letter 128.

7   Much of the following is adapted from my article in *First Things*, "Life is Full of Failure. Bio Blurbs Should be Too," May 14, 2014, https://www.firstthings.com/web-exclusives/2014/05/life-is-full-of-failure-bio-blurbs-should-be-too.

8   See Joseph Epstein, "The Art of Biography," *The Wall Street Journal*, January 1, 2016. For more on the virtues and pitfalls of incorporating failure into storytelling, see Giles Harvey, "Cry Me a River: The Rise of the Failure Memoir," *New Yorker*, March 25, 2013.

9   A few years after this article was originally written, Johannes Haushofer, a professor at Princeton, received national attention for a similar idea. On his academic page he published a CV consisting exclusively of his failures—all of the programs, fellowships, and awards he did not receive over the course of his career. See "CV of Failures: Princeton Professor Publishes Resume of

His Career Lows," *The Guardian*, April 29, 2016. The actual CV of failures can be found at https://www.princeton.edu/~joha/Johannes_Haushofer_ CV_of_Failures.pdf. Professor Haushofer credits an earlier article by Melanie Stefan entitled "A CV of Failures," published in *Nature* 468 (November 2010).

10   On the attribution of this saying see William Safire, "Let a Simile Be Your Umbrella," *New York Times*, February 11, 1996.

11   Gary A. Anderson, *Sin: A History* (New Haven: Yale University Press, 2010), 6.

12   Joseph Lam, *Patterns of Sin in the Hebrew Bible* (New York: Oxford University Press, 2016), 3.

13   Lam, *Patterns of Sin*, 4.

14   Anderson, *Sin: A History*, 105.

15   Anderson, *Sin: A History*, 110.

16   *Hayyei Moharan* II 11:4, as cited in Arthur Green, *Tormented Master: The Life and Spiritual Quest of Rabbi Nahman of Bratslav*, Third Printing (Woodstock, VT: Jewish Lights Publishing, 2004), 47.

17   Green, *Tormented Master*, 47.

18   For more biblical scholarship on *het* as missing the mark, see Lam, *Patterns of Sin*, 221n12.

19   Lam, *Patterns of Sin*, 6.

20   Cited by Lam, *Patterns of Sin*, 156.

21   See *Yoma* 35b and 36b.

22   See also Malbim's comment to Ex. 34:7.

23   Some later commentaries question the rationale of Rabbi Meir. See the comments of *Gevurot Ari*, *Maharsha*, and *Sefat Emet* on *Yoma* 36b and Malbim's comment on Lev. 16:21.

24   Karl Menninger, *Whatever Became of Sin?* (New York: Hawthorne Books, 1973), 50.

25   For a more comprehensive overview on early rabbinic attitudes towards sin, see A. Büchler, *Studies in Sin and Atonement in the Rabbinic Literature of the First Century* (London: Oxford University Press, 1928). For more on the relationship between sin and punishment in rabbinic thought, see the comprehensive Hebrew work by Aharon Shemesh entitled *Punishments and Sins: From Scripture to the Rabbis* (Jerusalem: Magnes Press, 2003).

26   See Meir Zvi Grossman, "Le-Mashmuatam shel ha-Bituyim 'aveirah' ve-'dvar aveirah' bi-Leshon Hakhamim," *Sinai* 100, no.1 (1987): 260–272, which notes that the phrase *aveirah* does not appear in biblical literature. Grossman provides a comprehensive presentation of its evolving usage in rabbinic literature, specifically focusing on the sexual connotations of the word.

27   *Avot* 2:2.

28   Steven D. Fraade, "The Innovation of Nominalized Verbs in Mishnaic Hebrew as Marking an Innovation of Concept," in *Studies in Mishnaic Hebrew and Related Fields,* eds. Elitzur A. Bar-Asher Siegal and Aaron J. Koller (Jerusalem: Magnes Press, 2017), 129–148.

29   Grossman, "Le-Mashmuatam," 260–272.

30   See Grossman, ibid.

31   On canonization as a concept in the development of Jewish law see Moshe Halbertal, *People of the Book* (Cambridge, MA: Harvard University Press, 1997).

32   See Sacha Stern, *Time and Process in Ancient Judaism* (Portland, OR: The Littman Library of Jewish Civilization, 2007) for an introduction to the rabbinic view of time. For more on the development of the words for time in rabbinic literature, see Jeffrey Woolf, "Time Awareness as a Source for Spirituality in the Thought of Rabbi Joseph B. Soloveitchik," *Modern Judaism* 32, no. 1 (February 2012).

33   This phrase features prominently in the works of Rabbi Yitzhak Hutner. For more on this phrase, in particular in the thought of Rabbi Hutner, see Shmuel Vigoda's "'Be-Hevlei Ha-Zman' Ha-Adam ve-Hazman be-Haguto shel ha-Rav Yitzhak Hutner" in *Be-Darkhe Shalom,* ed. Binyamin Ish Shalom (Jerusalem: Beit Morashah, 2007).

34   For a historical consideration of the Jewish community's lapse of donning *tefillin* in the Medieval period, see Ephraim Kanarfogel, "Not Just Another Contemporary Jewish Problem: A Historical Discussion of Phylacteries," *Gesher* 5 (1976): 106–121.

35   *Sefer ha-Hinukh* 421.

36   Ibid.

37   See Maimonides, *Mishneh Torah, Hilkhot Teshuvah,* 2:2.

38   Alan Lightman, *Einstein's Dreams* (New York: Pantheon Book, 1993), 69.

39   Ibid., 68.

40   Franz Boas, *Introduction [To Handbook of American Indian Languages]* (Washington DC: Government Print Office, 1911), 26.

41   See Gen. 2:25–3:24.

42   For differing approaches on the dating of Adam's sin see F.R. Tennant's *The Sources of the Doctrines of the Fall and Original Sin* (Cambridge: At the University Press, 1903), 151n6. It should be noted that Tennant was hostile to rabbinic thought, but his volume remains one of the most comprehensive works on original sin. In addition to the sources cited above, see also the Book of Jubilees 3:17 which explicitly states that Adam was in Eden for seven years before sinning.

43   See Alan Jacobs, *Original Sin: A Cultural History* (New York: HarperCollins Publishers, 2008), 43. Jacobs also notes the depiction in C.S. Lewis's *Perlandra* of the temptation going on "day after agonizing day." Ibid.

44   *Sanhedrin* 38b. For alternate versions of the events on that day, see *Vayikra Rabbah,* beginning of *Parshah* 29 (on *Emor*), and *Avot De-Rebi Natan* 1:8. For an explanation see Maharal's *Tiferet Yisrael* ch. 16. See however, *Perushei Rav Saadiah Gaon la-Bereishit* (New York: Beit ha-Midrash la-Rabbanim ba-America, 1984), 296-301, who seems to present an alternative timeline to the account in *Sanhedrin.* See, in particular, at footnote 505 therein. I am indebted to Rabbi Abraham Lieberman for pointing this out to me.

45   John Milton, *Paradise Lost,* ed. Barbara K. Lewalski (Malden, MA: Blackwell Publishing, 2007), 104.

46   Nahmanides commentary to Gen. 2:9. Translation from Oded Yisraeli, "Adam's Sin: Its Meaning and Essence," in *Temple Portals: Studies in Aggadah and Midrash in the Zohar,* trans. Liat Keren (Jerusalem: Magnes Press, 2016), 56. For a more robust presentation of the approach of Nahmanides to the sin of Adam, particularly the connection between his sin and the subsequent punishment of death, see Moshe Halbertal's "Mavet, Het, Hok, ve-Geulah be-Mishnat ha-Ramban," *Tarbiz* 71, no. 1-2 (2002): 133–162. For a more general discussion of Nahmanides approach to biblical exegesis see Elliot R. Wolfson, "By Way of Truth: Aspects of Nahmanides' Kabbalistic Hermeneutic," *AJS Review* 14, no. 2 (Autumn 1989): 103–178.

47   William Safire, *The Right Word in the Right Place at the Right Time* (New York: Simon & Schuster, 2004), 232.

48   Ora Wiskind-Elper, *Wisdom of the Heart: The Teachings of Rabbi Ya'akov of Izbica-Radzyn* (Philadelphia: The Jewish Publication Society, 2010), 185.

49   Ibid., 181–182. Note that my translation is different, particularly my translation of the term *bushah*/בושה as shame, rather than Wiskind-Elper's translation of the term as humility.

50   Shaul Magid, *From Metaphysics to Midrash: Myth, History, and the Interpretation of Scripture in Lurianic Kabbala* (Bloomington, IN: Indiana University Press, 2008), 71.

51   For more on the emotion of shame and its role in kabbalistic literature, see Jonathan Garb's "Shame as an Existential Emotion in Modern Kabbalah," *Jewish Social Studies*, 21, no. 1 (Fall 2015): 89–122. See also, Jonathan K. Crane, "Shameful Ambivalences: Dimensions of Rabbinic Shame," *AJS Review*, 35, no. 1 (April 2011): 61–84.

52   For a more comprehensive consideration of Cohen's approach to sin see Michael Zank's *The Idea of Atonement in the Philosophy of Hermann Cohen* (Providence, RI: Scholars Press, 2000). See also Annika Thiem's "Specters of Sin and Salvation: Hermann Cohen, Original Sin, and Rethinking the Critique of Religion," *Idealistic Studies* 40, no. 1/2 (2010): 117–138.

53   Scott Edgar, "Hermann Cohen", in *The Stanford Encyclopedia of Philosophy* (Fall 2015 Edition), ed. Edward N. Zalta, last revised September 17, 2015, https://plato.stanford.edu/archives/fall2015/entries/cohen/.

54   Hermann Cohen, *Religion of Reason: Out of the Sources of Judaism*, trans. Simon Kaplan (New York: Frederick Unger, 1972), 22.

55   Ibid., 20.

56   Alan Turing, "Computing Machinery and Intelligence," *Mind* 59:236 (October 1950): 433–460.

57   Brian Christian, The *Most Human Human* (New York: Doubleday, 2011), 11.

58   Eric Chinski, "Brian Christian on 'The Most Human Human,'" *The Paris Review*, March 14, 2011, https://www.theparisreview.org/blog/2011/03/14/brian-christian-on-the-most-human-human/.

59   Wiskind-Elper, *Wisdom of the Heart*, 181.

60   See N.P. Williams, *The Ideas of the Fall and of Original Sin: A Historical and Critical Study* (London: Longmans, Green and Co., Ltd., 1927), and F.R. Tennant, *The Sources of the Doctrines of the Fall and Original Sin* (Cambridge: At the University Press, 1903). For a more popular presentation of the doctrine with more contemporary context see Alan Jacobs, *Original Sin: A Cultural History* (New York: HarperCollins Publishers, 2008), as well as Paula Fredriksen, *Sin: The Early History of an Idea* (Princeton, NJ: Princeton University Press, 2012).

61   Alan Jacobs, *Original Sin*, 48–54.

62   Joel E. Rembaum, "Medieval Jewish Criticism of the Christian Doctrine of Original Sin," *AJS Review* 7/8 (1982-83): 353–382. This citation appears on

page 377. For more on medieval polemics see also Hyam Maccoby, *Judaism on Trial* (Portland, OR: The Littman Library of Jewish Civilization, 1993). For more on the rabbinic conceptualization of sin, in particular the concepts of good and evil inclinations, see Steven T. Katz, "Man, Sin, and Redemption in Rabbinic Judaism," in *The Cambridge History of Judaism: Volume IV The Late Roman-Rabbinic Period*, ed. Steven T. Katz (Cambridge: Cambridge University Press, 2006). More on the evolution of the rabbinic conception of the evil inclination can be found in Ishay Rozen-Zvi's *Demonic Desires: Yetzer Hara and the Problem of Evil* (Philadelphia: University of Pennsylvania Press, 2011). For an interesting contrast on the development of the concept of original sin in Christian and rabbinic thought, see Jeremy Cohen, "Original Sin as the Evil Inclination: A Polemicist's Appreciation of Human Nature," *Harvard Theological Review* 73 (1980): 495-520. See also Stanley E. Porter's "The Pauline Concept of Original Sin, In Light of Rabbinic Background," *Tyndale Bulletin* 41, no. 1 (1990): 3–30.

63   See Daniel J. Lasker, *Jewish Philosophical Polemics against Christianity in the Middle Ages,* 2nd ed. (Portland, OR: The Littman Library of Jewish Civilization, 2007), xx.

64   Lasker, *Jewish Philosophical Polemics*, 107.

65   See *Responsa Raavad* 11. See also Louis Jacobs's *Theology in the Responsa* (Portland, OR: The Littman Library of Jewish Civilization, 2005), 49–50. For a more extensive analysis of the approach of the Raavad in regards to original sin, see Byron L. Sherwin's *Studies in Jewish Theology: Reflections in the Mirror of Tradition* (Portland, OR: Vallentine Mitchell, 2007), 240–248.

66   For more, see Alan Cooper, "A Medieval Jewish Version of Original Sin: Ephraim Luntschitz on Lev. 12," *Harvard Theological Review* 97, no. 4 (October 2004): 445–59.

67   For a broader and more extensive discussion of the story of Adam's sin within Lurianic Kabbalah, see Shaul Magid, "From Theosophy to Midrash: Lurianic Exegesis and the Garden of Eden," *AJS Review* 22/1 (1997): 37–75.

68   Lasker, *Jewish Philosophical Polemics*, 226n19.

69   Allison P. Coudert, *The Impact of the Kabbalah in the Seventeenth Century: The Life and Thought of Francis Mercury van Helmont* (Leiden: Brill, 1999).

70   See Gershom Scholem, *Kabbalah* (Jerusalem: Keter Publishing House, 1974), 416. For more on the Christian kabbalah movement, see Scholem, 196.

71   For more on Leibniz and Kabbalah, see Allison Coudert, "Leibniz and the Kabbalah," in *The Impact of the Kabbalah*, 308–329.

72   For a more detailed discussion on the effect of Lurianic mysticism on the divide between original sin in Jewish and Christian thought, see Shaul Magid's *From Metaphysics to Midrash*, 36–37. He summarizes his thesis as follows, "It is my contention that Lurianic exegesis actually brings Judaism and Christianity closer together, perhaps because his mystical fraternity flourished at a time when New Christians were returning to Judaism, thinning the opacity between these two competing religions."

73   Coudert, *The Impact of the Kabbalah*, 347.

74   Rabbi Dr. Simcha Willig, email message to the author, August 18, 2010. For a moving dialogue that encapsulates this theme, see Saki Santorelli, *Heal Thy Self: Lessons on Mindfulness in Medicine* (New York: Random House, 1999), 29. There, he responds to someone who desired to "get back to being who I used to be." For more on resilience see Angela Duckworth, *Grit: The Power of Passion and Perseverance* (London: Vermilion, 2016). See also Ben Sherwood's *The Survivor's Club: The Secrets and Science that Could Save Your Life* (New York: Grand Central Publishing, 2009).

75   United States of America v. Gilberto Valle, 807 F.3d 508, 511 (2nd Cir. 2015). I am grateful to Ms. Debbie Stone for first introducing me to the details of this case. This case was later featured in Russ Mayberry, dir., *Thought Crimes: The Case of the Cannibal Cop*, aired April 24, 2015, HBO.

76   Edward Coke, *Institutes, Part II* (1797 edition), chapter 1, Folio 10.

77   For a longer rabbinic discussion on the implications of creating Halakhic categories through thought see Yosef Buxbaum, ed., *Sefer ha-Zikaron le-Maran ha-Gerah Shmulevitz Zatzal* (Jerusalem: Moriah, 1980), 161–163.

78   See *Kiddushin* ad loc. where the Talmud derives this based on Ezekiel 14:5.

79   See Maimonides, *Guide for the Perplexed* 3:8 who explains this passage in *Yoma* to be emphasizing the general elevation of the mind over the body. Since the mind is superior to the body, the thoughts of the mind also have graver repercussions than physical actions.

80   See *Sefer Yereim* 8. See however Maimonides, *Sefer ha-Mitzvot, Shoresh* (Foundation) 4, who does not include this in his count of the commandments. His reason, it should be noted, is not because it can only be transgressed in thought, but rather because it is a general prohibition that includes within it all religious violations.

81   In the first presentation of the Ten Commandments, the prohibition (Ex. 20:14) is phrased with the Hebrew term לא תחמוד—do not covet, which, as explained by the Midrash (*Mekhilta*) is a prohibition that is only violated once an action, such as theft or even purchase according to some, has been carried out. The terms of this prohibition fall outside of the scope of our

discussion, but according to most some action is necessary in order to be held accountable for this sin. The second presentation of the Ten Commandments features a different term, namely לא תתאוה, which according to many applies even to thought alone. For more see *Sefer ha-Hinukh* 38, 416; Maimonides, *Sefer ha-Mitzvot, Mitzvah* (Commandment), 266.

82   See *Hiddushei Aggadot* of the Maharal on *Kiddushin* 39b.

83   See also Rabbi Yosef Engel (1858–1920) in his Talmudic glosses known as *Gilyonei ha-Shas, Kiddushin,* in which he echoes the distinction of Rabbi Loew. Menachem Meiri (1249–1306) also seems to make a similar distinction. Rabbeinu Bahya (1255–1340) in his biblical commentary (Deut. 29:18) also notes the contradiction between the Talmud in *Kiddushin* and the passage in *Yoma.* He resolves the contradiction by explaining that the Talmud in *Yoma,* describing the gravity of thinking about sin, only refers to someone who actually follows through with their fantasies. But, according to Rabbeinu Bahya, if the thoughts never materialize to action, the person will not be held responsible. One additional Mishnaic case has generated some discussion regarding liability for thought alone, namely the opinion of Beit Shammai that a bailee becomes liable for misappropriation of a deposit even through thought alone (*Bava Metzia* 43b, *Kiddushin* 42b). Seemingly, this would be an example of one being culpable for a thought crime. Rashi explains the opinion of Beit Shammai in this vein. See, however the comments of Tosafot (*Bava Metzia* s.v. "*ha-hosheiv*") and Ritva, among others, who explain that according to Beit Shammai one is only culpable if words were spoken—thought alone, however, would not make one liable. Rabbi Yosef Engel, *Gilyonei ha-Shas,* in his comments on *Bava Metzia,* 43b explains that Rashi's explanation of Beit Shammai also concedes that in order to be found culpable in court the bailee must have articulated his plans for misappropriation.

84   Rex v. Scofield, Cald. 397 (1784). Dr. Gideon Yaffe notes this was not always the case. Yaffe, *Attempts* (Oxford, Oxford University Press, 2012), 1.

85   See Gideon Yaffe, "Criminal Attempts," *The Yale Law Journal* 124, no. 92 (2014): 101–103.

86   Yaffe, "Criminal Attempts," 101.

87   Yaffe, *Attempts,* 21.

88   Yaffe, "Criminal Attempts," 115.

89   See chapter 5 in Yaffe, *Attempts.*

90   See People v. Jaffe, 185 N.Y. 497, 78 N.E. 169 (1906).

91   People v. Dlugash, 41 N.Y.2d 725, 395 N.Y.S.2d 419, 363 N.E.2d 1155 (1977).

92   United States v. Crow, 164 F. 3d 229 (5th Cir. 1999).

93   United State v. Thomas, 13 U.S.C.M.A. 278 (1962).

94   Kadish et al., *Criminal Law and Its Processes: Cases and Materials,* 9th ed. (New York: Wolters Kluwer Law & Business, 2012), 646.

95   United State v. Thomas, 13 U.S.C.M.A. 278 (1962).

96   *Sanhedrin* 58b.

97   See Rama on *Hoshen Mishpat* 34:4, and the comment of the Vilna Gaon.

98   Jacob Bazak, "An Unsuccessful Attempt to Commit a Crime," in *Jewish Law Association Studies XVIII: The Bar-Ilan Conference Volume,* ed. Joseph Fleishman (The Jewish Law Association, 2008), 11.

99   Translation from the William Davidson Talmud available to the public on the invaluable website *Sefaria.*

100   For more on the legacy of the work *Ohr ha-Hayyim,* see David Assaf, "'A Heretic Who Has No Faith in the Great Ones of the Age': The Clash Over the Honor of the Or Ha-Hayyim," *Modern Judaism* 29, no. 2 (2009): 194–225.

101   See *Sefer Hasidim* 1425, and the comments of the Maharal Diskin on Gen. 50:20, in which he explains this verse to mean that Joseph's brothers do not need to apologize to Joseph, but still require absolution before God since they did attempt to commit a sin.

102   This question on the comments of *Ohr ha-Hayyim* is further strengthened based on a related case of attempt found in the Talmud in *Menahot* 64a. The case in *Menahot* involves someone who went fishing on Shabbat, which is forbidden, but upon raising his fish net found the body of a live baby. While attempting to violate Shabbat, the life of a child was saved. In one analysis of the case the Talmud explains that the liability of the fisherman depends on a dispute between Rabbah and Ravah who debate whether the fisherman should be assessed based on his criminal intent (Ravah) or the life-saving outcome (Rabbah). Maimonides, *Mishneh Torah, Hil. Shabbat* 2:16 rules in accordance with Ravah but nonetheless concludes that the fisherman has some measure of liability (see *Pri Megaddim* on *Orah Hayyim* 328:8). Once again we see here that an impossible attempt, much like the brothers of Joseph, still carries liability. Why, then, does the Ohr ha-Hayyim conclude that the brothers of Joseph were innocent though their attempt did not result in the crime they had intended? See *Binyan Shlomo* on *Hoshen Mishpat* 2:5, and Jacob Bazak, "An Unsuccessful Attempt to Commit a Crime," 13 for further analysis of this Talmudic passage and its implications for the principle of attempt.

103 See *Kli Hemdah*'s comment on *Parshat Va-Yehi* 3–4.

104 Many commentaries explain that Joseph's brothers were in fact convinced of Joseph's guilt and deserved punishment. See the comment of Seforno on Gen. 37:18 where he explains that Joseph's brothers viewed him as an assailant, justifying their actions on the Talmudic principle (*Sanhedrin* 72a) that someone who attempts to attack you can be pre-emptively punished.

105 Stephen Hawking, *A Brief History of Time* (New York: Bantam Books, 1988), vi–vii.

106 Michael Higger, "Intention in Talmudic Law" (PhD diss., Columbia University, 1927).

107 Shana Strauch-Schick, "Intention in Talmudic Law: An Intellectual History" (PhD diss., Yeshiva University, 2011).

108 See Malbim's *Sefer ha-Carmel*, entry *Zayin Daled*.

109 See *Sanhedrin* 8b.

110 Higger, "Intention," 56.

111 See the Responsa of Rabbi Akiva Eiger, 1:8, where he differentiates between an action performed while *mitasek* on Shabbat versus all other such actions. According to Rabbi Eiger, actions performed while *mitasek* are considered a sin—they are just exempt from a sacrificial obligation of penance. On Shabbat, however, an action performed while *mitasek* is not even considered a sin at all since on Shabbat actions require a higher level of intentionality to be considered a wrongdoing. This distinction has been widely debated among later rabbinic authorities.

112 See *Bava Kamma* 28b. See entry in the *Encyclopedia Talmudit*, vol. 1, *Oness*, paragraphs 347–350. See also Maimonides, *Mishneh Torah, Hil. Yesodei ha-Torah* 5:4, which cites an additional source from the interpretation of *Torat Kohanim* to the prohibition of delivering a child to idolatry (See Lev. 20:3).

113 See *Yad ha-Melech*'s comment on Maimonides, *Hil. Yesodei ha-Torah* 5:6.

114 See *Respona Rivash* 387.

115 Maimonides, *Hil. Yesodei ha-Torah* 5:6.

116 For more on the history of this letter, known as *Iggeret ha-Shemad*, and its relation to the rest of Maimonides' writings see Haym Soloveitchik, *Collected Essays Vol. 2* (Portland, OR: The Littman Library of Jewish Civilization, 2014), 288–364.

117 For a consideration of homosexuality in light of the exemption of duress in Jewish law, see Chaim Rapoport, *Judaism and Homosexuality: An Authentic*

Orthodox View (Portland, OR: Vallentine Mitchell, 2004), 61–67. In particular, see ibid., 65, where he cites the views of Rabbi Zadok Ha-Kohen in this legal discussion.

118   The Talmud in *Yevamot* 53b cites the opinion of Rava that male sexual arousal necessarily always involves implicit consent, so male sex acts are not subject to the exemption of coercion in Jewish law. For further discussion and additional views on this see the comments of Tosafot on *Yevamot* 53b–54a, s.v. "*eyn oness*"; Maimonides, *Mishneh Torah, Hil. Issurei Biah* 1:9; *Mishnah Sanhedrin* 20:3. See also the literature cited by Rapoport, *Judaism and Homsexuality*, 61–67.

119   Philippa Foot, "The Problem of Abortion and the Doctrine of Double Effect," *Oxford Review* 5 (1967): 5–15.

120   Kwame Anthony Appiah, *Experiments in Ethics* (Cambridge: Harvard University Press, 2008), 91.

121   For an unexpected but entertaining application of the Trolley Problem, see Robert Carlock, dir., *Unbreakable Kimmy Schmidt*, Season 3, episode 12, "Kimmy and the Trolley Problem!" aired May 19, 2017 on Netflix.

122   See his comments on *Yoma* 83a in his *Tosefet Yom ha-Kippurim*.

123   Vincent v. Lake Erie Transportation Co., 109 Minn. 456, 124 N.W. 221 (1910).

124   Regarding Halakhic direction in minimizing the violation of *Halakhah*, see Benjamin Brown, "'Ha-Ba'al Bayit'- R' Yisrael Meir Ha-Kohen, 'Ha-Hafetz Hayyim'," in *The Gdoilim*, ed. Benjamin Brown and Nissim Leon (Jerusalem: Magnes Press, 2017), 140. Note particularly its discussion of the work *Mahaneh Yisrael (The Camp of Israel)* by Rabbi Yisrael Meir Kagan (Vilna, 1881), which is a Halakhic compendium for Jewish soldiers in the Russian army. The volume includes a lot of Halakhic direction for soldiers in compromising situations such as someone who cannot pray all of the normal prayers or who only has access to non-kosher food. For an abbreviated English adaptation of *Mahaneh Yisrael* published by a student of Rabbi Kagan's on behalf of Jewish-American soldiers serving in World War II, see Rabbi Moses M. Yoshor, *Israel in the Ranks* (New York: Yeshivah Chofetz Chaim, 1943).

125   See Rabbi Wasserman's *Kovetz Ma'amarim*, 40–41.

126   See Shaul Magid, *Hasidism on the Margin: Reconciliation, Antinomianism, and Messianism in Izbica/Radzin Hasidism* (Madison: University of Wisconsin Press, 2003), xx and xxn18; Morris M. Fairstein, *All Is in the Hands of Heaven: The Teaching of Rabbi Mordechai Joseph Liener of Izbica* (Hoboken, NJ: Ktav Publishing House, 1989); and idem., "Kotsk-Izbica Dispute: Theological or Personal?" *Kabbalah* 17 (2008): 75–79.

127 For decades, the role of Rabbi Yaakov Leiner, author of the *Beit Yaakov*, was overlooked in the academic and religious community, a sentiment I personally heard bemoaned years ago by the *Rosh Yeshiva* of Yeshivat Kerem B'Yavneh, Rabbi Mendel Blachman. The academic community is indebted to Ora Wiskind-Elper, whose *Wisdom of the Heart: The Teachings of Rabbi Ya'akov of Izbica-Radzyn* (Philadelphia: The Jewish Publication Society, 2010) masterfully presents the Hasidic approach of the *Beit Yaakov*.

128 As opposed to his father, Rabbi Gershon Henokh has received careful attention regarding his role in radicalizing Izbica Hasidut. The messianic activities of Rabbi Gershon Henokh, including his efforts to renew the practice of wearing *tekhelet* as well as assembling a Talmudic commentary on the Order of *Tahorot*, which deals with ritual impurity, brought additional controversy and attention to Izbica Hasidut. For more on his life and theology see Shaul Magid, "'A Thread of Blue': Rabbi Gershon Henoch Leiner of Radzyń and his Search for Continuity in Response to Modernity," *Polin* 11 (1998), as well as his more comprehensive *Hasidism on the Margin*.

129 The works of Rabbi Zadok were first presented in English to the academic community by my teacher Rabbi Yaakov Elman. See Yaakov Elman, "R. Zadok Hakohen on the History of Halakhah," *Tradition* 21, no. 4 (Fall 1985): 1–26; Yaakov Elman, "Reb Zadok Hakohen of Lublin on Prophecy in the Halakhic Process," *Jewish Law Association Studies* 1 (1985): 1–16; Yaakov Elman, "The History of Gentile Wisdom According to R. Zadok ha-Kohen of Lublin," *Journal of Jewish Thought and Philosophy* 3, no. 1 (1993): 153–187; Yaakov Elman, "Progressive Derash and Retrospective Peshat: Nonhalakhic Considerations in Talmud Torah," in *Modern Scholarship in the Study of Torah: Contributions and Limitations,* ed. Shalom Carmy (Northvale, NJ: Jason Aronson, 1996), 227–87; and Yaakov Elman, "The Rebirth of Omnisignificant Biblical Exegesis in the Nineteenth and Twentieth Centuries," *Jewish Studies Internet Journal* 2 (2003): 199–249. Two other crucial works on Rabbi Zadok bear mentioning, Alan Brill, *Thinking God: The Mysticism of Rabbi Zadok of Lublin* (Jersey City, NJ: Ktav Publishing House, 2002) and the incisive dissertation of the elusive Amira Liwer, "Oral Torah in the Writings of Reb Zadok ha-Kohen of Lublin" (PhD diss., Hebrew University, 2006; Hebrew).

130 My decision to exclude Rabbi Leible Eiger from this collective Hasidic legacy is deliberate. The style and focus of his works is markedly different than the other Hasidic leaders mentioned. Nonetheless, his scholarship and contextual role within the larger Izbica tradition merits attention and sadly remains a glaring desideratum within the academic community. For more on the life of Rabbi Leible, see Shimon Hirschler, *Yehudah le-Kadsho*, 3 vols. (Tel Aviv: Shem Olam, 1999).

131 For example, see *Mei ha-Shiloah*, vol. 1 (Mishur, 1990), 27, 245. For instances of this phrase in the work of Rabbi Zadok, see his *Resisei Laylah* (Machon Har Bracha, 2002), 41, 50. See also his *Dover Tzedek* (Machon Har Bracha, 2007), 9.

132 Fairstein, *All Is in the Hands of Heaven*, 36.

133 Herzl Hefter, "'In God's Hands': The Religious Phenomenology of R. Mordechai Yosef of Izbica," *Tradition* 46, no. 1 (Spring 2013): 50.

134 All of the former examples are discussed by Herzl, "In God's Hands." The story of Aher is interpreted in this context in Rabbi Zadok's *Sefer Zikhronot* (Machon Har Bracha, 2002), 293:11.

135 See "In God's Hand's," 52–54, for interesting parallels in the writings of Rudolf Otto. For a much more comprehensive examination of the role of free will in Izbica see Aviezer Cohen, "Self-Consciousness in Mei ha-Shiloah as the Nexus Between God and Man" (PhD diss., Ben-Gurion University of the Negev, 2006; Hebrew).

136 See for instance Rabbi Zadok's *Tzidkat Ha-Tzadik* 40, which cites the Lurianic work *Arbeh Me'ot Shekel* 91b. It is interesting to note that Rabbi Zadok, rather than citing his rebbe, invokes this Lurianic work as a basis for the more radical determinism found in Izbica. See also *Likkutei Ma'amarim* (Machon Har Bracha, 2007), 183. In some instances Rabbi Zadok also cites a parable of the Baal Shem Tov to explain this concept, see *Pri Tzadik Bamidbar*, Rosh Chodesh Av.

137 Magid, *Hasidism on the Margin*, 248.

138 See also Brill, *Thinking God*, 199–200 where he suggests that the more radical applications of Hasidut in everyday life only flourished as a rejection of the "bourgeois morality in the 1930s." In this view, subversive extra-Halakhic notions only emerged when "the traditional way of life began to break down in confrontation with the libertine secular life of the cities."

139 Notably, in Rabbi Zadok's first Hasidic work, *Tzidkat Ha-Tzadik*, passages 162–163, were censored by his students. For more see Brill, *Thinking God*, 181. For other examples of students censoring the work of their teacher, see Marc Shapiro, *Changing the Immutable: How Orthodox Judaism Rewrites its History* (Portland, OR: The Littman Library of Jewish Civilization, 2015), 160–183, which discusses this phenomenon in the works of Rabbi Kook.

140 See Hefter, "'In God's Hands,'" 52.

141 *Pri Tzadik*, Nasso 15, citing Rabbi Mordekhai Yosef Leiner.

142 For a similar distinction, see Wiskind-Elper, *Wisdom of the Heart*, 102–103.

143　Rabbi Elliot Cosgrove, "Religion Beyond the Limits of Reason Alone," in *Go Forth! Selected Sermons by Rabbi Elliot J. Cosgrove* (Park Avenue Synagogue, 2013), http://pasyn.org/resources/sermons/%5Bfield_dateline-date%5D-52.

144　Jennie Rosenfeld, "Talmudic Re-Readings: Toward a Modern Orthodox Sexual Ethic" (PhD diss., The City University of New York, 2008), 122.

145　See ibid., 108–109, where Rosenfeld notes the centrality of this phrase in Rabbi Zadok's thought and also mentions the strange context, a discussion around the marriage right of a woman who is half-slave and half-free, which appears in Tractate *Gittin*. See my *B-Rogez Rahem Tizkor* (Brooklyn: HaDaf Printing, 2015), 47–50. See also the end of chapter 9 in this work for a suggested explanation of this phrase's strange contextual appearance as well as a discussion on the permissibility of voluntarily entering into situations of religious struggle.

146　See Shmuel Ettinger, "The Hasidic Movement—Reality and Ideals," in *Essential Papers on Hasidism: Origins to Present*, ed. Gershon David Hundert (New York: New York University Press, 1991), 226–243.

147　Haym Soloveitchik, "Rupture and Reconstruction: The Transformation of Contemporary Orthodoxy," *Tradition* 28, no. 4 (Summer 1994): 64–130.

148　Soloveitchik, "Rupture and Reconstruction," 66.

149　Ibid., 72.

150　Ibid., 65.

151　Ibid., 103.

152　See Steven Schwarzchild, "An Introduction to the thought of R. Isaac Hutner," *Modern Judaism* 5, no. 3 (February 1985): 235–277. Some added consideration regarding Rabbi Hutner's connection to Rabbi Zadok can be found in the exhaustive work of Rabbi Shlomo Kasirer, "Repentance in the Thought of R. Isaac Hutner" (PhD diss., Bar-Ilan University, 2009; Hebrew), 198–199.

153　*Pahad Yitzhak: Igrot U-Ketavim*, Letter 9.

154　*Igrot Moshe, Orah Hayyim*, 2:95. See also *Igrot Moshe, Yoreh Deah* 2:33 regarding removing a *yarmulke* at, what seems to be describing a nightclub. In a recent collection of Rabbi Shlomo Aviner's text message responses to Halakhic questions, he cites this ruling of Rabbi Moshe as precedent for his own similar conclusion. See *Piskei Shlomo*, vol. 1 (Beit El, 2013), 15.

155　See Rabbi Hershel Schachter's *B-Ikvei Ha-Tzon* (Jerusalem: 1997), 3, in which he explains that proper intent when committing a legally justified violation is absolutely required. If the violation is committed even when justified without the proper intent, the mitigating factors are disqualified. This logic may also be at play in Rabbi Feinstein's conclusion, namely, that the person will not have the necessary motivation that may have justified the removal of the *yarmulke*. For more, see my *B-Rogez Rahem Tizkor*, 84–85, as well as my discussion in the next chapter.

156   See *Akeidat Yitzhak, Va-Yera* 20.

157   This tale can be found in Rabbi Avraham Michaelson's *Shemen ha-Tov* (Petrokov, 1905), 60a–b. This story was brought to my attention by Marc Shapiro in "Further Comments," *The Seforim Blog* (blog), May 6, 2010, http://seforim.blogspot.com/2010/05/marc-shapiro-further-comments.html.

158   See *Sanhedrin* 74a–b as well as *Yoma* 82a—where the source for this exception is derived.

159   See comments of the Rama to *Shulkhan Arukh: Yoreh Deah* 157:1.

160   See *Shevut Yaakov* 2:117.

161   *Nodeh B-Yehudah, Yoreh Deah (Mahadura Tanina)* 161. For more on the unique Halakhic status of saving the entire Jewish people, see Yosef Aryeh Lorentz, *Mishnat Pikuach Nefesh* 63, where he cites an intriguing explanation from Rabbi Yitzhak Hutner. For Rabbi Hutner's reasoning behind this distinction, see Dovid Lichtenstein, "Seducing the Enemy," in *Headlines 2: Halachic Debates of Current Events* (New York: OU Press, 2017), 329–342.

162   See Rabbi Avraham Yitzhak Ha-Kohen Kook, *Mishpat Kohen* 144, as well as Rabbi Ari Yitzhak Shvat, "Gilui Arayot li-ma'an Bitahon ha-Medinah," *Techumim* 30 (2010): 68–81.

163   See Gavri Butler, "The Honeytrap: Seduction for National Defense in the State of Israel: A Theoretical Approach," in *Essays for a Jewish Lifetime: Burton D. Morris Jubilee Volume*, eds. Menachem Butler and Marian E. Frankston (New York: Hakirah Press, forthcoming in 2018). Compare Michal Shmulovich, "What the Mossad's female agents do—and don't do—for the sake of Israel," *Times of Israel*, September 15, 2012, https://www.timesofisrael.com/what-the-mossads-female-agents-do-and-dont-do-for-the-sake-of-israel/.

164   See *Yalkut Shimoni* 9 on Joshua.

165   Yuval Blankovsky, *Het l-Shem Shamayim* (Jerusalem: Magnes Press, 2017).

166   Blankovsky, *Het l-Shem Shamayim*, 6, citing Tzvi Heber, "Aveirah l-Shem Shamayim," *Ma'aliot* 21, no. 5759/1999: 205–228.

167 See Blankovsky, *Het l-Shem Shamayim*, 6n33, which cites several sources that align with this view, including the comment of Maharik in *shoresh* 167, Netziv on Gen. 27:9, and Rabbi Kook in *Mishpat Kohen* at 143–144.

168 For what proceeds, see Rabbi Hershel Schachter, *B-Ikvei Ha-Tzon*, 3:14–18.

169 See *Shabbat* 4a and Tosafot there s.v. "*Ve-Ki.*"

170 For more on the need for repentance on an *aveirah l-shmah*, see Rabbi Zadok of Lublin's *Tzidkat Ha-Tzadik,*128, as well as his *Mahshavat Harutz* 20:29.

171 See Rabbi Moshe Feinstein's *Igrot Moshe*, vol. 4, at *Orah Hayyim* 2:95 where Rabbi Feinstein was asked about removing a *yarmulke* before entering an inappropriate place. His response, insisting that in order to permit such an action you would need to have proper intentions while removing a head covering, may be in line with the logic posited by Rabbi Schachter.

172 See, however, Jerry Rabow, *50 Jewish Messiahs* (Jerusalem: Gefen Publishing House, 2002), 131–32, in which he considers Eve Frank, the daughter of Jacob Frank, to be a Jewish female false messiah.

173 See Gershom Scholem, *Kabbalah* (Jerusalem: Keter Publishing House, 1974), 259, which mentions five factors that "contributed to the overwhelming success of the messianic awakening."

174 See Leon Festinger, Henry W. Riecken, and Stanley Schachter, *When Prophecy Fails* (London: Pinter and Martin Ltd., 2008), 9–13, where he bases much of his renowned theory of cognitive dissonance on the story of Shabbtai Zevi, particularly the continued allegiance of his followers even following his apostasy and death.

175 Gershom Scholem, *The Messianic Idea in Judaism: And Other Essays on Jewish Spirituality* (New York: Schocken, 1995), 110.

176 Maimonides, *Mishneh Torah, Hil. Malakhim U-Milhamoteihem*, chapter 11.

177 See *Nazir* 23a.

178 Gershom Scholem, *Sabbatai Sevi: The Mystical Messiah* (Princeton: Princeton University Press, 1973), 813. See also Nehemia Polen, "Dark Ladies and Redemptive Compassion: Ruth and the Messianic Lineage in Judaism," in *Scrolls of Love: Ruth and the Song of Songs*, ed. Peter S. Hawkins (New York: Fordham University, 2006), 59–74.

179 See Isaiah Tishby, *Messianic Mysticism: Moshe Hayim Luzzato and the Padua School* (Portland, OR: The Littman Library of Jewish Civilization, 2014), 248–253. For more on this see also Ruth Kara-Ivanov Kaniel, "'Gedolah Aveirah Lishmah': Mothers of the Davidic Dynasty, Feminine Seduction and the Development of Messianic Thought, From Rabbinic Literature to

Rabbi Moses Haim Luzzato," *Nashim: A Journal of Jewish Women's Studies and Gender Issues* 24 (2013): 27–52.

180   See Mordechai L. Wilensky, "Hasidic-Mitnaggedic Polemics in the Jewish Communities of Eastern Europe: The Hostile Phase," in *Essential Papers on Hasidism: Origins to Present,* ed. Gershon David Hundert (New York: New York University Press, 1991), 259–261.

181   See Elijah Schochet, *The Hasidic Movement and the Gaon of Vilna* (Northvale, NJ: Jason Aronson, 1993), 52.

182   See Shaul Magid, "Deconstructing the Mystical: The Anti-Mystical Kabbalism in Rabbi Hayyim of Volozhin's Nefesh Ha-Hayyim," *The Journal of Jewish Thought and Philosophy* 9 (2000): 21–67. Note also Avinoam Fraenkel, *Nefesh HaTzimtzum, Vol. 1: Rabbi Chaim Volozhin's Nefesh HaChaim with Translation and Commentary* (Jerusalem: Urim Publications, 2015), 46. For another commendable translation of *Nefesh ha-Hayyim* see Eliezer Lipa (Leonard) Moskowitz's *The Soul of Life: The Complete Neffesh Ha-Chayyim* (Teaneck, NJ: New Davar Publications, 2014).

183   *Nefesh ha-Hayyim* in *Shaar* 3.

184   Many point out the difficulty in Rabbi Hayyim's hypothesis, since the entire concept of *aveirah l-shmah* originates from the story of Yael which follows the Sinai revelation. See Rabbi Hershel Schachter, *B-Ikvei Ha-Tzon* 3 and my *B-Rogez Rahem Tizkor,* chapter 10.

185   Yehoshua Mondshine, "The Fluidity of Categories in Hasidism," in *Hasidism Reappraised,* ed. Ada Rapoport-Albert (Portland, OR: The Littman Library of Jewish Civilization, 1996), 315.

186   Ibid., 313.

187   Richard Pindell, "Somebody's Son," in *Choices,* ed. Burton Goodman (New York: Glencoe McGraw-Hill, 2002), 142. "Somebody's Son" was originally published in *American Girl* (August 1966): 28–47.

188   Pindell, "Somebody's Son," 145.

189   See the comment of Tosafot on *Shavuot* 9a, s.v. "*Se'ir*".

190   See Dov Weiss, *Pious Irreverence: Confronting God in Rabbinic Judaism* (Philadelphia: University of Pennsylvania Press, 2017), 180–181, for a discussion of the story in *Hullin.* See also ibid.n76 for a concise presentation of some of the rabbinic apologetics to this story. For more on the ease in which this passage can be misunderstood see Rabbi Yehudah Loew's *Gur Aryeh* to Numbers 28:15 as well as his *Be'er ha-Golah* 4, which describes people "astonished and bewildered" when reading this passage.

191 Weiss, *Pious Irreverance*, 20.

192 Ibid., 110–113.

193 Ibid., 113.

194 Ibid., 111.

195 Ibid., 184.

196 Ibid.

197 Ibid., 188n9.

198 Nehemia Polen, *The Holy Fire* (Lanham, MD: Rowman & Littlefield, 2004), 94–105. In particular see his interpretation of Sarah's death following Yitzhak's sacrifice at ibid., 96–97. See also Erin Leib, "God in the Years of Fury: Theodicy and Anti-Theodicy in the Holocaust Writings of Rabbi Kalonymus Kalman Shapira" (PhD diss., University of Chicago, 2014), 37–40.

199 Polen, *The Holy Fire*, 155.

200 See *Pesikta Rabbati* 33; Weiss, *Pious Irreverance*, 157–159.

201 *Genesis Rabbah* 55:3; Weiss, *Pious Irreverance*, 159–160.

202 *Berakhot* 6a.

203 Jerusalem Talmud *Rosh Hashanah* 1:2.

204 Weiss uses some of these sorts of examples to challenge the notion that the rabbinic conception of God was perfect. I find his thesis in this regard quite radical. Readers can draw their own conclusions. I, however, have opted to provide a different approach to this question.

205 Rabbi Joseph B. Soloveitchik, *Halakhic Man* (Philadelphia: The Jewish Publication Society of America, 1983), 107.

206 See Weiss, *Pious Irreverence*, 34 on the concept of hurling words heavenward (*metiakh devarim kelapei ma'alah*).

207 See *Pri Tzadik, Va-Yelekh* 16.

208 For more on the repentance of God, see chapter 8 of my *B-Rogez Rahem Tizkor*.

209 For a remarkable consideration of analogies as a sign of humanity see Douglas Hofstadter and Emmanuel Sander, *Surfaces and Essences: Analogy as the Fuel and Fire of Thinking* (New York: Basic Books, 2013).

210 W. Granger Blair, "Monk Sues in High Court in Israel for Right to Settle as a Jew," *New York Times*, November 20, 1962.

211   The Law of Return was enacted by Israel's Knesset on July 5, 1950.

212   Baruch Litvin, *Jewish Identity: Modern Responsa and Opinions*, ed. Sidney B. Hoenig (New York: Shulsinger Bros. Inc., 1965).

213   See *Arukh* s.v. *"shemad"* and Saul Lieberman, *Tosefta ki-Pshutah*, vol. 2 (New York: The Jewish Theological Seminary Press, 2012), 402n45.

214   See Talmud *Hullin* 4b–5a.

215   Louis Jacobs, "Attitudes Towards Christianity in the Halakhah," in *Judaism and Theology: Essays on the Jewish Religion* (Portland, OR: Vallentine Mitchell, 2005), 102–116.

216   Regarding conversion to Islam in Medieval Halakhic literature, see the incisive but contentious analysis of Haym Soloveitchik, "Maimonides' Iggeret ha-Shemad: Law and Rhetoric," in *Collected Essays vol. II* (Portland, OR: The Littman Library of Jewish Civilization, 2014), 288–330.

217   For a full overview on the varied rabbinic opinions on this issue, see Ephraim Kanarfogel, "Returning to the Jewish Community in Medieval Ashkenaz: History and Halacha," in *Tumim: Studies in Jewish History and Literature— Presented to Dr. Bernard Lander Volume One* ed. Michael A. Shmidman (Jersey City, NJ: Ktav Publishing, 2007), 69–97.

218   See *Yoreh Deah* 268.

219   See, for example, *Hagaot Ashrei, Moed Katan* 3:59.

220   See Rabbi Shlomo Kluger's *Teshuvot Tuv Ta'am va-Da'at (Mahadura Telitai)* 2:232.

221   *Teshuvot Hatam* Sofer 326.

222   *Teshuvot Rashi* 168–175.

223   See the comment of Mordekhai to *Yevamot* 29. See Deut. 25:5, which mentions the term *ahim*, brothers, to introduce the law of levirate marriage. Based on this term, some insist that the laws of levirate marriage have a higher standard of brotherhood that would exclude an apostate, even if for other considerations the apostate would be considered a Jew.

224   There was a minority Geonic opinion that someone who converts is no longer considered a Jew. See *Tur Even ha-Ezer* 44.

225   *Sanhedrin* 44a.

226   Jacob Katz, *Exclusiveness and Tolerance: Studies in Jewish-Gentile Relations in Medieval and Modern Times* (Oxford: Oxford University Press, 1961).

227   Ibid., 71.

228 See de Medina's discussion of *Bekhorot* 36a and *Yevamot* 46b, in which he marshals further proof for an apostate's loss of Jewish identity.

229 Israel Shenker, "Responsa: The Law As Seen By Rabbis for 1,000 Years," *New York Times*, May 5, 1975.

230 Aside from the example to follow, there are several other instances where Rabbi Feinstein was adamant regarding the immutability of Jewish identity. See *Dibrot Moshe* to *Yevamot* 89, where he discredits a rabbinic opinion that Jewish identity can be legally dissolved.

231 *Igrot Moshe, Even ha-Ezer* 4:83.

232 Dan Harris, Eric Johnson, and Mary Flynn, "Atheists Break Out New Ritual Tool: The Blow-Dryer," *ABC News*, July 16, 2010, https://abcnews.go.com/Nightline/atheists-conduct-de-baptisms/story?id=11109379.

233 There is some discussion in Jewish law whether converting to another religion is preferred to atheism. This question has practical ramifications in the laws of *yibum*. When a woman's husband dies without children, the Torah asks that she either marry one of his brothers or, more common today, perform a ceremony known as *halitzah*, which allows her to marry whomever she wants. In a situation where one brother has converted to another religion and another brother is an atheist, contemporary Halakhic authorities debate which is preferable. See Rabbi Yechiel Yaakov Weinberg's *Responsa S'reidi Eish, Even ha-Ezer*, 1:114–115. His animated disagreement with Rabbi Yosef Rosen, known as the Rogatchover Gaon, is fascinating.

234 "Excerpts from Israeli Court Opinion in Monk's Case," *New York Times*, December 7, 1962.

235 Ibid.

236 This point is an important consideration when considering racial identity. The 2015 controversy surrounding Rachel Dolezal, a white woman who self-identified as black, has many parallels with the role of the Jewish community in shaping Jewish identity. See "Beyond the Jewfro: Rachel Dolezal Story Touches Historic Nerve for Jews," *Haaretz*, June 15, 2015. See also Avraham Osipov-Gipsh, "Am I Like Rachel Dolezal?" *Tablet*, June 19, 2015, http://www.tabletmag.com/jewish-news-and-politics/191559/rachel-dolezal, which questionably advocates that communities should have no say over the boundaries for those who want to identify with them.

237 Aharon Lichtenstein, "Brother Daniel and the Jewish Fraternity," *Judaism* 12, no. 3 (Summer 1963).

238 *Pri Tzadik, Tetzaveh* 12.

239 See *Hokhmah U-Mussar* 1:53.

240 "Excerpts from Israeli Court Opinion in Monk's Case," *New York Times*, December 7, 1962.

241 As told to the author by Rabbi Yossel "Joe" Kanofsky. I am indebted to him for introducing me to this short story.

242 See Lev. 4:22. See the comments of Rashi and Seforno ad loc.

243 For more on the inevitability of failure in the context of leadership see Rabbi Jonathan Sack's essay, "The Sins of a Leader," in his *Covenant and Conversation—Leviticus: The Book of Holiness* (Jerusalem: Koren Publishers, 2015). For a Halakhic discussion of the parameters of sin as a disqualification from leadership see Nahum Rakover, "Should Transgression Disqualify One from Public Office," in *Jewish Law Association Studies XII: The Zutphen Conference Volume*, ed. Hillel Gamoran (Binghamton: Binghamton University, 2002), 141–157.

244 Jacob J. Schacter, "On the Morality of the Patriarchs: Must Biblical Heroes Be Perfect?" in *Jewish Education in Tradition: Proceedings of the First International Conference on Jewish Education*, ed. Zvi Grumet (Teaneck, NJ: Ben Yehuda Press, 2007), 1–9. For a thorough discussion on the unreliability of rabbinic biography in general, particularly in evaluating sin, see Alon Goshen-Gottstein, *The Sinner and the Amnesiac: The Rabbinic Invention of Elisha ben Abuya and Eleazar ben Arach* (Stanford: Stanford University Press, 2000).

245 Zev Eleff, "Psychohistory and the Imaginary Couch: Diagnosing Historical Biblical Figures," *Journal of The American Academy of Religion* 80, no. 1 (March 2012): 94–136.

246 See *Moed Katan* 17a.

247 See Maimonides, *Mishneh Torah, Hilkhot Talmud Torah*, 4:1; *Shulkhan Arukh: Yoreh Deah, Hilkhot Talmud Torah* 246:8. There have been a few exhaustive reviews of the laws regarding learning from a disgraced rabbi in contemporary Jewish law. For example, see Yaakov Shmuel Spiegel, "How is Elisha b. Avuya Mentioned in the Mishnah and Learning from Works Whose Authors Went to Bad Environs," in *M-Orot L-Yehudah: Pirkei Hagut v-Hinukh*, ed. Moshe Rachimi (Elkanah-Rehovot: Mikhlelet Orot Yisrael, 2012; Hebrew). See also Dovid Lichtenstein, "The Disgraced Rabbi," in *Headlines 2: Halachic Debates of Current Events* (New York: OU Press, 2017), 95–120.

248 See Rabbi Yehudah Loew's (Maharal) *Tiferes Yisrael*, chapter 12.

249 See the comment of Rabbi Yaakov Tzvi Mecklenburg in his *Ha-Ketav Ve-HaKabbalah* on Numbers 22:5.

250 For more on the angelic capacity for free will, see Marc Shapiro, *The Limits of Orthodox Theology: Maimonides' Thirteen Principles Reappraised* (Portland, OR: The Littman Library of Jewish Civilization, 2011), 78–86.

251 See Maharal, *Netivot Olam: Netiv Ha-Torah*, chapter 14. For more on these and other distinctions and considerations, see Lichtenstein, *Headlines 2*, 95–120.

252 See *Hagigah* 14b. It is unclear whether the exception allotted to Rabbi Meir, namely that his greatness afforded him the right to learn directly from a disgraced rabbi, is accepted in Jewish law. See the comment of *Siftei Kohen* on *Yoreh Deah* 246. See also Rabbi Ovadia Yosef, *Yabia Omer* 7:19.

253 See Norman K. Swazo, "Rabbi Elisha Ben Abuyah 'At the Mind's Limit': Between Theodicy and Fate." *Philosophy and Literature* 38, no. 1 (2014): 153–168, who has a long analysis of Steinberg's work. He concludes that Steinberg, in effect attempted to redeem *Aher* himself. In the closing paragraph of his article he writes, "Situating us as witnesses in a modern court of reason, Steinberg, I submit, rules on the question of Elisha's salvation."

254 See Gedaliahu G. Stroumsa, "Aher: A Gnostic," in *The Rediscovery of Gnosticism, volume 2*, ed. Bentley Layton (Leiden: Brill Academic Publishing, 1997), 808.

255 See also the Tosefta on *Hagigah* 2:3–4.

256 See Jay Rovner, "Structure and Ideology in the Aher Narrative (bHag 15a and b)," *JSIJ* 10 (2012): 1–73.

257 Jeffrey L. Rubinstein, "Elisha ben Abuya: Torah and the Sinful Sage," *The Journal of Jewish Thought and Philosophy* 7 (1998): 142n7 does point out that in some manuscripts *Aher* is identified as Elisha in this passage. The ambiguity of his name in this passage may relate, as we will discuss, to the very ambiguity of his fate.

258 *Hagigah* 15a.

259 Jerusalem Talmud *Hagigah* 2:1.

260 Rubinstein, "Elisha ben Abuya," 172.

261 See *Hagigah* 15a–b.

262 See Rubinstein, "Elisha ben Abuya," 200n128, for a fascinating explanation for the differing narratives based on the Aristotelian theory of tragedy.

263 Rubinstein, 156–157.

264 *Hagigah* 15b.

265 See the comments of Rabbi Zvi Hirsch Chajes to *Sanhedrin* 11a in his *Hagaot Maharatz Hayes*, where he considers the act of asking a child at random what he learned in school a form of *Bat Kol* (which can be loosely translated as a "heavenly whisper").

266 Rovner, "Structure and Ideology," 32. See also Rabbi Joseph Trani, the Maharit, at 2:8 of his responsa.

267 Rovner, 35.

268 Rubinstein, "Elisha ben Abuya," 158.

269 See Talmud *Ketubot* 62b. See also Talmud *Pesakhim* 49b where Rabbi Akiva said of himself that before he became immersed in Torah he would have bitten a Torah scholar. For more on his life see *Encyclopedia Judaica*, 2nd ed. (2006), s.v. "Akiva Ben Joseph." More recently, Barry W. Holtz authored a biography on Rabbi Akiva as part of Yale's "Jewish Lives" Series. See Barry W. Holtz, *Rabbi Akiva: Sage of the Talmud* (New Haven, CT: Yale University Press, 2017). For an illuminating piece on the optimism of Rabbi Akiva, see Meir Soloveichik, "Rabbi Akiva's Optimism," *Azure* 30 (Autumn 2007).

270 *Makkot* 24b.

271 Rabbi Hershel Schachter records this explanation in the name of Rabbi Joseph Dov Soloveitchik in his *Mi-Pninei Ha-Rav* (Jerusalem: Hotzaot Beit Hamidrash Dflatbush, 2001), 216.

272 Kim Severson, "Mixing Drinks with Work and Staying Sober, Too," *New York Times*, June 23, 2009.

273 Some commentaries contextualize this passage of Talmud to be referring only to loftier levels of repentance; see Rabbeinu Nissim of Gerona in his *Derashot Ha-Ran*, chapter 6, see also Rabbeinu Yonah's *Shaarei Teshuvah* at 1:49.

274 For more on the Hasidei Ashkenaz see the discussion found in chapter 13 "To Whom it May Concern: Rabbinic Correspondence on Sin and Failure" in this work.

275 See A. Rubin, "The Concept of Repentance Among the Hasidey Ashkenaz," *The Journal of Jewish Studies* 16 (1965): 161–176. See also Talya Fishman, "The Penitential System of Hasidei Ashkenaz and the Problem of Cultural Boundaries," *The Journal of Jewish Thought and Philosophy* 8 (1999): 207–209. There she also cites *Avodah Zarah* 17b as another possible source that advocates placing oneself into situations of temptation.

276 *Sefer ha-Rokeah* 206.

277 Fishman, "The Penitential System of Haside Ashkenaz," 209.

278   Rubin, "The Concept of Repentance," 166n21.

279   See Brill, *Thinking God*, 108. See also Norman Lamm, *The Religious Thought of Hasidism* (Hoboken, NJ: Ktav Publishing House, 1999), 370, which presents a comparison of their respective approaches to repentance and the need to repent for previous acts of repentance.

280   See Green, *Tormented Master*, 266, which cites a moving example of the fervor with which this slogan was held by contemporary Bratslav Hasidim during the torments of World War II. Green found in the diary of Emanuel Ringelblum a description of life in the Warsaw ghetto. The diary describes, "In the prayer-house of the Hasidim from Bratslav on Nowolipie Street there is a large sign: 'Jews, Never Despair!' The Hasidim dance there with the same religious fervor as they did before the war."

281   *Likutei Moharan* is the foundational work of Bratslav Hasidut. Most of the work was compiled by Rabbi Nahman though some segments were added or edited by Rabbi Nathan.

282   I have decided to cite the passage in the original Hebrew, with my own translation following. The original language will help facilitate linguistic comparisons to Rabbi Zadok's work.

283   See *Likutei Moharan* II:78.

284   See Rabbi Zadok's *Divrei Sofrim* 16.

285   Shilo Pachter, "Shmirat Habrit: The History of the Prohibition of Wasting Seed" (PhD diss., Hebrew University, 2006; Hebrew), 244–275.

286   *Shivhei Moharan* 11–12, translated in Green, *Tormented Master*, 27. See also *Shivhei* 2, in *Tzadik: A Portrait of Rabbi Nachman*, trans. Avraham Greenbaum (Jerusalem: Breslov Research Institute, 1987), 247, which depicts Rabbi Nahman's efforts to experience the holiness of Shabbat as a child. After intensely preparing himself to accept Shabbat, "he wanted to see something but he saw nothing." Pained by his sense of distance from the awesome holiness of Shabbat he crawled underneath the table and cried for several hours.

287   Green, *Tormented Master*, 288.

288   See Green's discussion of Rabbi Nahman's approach to religious ecstasy in *Tormented Master*, 142. He writes, "Nahman, plagued as he was by inner tensions, could not accept the rather facile advocacy of joy that was his Hasidic heritage."

289   See, for example, *Likutei Moharan* II:12.

290 See *Shivhei Moharan* (Brooklyn: Moriah, 1974), 3–7. Also see the commendable translation of Avraham Greenbaum in *Tzadik: A Portrait of Rabbi Nachman* (Jerusalem: Breslov Research Institute, 1987), 247–253. Aside from the chapter dedicated to the triumphs that emerge from Rabbi Nahman's spiritual struggles, the entire biography is replete with similar examples that occurred throughout Rabbi Nahman's life.

291 See Elchanan Dov's biographical sketch appended to Rabbi Zadok's *Otzar He-Melekh* (Bnei Brak: Yahadus, 1968), 3 and its reference to *Midrash Tanhuma* Noah 3 in this regard.

292 First printed in 1922.

293 See Brill, *Thinking God*, 27 for a translation.

294 Brill speculates that it relates to Rabbi Zadok's sinful past, suggesting that "the moral weakness he experienced during adolescence and marriage is likely to have been his own sexual desire or perhaps masturbation." Brill, *Thinking God*, 27.

295 Rabbi Zadok returns to this point countless times in his writings. Of particular interest in this context may be *Tzidkat Ha-Tzadik* 76 that reiterates many of the themes discussed in this dream.

296 See *Tzadik: A Portrait of Rabbi Nachman*, 248.

297 Ibid., 249.

298 See Jerusalem Talmud *Sanhedrin* 2:3 and Babylonian Talmud *Sanhedrin* 107a.

299 An early Hasidic work written by Rabbi Yaakov Yosef of Ostroh (1738–1791).

300 Written by Rabbi Shlomo Ephraim ben Aaron Luntschitz (1550–1619).

301 There the story is cited that King David would have concubines brought before him every day and would treat them as if they were prohibited to him by Jewish law, despite the fact that they were permitted. He would say to his evil inclination, "Do you desire something which is forbidden to you? By your life! I will make you desire something which is permitted to you."

302 *Takanat ha-Shavin* 9.

303 For more on the Talmudic phrase "[w]here penitents stand, even the wholly righteous cannot stand," see Nahum Rakover, "Where Penitents Stand, Even the Wholly Righteous Cannot Stand," in *Between Rashi and Maimonides: Themes in Medieval Jewish Thought, Literature and Exegesis*, eds. Ephraim Kanarfogel and Moshe Sokolow (New York: Yeshiva University Press, 2010), 167–190.

304 Sim B. Sitkin, "Learning through Failure: The Strategy of Small Losses," in *Research in Organizational Behavior*, Vol. 14, eds. L.L. Cummings and B.M. Staw (Greenwich, CT: JAI Press, 1992), 231–266.

305 Ibid., 243.

306 Ibid., 232.

307 See Jennie Rosenfeld, "Talmudic Re-Readings: Toward a Modern Orthodox Sexual Ethic," 108. Her discussion focuses on the interpretation of this passage in the works of Rabbi Zadok. She notes, "R. Zadok clearly reads against the literal meaning of this text in that the statement is more the academic observation of a rabbinic decisor than a practical observation about the role of sin in the life of the individual; the stumbling referred to is in rendering an incorrect ruling rather than in taking an incorrect or sinful action." I have taken for granted that the context of Talmudic passages should be taken into account in their interpretation. This, however, is a much larger discussion. See the literature cited by Jeffrey L. Rubinstein, "Elisha ben Abuya: Torah and the Sinful Sage," *The Journal of Jewish Thought and Philosophy* 7 (1998): 207n142.

308 See *B-Rogez Rahem Tizkor*, 47–50, where I first presented the contextual connection of this passage to the broader Talmudic discussion.

309 This phenomenon, of course, is not limited to the children of Jewish clergy. There is an extensive body of literature that discusses the corollary of this phenomenon in the Christian world, where it is often referred to as "Preacher's Kid." See, for example, the memoirs of Franklin Graham, son of the famed evangelist Billy, *Rebel with a Cause* (Nashville, TN:Thomas Nelson Publishers, 1995). For more, see Carol Anderson, "The Experience of Growing Up in a Minister's Home and the Religious Commitment of the Adult Child of a Minister," *Pastoral Psychology* 46, no. 6 (1998): 393–411. Testimonials of children of rabbis are uncommon but not rare. For a touching anecdote, see Jerome R. Mintz, *Hasidic People: A Place in the New World* (Cambridge, MA: Harvard University Press: 1992), 19–20 which quotes Rabbi Israel Friedman, the child of the Boyaner Rebbe, who decided to become a social worker instead of a Hasidic Rebbe like his father. "When I said I would go into social work," Rabbi Friedman recalls, "my father said, 'That's the next best thing to being a Rebbe.'" More recently, Shulamit Kitzis published a volume exploring the experience of children of rabbis in the religious Zionist community. See Kitzis, *Demut Deyokno: Avot Rabanim ba-Tzionit ha-Datit ba-Eynei Yildeihem* (Israel: Resling, 2017). Dr. Kitzis is herself the child of the esteemed Rabbi Shimon Gershon Rosenberg, known as Rav Shagar.

310 Irving N. Levitz, "Children of Rabbis," *Tradition* 23, no. 2 (Winter 1988): 76–87.

311   Ibid., 79.

312   Ibid., 77.

313   David Assaf, *Untold Tales of the Hasidim: Crisis & Discontent in the History of Hasidism* (Lebanon, NH: Brandeis University Press, 2010).

314   Ibid., 30.

315   In a recent article on *The Lehrhaus* web site, Elli Fischer couches the phenomenon of Rabbi's Children in an earlier biblical figure—Yitzhak, the son of Avraham. See his "The Patron Saint of Rabbi's Kids," *The Lehrhaus*, December 1, 2016, http://www.thelehrhaus.com/commentary-short-articles/patron-saint-of-rabbis-sons.

316   See Rabbi Moshe Sofer's comment, in his *Torat Moshe*, on Numbers 1:3.

317   See Rabbi Avraham Shmuel Sofer's comment, in his *Ktav Sofer*, on the Torah portion of *Shemini*, where he explains that Aaron's children were reluctant to get married in order to avoid having children and repeating the parental mistakes they witnessed Moshe make.

318   Interestingly, Moshe's grandson may have served as an idolatrous priest. See Rashi's comment on Judges 18:30. See also *Bava Batra* 109b.

319   See his introduction to *Tiferet Yisrael*.

320   See Rabbi Shlomo Rabinowicz of Radomsk's (1801–1866) *Tiferet Shlomo, Moadim,* 6, and Rabbi Aryeh Zvi Fromer of Koziegłowy's (1884–1943) Responsa *Eretz Ha-Tzvi* 20. They both pose this question, though they offer different approaches than what proceeds here.

321   See *Sefer Haredim* 12:18, Responsa *Dvar Avraham* 1:31, and the presentation of Rabbi Soloveitchik in *Shiurei Ha-Rav, Tefillah u-Kriat Shema* 22.

322   See his *Imrei Emet* on the Torah portion of *Nasso* for the year 5624.

323   For more on this approach to the Kohanic blessings see my *B-rogez Rahem Tizkor*, 21–30. See there also the explanation in line with this approach of the Talmudic custom to pray for one's dreams during the blessings of the Kohanim.

324   Special appreciation must be given to Rabbi Baruch Dov Braun. I never would have met the Jonah described in this chapter were it not for his analysis. My continued admiration and deepest gratitude to Rabbi Braun for making this introduction. Jonah has always fascinated scholars. For other approaches to the personality of Jonah, see in particular Ze'ev Haim Lifshitz, *The Paradox of Human Existence: A Commentary on the Book of Jonah* (Northvale, NJ: Jason Aronson, 1994), Rabbi Avraham Rivlin, *Yonah:*

Nevuah va-Tokhahah (Israel: Hotzaot Yeshivat Kerem B'Yavneh, 5766), and, most recently, Dr. Erica Brown, *Jonah: The Reluctant Prophet* (Jerusalem: Maggid Books, 2017).

325   *Midrash Shokher Tov* 26:7.

326   David Hume, *The Natural History of Religion* (London: A. and H. Bradlaugh Bonner, 1889), 9–10.

327   This is a translation of his original statement in German, *"Die Religion . . . ist das opium des volkes."* The quote comes from Karl Marx's 1843 work *A Contribution to the Critique of Hegel's Philosophy of Right.*

328   Gordon Allport and J. Michael Ross, "Personal Religious Orientation and Prejudice," *Journal of Personality and Social Psychology* 5:4 (1967): 432–443. Since the publication of this article, there has been an explosion of literature on religious motivation. For an academic discussion of religious motivation in the Jewish context see, in particular, Aryeh Lazar and Shlomo Kravetz, "A Motivational Systems Theory Approach to the Relation Between Religious Experience and Motives," *The International Journal for the Psychology of Religion* 15:1 (2005): 63–72. Dr. Lazar has worked on religious motivation studies within the Israeli population. See his dissertation, "The Structure of the Motivation for Religious Behavior among Jews: A Comparison of Two Structure Models" (PhD diss., Bar-Ilan University, 1999).

329   Christian Wiman, *My Bright Abyss: Meditations of a Modern Believer* (New York: Farrar, Straus and Giroux, 2013), 146.

330   Ibid.

331   Ibid., 7.

332   For the primary theories regarding proper corporate apologies see Keith Michael Hearit, *Crisis Management by Apology* (New York: Routledge, 2010); W. Timothy Coombs, *Ongoing Crisis Communication: Planning, Managing, and Responding* (Thousand Oaks, CA: Sage, 2012); Uriel Rosenthal, R. Arjen Boin and Louise K. Comfort, *Managing Crises: Threats, Dilemmas, Opportunities* (Springfield, IL: Charles C. Thomas, 2001); and Alfred A. Marcus and Robert S. Goodman, "Victims and Shareholders: The Dilemmas of Presenting Corporate Policy During a Crisis," *The Academy of Management Journal* 34:2 (June 1991). For an anthology of poor apologies see Paul Slansky and Arleen Sorkin, *My Bad: The Apology Anthology* (New York: Bloomsbury 2006). Nearly all discussions of apologies in a religious context include a reference to Simon Wiesenthal's *The Sunflower: On the Possibilities and Limits of Forgiveness* (New York: Schocken Books, 1976), a moving volume that considers the possibility of forgiving Nazis in the aftermath of the Holocaust.

333 See Richard E. Mooney, "Editorial Notebook; 'If This Sounds Slippery . . .' How to Apologize And Admit Nothing," *New York Times*, November 30, 1992, http://www.nytimes.com/1992/11/30/opinion/editorial-notebook-if-this-sounds-slippery-how-to-apologize-and-admit-nothing.html.

334 Ibid.

335 See John M. Broder, "Familiar Fallback for Officials: 'Mistakes were Made'," *New York Times*, March 14, 2007.

336 See Hearit, *Crisis Management by Apology*, 30–31.

337 See Robert L. Ulmer, Timothy L. Sellnow and Matthew W. Seeger, *Effective Crisis Communication: Moving from Crisis to Opportunity*, 2nd ed. (Thousand Oaks, CA: SAGE Publications, 2011), 3.

338 For a more comprehensive history on the concept of repentance see David A. Lambert's *How Repentance Became Biblical: Judaism, Christianity, & the Interpretation of Scripture* (New York: Oxford University Press, 2016). Regrettably, I only became aware of the volume during the final stages of the preparation of this manuscript.

339 See Pinchas H. Peli, ed. *Al ha-Teshuvah* (Jerusalem: World Zionist Organization, Department for Torah Education and Culture in the Diaspora, 1975), 15–18, translated into English in Pinchas H. Peli, ed. *On Repentance in the Thought and Oral Discourses of Rabbi Joseph B. Soloveitchik* (Northvale, NJ: Jason Aronson, 1996). See also Yitzchak Blau "Creative Repentance: On Rabbi Soloveitchik's Concept of Teshuva," *Tradition* 28, no. 2 (Winter 1994): 11–18. Rabbi Soloveitchik was not the only thinker who developed a dual typology for sin along these lines. See also Rabbi Elchanan Wasserman's *Kovetz Ha'arot: Dugmaot la-Biurei Agadot al Derekh Peshat* 3, which presents a similar dichotomy in his analysis of sin in Jewish though.

340 Pinchas Peli, "Repentant Man-A High Level in Rabbi Soloveitchik's Typology of Man," *Tradition* 18, no. 2 (Summer 1980): 140.

341 Stephen P. Garvey, "Punishment as Atonement," *UCLA Law Review* 46, no. 6 (August 1999): 1818.

342 See Samuel Levine, "Teshuva: A Look at Repentance, Forgiveness and Atonement in Jewish Law and Philosophy and American Legal Thought," *Fordham Urban Law Journal* 27, no. 5 (2000): 1677.

343 Ibid., 1693.

344 See comments of the Rama to *Shulkhan Arukh: Orah Hayyim* 343 and the discussion of the Radvaz in 6:2.

345 See the discussion of Tosafot to *Sanhedrin* 71b s.v. *"ben."* Many Halakhic commentaries discuss the legal culpability of a convert for the sins committed prior to conversion; for more see the sources cited in *Yalkut Meforshim* (Wagshal edition) to *Sanhedrin* ibid.

346 *Beit Elokim*. Cited in Rabbi Shraga Neuberger's pamphlet on repentance, *Sas Anokhi* no. 13, 20–21 which presents this passage as support for the idea of "Half *Teshuvah*" [חצי תשובה].

347 For more on the role of verbal confession, see Rabbi Simcha Zissel Broyde's *Sam Derekh: Parshat Nizavim* 9.

348 See Rabbi Avraham Genichovsky *Agan ha-Sahar (Mahadura Shlishit)*, edited by Rabbi Shmuel Fish (Israel: 5773), 105–106.

349 There is a lot of discussion in Halakhic literature regarding the limits of when to apply the presumption that the inner will of a Jew is to act in accordance with Jewish law. For instance, is this presumption still operative if the person in question has converted to another religion? For more on this assumption, see *Hagaot Maimoniyot, Hilkhot Gerushin* 2:20:4, as well as *Teshuvot Hatam Sofer* 4, *Even ha-Ezer* 2:60.

350 See chapter 6 in my *B-Rogez Rahem Tizkor*, where I first present this analysis.

351 John W. Collis, *Seven Fatal Management Sins: Understanding and Avoiding Managerial Malpractice* (Boca Raton, FL: CRC Press LLC, 1998), 151.

352 Pema Chödrön, *When Things Fall Apart: Heart Advice for Difficult Times* (Boulder, CO: Shambhala Publications, 1997), 102.

353 For more on the etymology of the word *mehilah* [מחילה] see Mitchell First's essay "What is the Origin of the Word מחילה" in his collection *Esther Unmasked* (New York: Kodesh Press, 2015), 30–41.

354 Shaun Usher, *Letters of Note: An Eclectic Collection of Correspondence Deserving of a Wider Audience* (San Fransisco: Chronicle Books, 2014), xvi.

355 Gordon A. Craig, "On the Pleasure of Reading Diplomatic Correspondence," *Journal of Contemporary History* 25, no. 3/4 (1991): 369–384.

356 Haym Soloveitchik, "Three Themes in the 'Sefer Hasidim,'" *AJS Review*, 1, no. 1 (1976): 315.

357 Haym Soloveitchik, "Re-evaluation of Eleventh-Century Ashkenaz," in *Collected Essays vol. II* (Portland, OR: The Littman Library of Jewish Civilization, 2014), 104–105.

358 Talya Fishman, "The Penitential System of Hasidei Ashkenaz and the Problem of Cultural Boundaries," *The Journal of Jewish Thought and Philosophy* 8 (1999): 201–229.

359 Ibid., 222.

360 On the difficulty of precisely identifying adherents to the school of Hasidei Ashkenaz, see Ephraim Kanarfogel, "German Pietism in Northern France: The Case of R. Isaac of Corbeil," in *Hazon Nahum: Studies in Jewish Law, Thought, and History Presented to Dr. Norman Lamm on the Occasion of his Seventieth Birthday*, eds. Yaakov Elman and Jeffrey Gurock (New York: Yeshiva University Press, 1997), 207–227.

361 *Teshuvot Mahari Weil* 123.

362 Ibid., 12.

363 For an English synopsis of the aforementioned responsa, see Louis Jacobs, *Theology in the Responsa* (Portland, OR: The Littman Library of Jewish Civilization, 2005), 101–102.

364 Michael Rosen, *The Quest for Authenticity: The Thought of Reb Simhah Bunim* (Jerusalem: Urim Publications, 2008), 27. For some of the relevant academic discussions as to the precise contribution of the Baal Shem Tov see ibid.n1.

365 See https://twitter.com/DBashIdeas/status/517164309915639809.

366 Louis Jacobs, *Their Heads in Heaven: Unfamiliar Aspects of Hasidism* (Portland, OR: Vallentine Mitchell, 2005), 76. For more discussion of the role of the *Tzadik* in the thought of Rabbi Elimelekh of Lizhensk, see also Ada Rapoport-Albert, "God and the Zaddik as the Two Focal Points of Hasidic Worship," *History of Religions* 18, no. 4 (May 1979): 321.

367 Rabbi Elimelekh of Lizhensk's *Noam Elimelekh* to *Metzora* as translated in Rabbi Norman Lamm, *The Religious Thought of Hasidism* (Hoboken, NJ: Ktav Publishing House, 1999), 356–357. See there for more discussions of Rabbi Elimelekh's conception of the T*zadik*.

368 For more on the approach of Rabbi Shneur Zalman to sin, see Rabbi Dr. Ariel Evan Mayse, "The Sacred Writ of Hasidism: Tanya and the Spiritual Vision of Rabbi Shneur Zalman of Liady" in *Books of the People: Revisiting Classic Works of Jewish Thought*, ed. Stuart Halpern (Jerusalem: Maggid Books, 2017), 109–156.

369 Shaul Magid, "The Absence of God in Rabbi Nahman of Bratzlav's 'Likkutei MoHaRan'," *The Harvard Theological Review* 88, no. 4 (Oct. 1995): 503. This, of course, is far from a comprehensive overview of Rabbi Nahman's approach to sin and repentance. Such a disclaimer is practically absurd

given the brevity of his treatment here and the expansiveness of his own writing. For more secondary literature on Rabbi Nahman's approach to sin and repentance, see Arthur Green's discussion of the role of confession in Rabbi Nahman's writing in his *Tormented Master: The Life and Spiritual Quest of Rabbi Nahman of Bratslav*, Third Printing (Woodstock, VT: Jewish Lights Publishing, 2004), 60n79.

370   See chapter 4 in this work, "What to Wear to a Sin."

371   See Alan Brill, *Thinking God: The Mysticism of Rabbi Zadok of Lublin* (Jersey City, NJ: Ktav Publishing House, 2002), 146–168.

372   Brill, 157.

373   See *Nodeh B-Yehudah, Orah Hayyim (Mahadura Kama)* 35. For an English presentation of many of the details of Rabbi Landau's response, see Louis Jacob's *Theology in the Responsa*, 175–176.

374   *Nodeh B-Yehudah, Orah Hayyim (Mahadura Kama)* 35.

375   Ibid.

376   For a fascinating comparison of the contributions of Rabbis Landau and Sofer, see Maoz Kahana, "*Mi-Prag la-Pressburg: Ketivah Hilkhatit ba-Olam Mishtaneh me-ha'Node B-Yehudah' el ha-'Hatam Sofer' 1730–1839*" (PhD diss., Hebrew University, 2010).

377   See *Teshuvot Hatam Sofer, Orah Hayyim* 1:173.

378   *Igrot Moshe* vol. 6 at *Orah Hayyim* 4:115.

379   For a discussion of the unique candor found in correspondence, see Marc B. Shapiro, "Scholars and Friends: Rabbi Jehiel Jacob Weinberg and Professor Samuel Atlas," *The Torah U-Madda Journal* 7 (1997): 105–121. For a discussion on the ethics of examining personal rabbinic correspondence, see Rabbi Jacob J. Schachter's follow up article, "Facing the Truths of History," *The Torah U-Madda Journal* 8 (1998): 200–276. For another fascinating example of the analysis of Jewish correspondence, although more academic than rabbinic, see Shaul Magid, "Between Zionism and Friendship: The Correspondence between Gershon Scholem and Joseph Weiss," *The Jewish Quarterly Review* 107, no. 3 (Summer 2017): 427–444.

380   To add some confusion for the uninitiated reader, Rabbi Moshe Feinstein's responsa are actually called *Igrot Moshe*, though nearly all of them are Halakhic responsa rather than rabbinic correspondence in the style of *igrot*. A notable exception, however, is the correspondence we referred to in the previous section, which bear the style of rabbinic correspondence rather than Halakhic correspondence.

381   For a brief synopsis of Rabbi Kanievsky's life, see Marc Shapiro's aptly ti-
tled "Ha-Tamim: R' Yaakov Yisrael Kanievsky, Ha-Steipler," in *The Gdoi-
lim*, ed. Benjamin Brown and Nissim Leon (Jerusalem: Magnes Press, 2017;
Hebrew), 663–674. See also, Benjamin Brown's biography on the Hazon
Ish, *Ha-Hazon Ish: Ha-Posek, Ha-Ma'amin, u-Manhig Ha-Mahapakha
Ha-Haredit* (Jerusalem: Magnes Press, 2011).

382   Yaakov Mordekhai Greenwald, ed., *Eitzot V-Hadrakhot: Meyusad al
Mikhtivei Maran Baal ha-'Kehilot Yaakov'* (Lakewood, NJ: Gottlieb Torah
Graphics, 1991).

383   Translation from David Greenberg and Eliezer Witztum, *Sanity and Sanctity: Mental Health Work among the Ultra-Orthodox in Jerusalem* (New Haven,
CT: Yale University Press, 2001), 245, based on the letter of Rabbi Kanievsky
found in *Kreina d-Igrassa*, vol. 1, ed. Avraham Yeshayahu Kanievski (Bnei
Brak, Israel: Avraham Yeshayahu Kanievski, 2011), Letter 267.

384   See *Kreina d-Igrassa*, Letters 105–114.

385   Ibid., Letters 105, 128.

386   Ibid., Letters 111, 136.

387   Ibid., Letters 282 and 291.

388   *Pahad Yitzhak: Igrot U-Ketavim*, Letter 112.

389   Ibid.

390   Ibid., Letter 155.

391   See ibid., Letter 9.

392   See ibid., Letter 96.

393   Matt Potter, *The Last Goodbye: A History of the World in Resignation Letters*
(London: Silvertail Books, 2016), ix.

394   Irvin D. Yalom, *Love's Executioner & Other Tales of Psychotherapy* (New
York: Perennial Classics, 2000).

INDEX

SELECTED BIBLIOGRAPHY

A note on the bibliography: This book was intended for different audiences, both scholarly and general. I never paid much attention to bibliographies until I became involved in scholarship. Nonetheless we have provided a selected bibliography for scholars or curious readers who may want to see the works of others on this topic. The focus of this bibliography is on secondary literature cited within. Most classic rabbinic works such as the Talmud, Maimonides, and others that are readily available in Jewish study halls have been omitted. This was done mainly because popular classic Jewish works have so many different editions through the ages that including them would make perusing the bibliography somewhat cumbersome. I hope you enjoy the selection below.

Allport, Gordon and Ross, J. Michael. "Personal Religious Orientation and Prejudice." *Journal of Personality and Social Psychology* 5, no. 4 (1967): 432–443.

Anderson, Carol. "The Experience of Growing Up in a Minister's Home and the Religious Commitment of the Adult Child of a Minister." *Pastoral Psychology* 46, no. 6 (1998).

Anderson, Gary A. *Sin: A History.* New Haven: Yale University Press, 2010.

Appiah, Kwame Anthony. *Experiments in Ethics.* Cambridge Massachusetts: Harvard University Press, 2008.

Assaf, David. "'A Heretic Who Has No Faith in the Great Ones of the Age': The Clash Over the Honor of the Or Ha-Hayyim." *Modern Judaism* 29, no. 2 (2009): 194–225.

———*Untold Tales of the Hasidim: Crisis & Discontent in the History of Hasidism.* Lebanon, NH: Brandeis University Press, 2010.

Bashevkin, David. "Life is Full of Failure. Bio Blurbs Should be Too." *First Things.*

———*B-Rogez Rahem Tizkor,* Brooklyn: HaDaf Printing, 2015.

———"A Radical Theology and a Traditional Community: On the Contemporary Application of Izbica-Lublin Hasidut in the Jewish Community." *Torah Musings.*

———"What to Wear to a Sin." *Torah Musings.*

———"Letters of Love and Rebuke from Rav Yitzchok Hutner." *Tablet Magazine.*

———"Rabbi's Son Syndrome: Religious Struggle in a World of Religious Ideals." *Jewish Action* 77, no. 4: 38–44.

———"Jonah and the Varieties of Religious Motivation." *Lehrhaus.*

Bazak, Jacob. "An Unsuccessful Attempt to Commit a Crime." In *Jewish Law Association Studies XVIII: The Bar-Ilan Conference Volume,* ed. Joseph Fleishman. The Jewish Law Association, 2008.

Blair, W. Granger. "Monk Sues in High Court in Israel for Right to Settle as a Jew." *New York Times,* November 20, 1962.

Blankovsky, Yuval. *Het l-Shem Shamayim.* Jerusalem: Magnes Press, 2017.

Blau, Yitzchak. "Creative Repentance: On Rabbi Soloveitchik's Concept of Teshuva." *Tradition* 28, no. 2 (Winter 1994): 11–18.

Boas, Franz. *Handbook of American Indian Languages.* Washington DC: Government Print Office, 1911.

Brill, Alan. *Thinking God: The Mysticism of Rabbi Zadok of Lublin.* Jersey City, NJ: Ktav Publishing House, 2002.

Broder, John M. "Familiar Fallback for Officials: 'Mistakes were Made'." *New York Times,* March 14, 2007.

Brown, Benjamin. *Ha-Hazon Ish: Ha-Posek, Ha-Ma'amin, u-Manhig Ha-Mahapakha Ha-Haredit.* Jerusalem: Magnes Press, 2011.

Brown, Benjamin and Leon, Nissim, eds. *The Gdoilim.* Jerusalem: Magnes Press, 2017.

Brown, Erica. *Jonah: The Reluctant Prophet.* Jerusalem: Maggid Books, 2017.

Büchler, A. *Studies in Sin and Atonement in the Rabbinic Literature of the First Century.* London: Oxford University Press, 1928.

Cameron, Samuel. *The Economics of Sin: Rational Choice or No Choice at All?* Northhampton, MA: Edgar Elgar Publishing, 2002.

Chinski, Eric. "Brian Christian on 'The Most Human Human.'" *The Paris Review.* Last modified March 14, 2011. https://www.theparisreview.org/blog/2011/03/14/brian-christian-on-the-most-human-human/.

Chödrön, Pema. *When Things Fall Apart: Heart Advice for Difficult Times.* Boulder, CO: Shambhala Publications, 1997.

Christian, Brian. The *Most Human Human.* New York: Doubleday, 2011.

Cohen, Aviezer. "Self-Consciousness in Mei ha-Shiloah as the Nexus Between God and Man." PhD diss., Ben-Gurion University of the Negev, 2006.

Cohen, Hermann. *Religion of Reason: Out of the Sources of Judaism,* trans. Simon Kaplan. New York: Frederick Unger, 1972.

Collis, John W. *Seven Fatal Management Sins: Understanding and Avoiding Managerial Malpractice.* Boca Raton, FL: CRC Press LLC, 1998.

Coombs, W. Timothy. *Ongoing Crisis Communication: Planning, Managing, and Responding.* Thousand Oaks, CA: Sage, 2012.

Cooper, Alan. "A Medieval Jewish Version of Original Sin: Ephraim Luntschitz on Leviticus 12." *Harvard Theological Review* 97, no. 4 (October 2004): 445–459.

Cosgrove, Elliot. "Religion Beyond the Limits of Reason Alone." In *Go Forth! Selected Sermons by Rabbi Elliot J. Cosgrove.* Park Avenue Synagogue, 2013.

Coudert, Allison P. *The Impact of the Kabbalah in the Seventeenth Century: The Life and Thought of Francis Mercury van Helmont.* Leiden: Brill, 1999.

Crane, Jonathan K. "Shameful Ambivalences: Dimensions of Rabbinic Shame." *AJS Review* 35, no. 1 (April 2011): 61–84.

Craig, Gordon A. "On the Pleasure of Reading Diplomatic Correspondence." *Journal of Contemporary History* 25, no. 3/4 (1991): 369–384

Delumeau, Jean. *Sin and Fear: The Emergence of a Western Guilt Culture 13th-18th Centuries.* Translated by Eric Nicholson. New York: St. Martin's Press, 1990

Duckworth, Angela. *Grit: The Power of Passion and Perseverance.* London: Vermilion, 2016.

Eleff, Zev. "Psychohistory and the Imaginary Couch: Diagnosing Historical Biblical Figures." *Journal of The American Academy of Religion* 80, no. 1 (March 2012): 94–136.

Elman, Yaakov. "R. Zadok Hakohen on the History of Halakhah." *Tradition* 21, no. 4 (Fall 1985): 1-26.

———"Reb Zadok Hakohen of Lublin on Prophecy in the Halakhic Process." *Jewish Law Association Studies* 1 (1985): 1–16.

———"The History of Gentile Wisdom According to R. Zadok ha-Kohen of Lublin." *Journal of Jewish Thought and Philosophy* 3, no. (1993): 153–187.

———"Progressive Derash and Retrospective Peshat: Nonhalakhic Considerations in Talmud Torah." In *Modern Scholarship in the Study of Torah: Contributions and Limitations,* ed. Shalom Carmy. Northvale, NJ: Jason Aronson, 1996.

———"The Rebirth of Omnisignificant Biblical Exegesis in the Nineteenth and Twentieth Centuries." *Jewish Studies Internet Journal* 2 (2003): 199–249.

Epstein, Joseph. "The Art of Biography." *The Wall Street Journal,* January 1, 2016.

Ettinger, Shmuel. "The Hasidic Movement - Reality and Ideals." In *Essential Papers on Hasidism: Origins to Present,* ed. Gershon David Hundert. New York: New York University Press, 1991.

Fairstein, Morris M. *All Is in the Hands of Heaven: The Teaching of Rabbi Mordechai Joseph Liener of Izbica.* Hoboken, NJ: Ktav Publishing House, 1989.

———"Kotsk-Izbica Dispute: Theological or Personal?" *Kabbalah* 17 (2008): 75–79.

Feiler, Bruce. "The Stories that Bind Us." *New York Times,* March 15, 2013.

Festinger, Leon. *When Prophecy Fails.* London: Pinter and Martin Ltd., 2008.

Finkelman, Yoel. *Strictly Kosher Reading.* Brighton, MA: Academic Studies Press, 2011.

First, Mitchell. *Esther Unmasked.* New York: Kodesh Press, 2015.

Fischer, Elli. "The Patron Saint of Rabbi's Kids." *Lehrhaus.* December 1, 2017.

Fishman, Talya. "The Penitential System of Hasidei Ashkenaz and the Problem of Cultural Boundaries," *The Journal of Jewish Thought and Philosophy* 8 (1999): 201–229

Fivush, Robyn, Bohanek, Jennifer G., and Duke, Marshall. "The Intergenerational Self: Subjective Perspective and Family History." In *Self Continuity: Individual and Collective Perspectives,* ed. Fabio Sani. New York: Psychology Press, 2008.

Foot, Philippa. "The Problem of Abortion and the Doctrine of Double Effect." *Oxford Review* 5 (1967): 5–15.

Fraade, Steven D. "The Innovation of Nominalized Verbs in Mishnaic Hebrew as Marking an Innovation of Concept." In *Studies in Mishnaic Hebrew and Related Fields*. Edited by Elitzur A. Bar-Asher Siegal and Aaron J. Koller. Jerusalem: Magnes Press, 2017.

Fraenkel, Avinoam. *Nefesh HaTzimtzum, Vol. 1: Rabbi Chaim Volozhin's Nefesh HaChaim with Translation and Commentary.* Jerusalem: Urim Publications, 2015.

Fredriksen, Paula. *Sin: The Early History of an Idea.* Princeton, NJ: Princeton University Press, 2012.

Garb, Jonathan. "Shame as an Existential Emotion in Modern Kabbalah." *Jewish Social Studies* 21, no. 1 (Fall 2015): 89–122.

Garvey, Stephen P. "Punishment as Atonement." *UCLA Law Review* 46, no. 6 (August 1999): 1801–1858.

Genichovsky, Avraham. *Agan ha-Sahar (Mahadura Shlishit).* Edited by Rabbi Shmuel Fish. Israel: 2013.

Goshen-Gottstein, Alon. *The Sinner and the Amnesiac: The Rabbinic Invention of Elisha ben Abuya and Eleazar ben Arach.* Stanford: Stanford University Press, 2000.

Graham, Franklin. *Rebel with a Cause.* Nashville, TN:Thomas Nelson Publishers, 1995.

Green, Arthur. *Tormented Master: The Life and Spiritual Quest of Rabbi Nahman of Bratslav.* Woodstock, VT: Jewish Lights Publishing, 2004.

Greenbaum, Avraham. *Tzadik: A Portrait of Rabbi Nachman.* Jerusalem: Breslov Research Institute, 1987.

Greenberg, David and Eliezer Witztum. *Sanity and Sanctity: Mental Health Work among the Ultra-Orthodox in Jerusalem.* New Haven, CT: Yale University Press, 2001.

Greenwald, Yaakov Mordekhai, ed. *Eitzot V-Hadrakhot: Meyusad al Mikhtivei Maran Baal ha-"Kehilot Yaakov."* Lakewood, NJ: Gottlieb Torah Graphics, 1991.

Grossman, Meir Zvi. "Le-Mashmuatam shel ha-Bituyim 'aveirah' ve-'dvar aveirah' bi-Leshon Hakhamim." *Sinai* 100, no. 1 (1987).

Halbertal, Moshe. *People of the Book.* Cambridge, MA: Harvard University Press, 1997.

———"Mavet, Het, Hok, ve-Geulah be-Mishnat ha-Ramban." *Tarbiz* 71, no. 1/2 (2002): 133–162.

Harvey, Giles. "Cry Me a River: The Rise of the Failure Memoir." *New Yorker*, March 25, 2013.

Haushofer, Johannes. "CV of Failures: Princeton Professor Publishes Resume of His Career Lows." *The Guardian*, April 29, 2016.

Hearit, Keith Michael. *Crisis Management by Apology.* New York: Routledge, 2010.

Heber, Tzvi. "Aveirah l-Shem Shamayim." *Ma'aliot* 21 (1999).

Hefter, Herzl. "'In God's Hands': The Religious Phenomenology of R. Mordechai Yosef of Izbica." *Tradition* 46, no. 1 (Spring 2013): 43–65.

Higger, Michael. "Intention in Talmudic Law." PhD diss., Columbia University, 1927.

Hirschler, Shimon. *Yehudah le-Kadsho.* Tel Aviv: Shem Olam, 1999.

Hoffman, Lawrence A. ed. *We Have Sinned: Sin and Confession in Judaism.* Woodstock, VT: Jewish Lights Publishing, 2012.

Hofstadter, Douglas and Sander, Emmanuel. *Surfaces and Essences: Analogy as the Fuel and Fire of Thinking*. New York: Basic Books, 2013.

Holtz, Barry W. *Rabbi Akiva: Sage of the Talmud*. New Haven, CT: Yale University Press, 2017.

Hume, David. *The Natural History of Religion*. London: A. and H. Bradlaugh Bonner, 1889.

Jacobs, Alan. *Original Sin: A Cultural History*. New York: HarperCollins Publishers, 2008.

Jacobs, Louis. *Theology in the Responsa*. Portland, OR: The Littman Library of Jewish Civilization, 2005.

———"Attitudes Towards Christianity in the Halakhah." In *Judaism and Theology: Essays on the Jewish Religion*. Portland, OR: Vallentine Mitchell, 2005.

———*Their Heads in Heaven: Unfamiliar Aspects of Hasidism*. Portland, OR: Vallentine Mitchell, 2005.

Kahana, Maoz. "*Mi-Prag la-Pressburg: Ketivah Hilkhatit ba-Olam Mishtaneh me-ha'Node B-Yehudah' el ha-'Hatam Sofer' 1730–1839*." PhD diss., Hebrew University, 2010.

Kamenetsky, Nathan. *Anatomy of a Ban*. Jerusalem: Private Printing Publishers, 2003.

Kasirer, Shlomo. "Repentance in the Thought of R. Isaac Hutner." PhD diss., Bar-Ilan University, 2009.

Kanarfogel, Ephraim. "Not Just Another Contemporary Jewish Problem: A Historical Discussion of Phylacteries." *Gesher* 5 (1976): 106–121.

———"Returning to the Jewish Community in Medieval Ashkenaz: History and Halacha." In *Tumim: Studies in Jewish History and Literature—Presented to Dr. Bernard Lander Volume One*. Edited by Michael A. Shmidman. Jersey City, NJ: Ktav Publishing, 2007: 69–97.

———"German Pietism in Northern France: The Case of R. Isaac of Corbeil." In *Hazon Nahum: Studies in Jewish Law, Thought, and History Presented to Dr. Norman Lamm on the Occasion of his Seventieth Birthday*. Edited by Yaakov Elman and Jeffrey Gurock. New York: Yeshiva University Press, 1997.

Kara-Ivanov Kaniel, Ruth. "'Gedolah Aveirah Lishmah': Mothers of the Davidic Dynasty, Feminine Seduction and the Development of Messianic Thought, From Rabbinic Literature to R. Moses Haim Luzzato." *Nashim: A Journal of Jewish Women's Studies and Gender Issues* 24 (2013).

Katz, Jacob. *Exclusiveness and Tolerance: Studies in Jewish-Gentile Relations in Medieval and Modern Times*. Oxford: Oxford University Press, 1961.

Kitzis, Shulamit. *Demut Deyokno: Avot Rabanim ba-Tzionit ha-Datit ba-Eynei Yildeihem*. Israel: Resling, 2017.

Klawans, Jonathan. *Impurity and Sin in Ancient Judaism*. New York: Oxford University Press, 2000.

Lam, Joseph. *Patterns of Sin in the Hebrew Bible*. New York: Oxford University Press, 2016.

Lamm, Norman. *The Religious Thought of Hasidism*. Hoboken, NJ: Ktav Publishing House, 1999.

Lasker, Daniel J. *Jewish Philosophical Polemics against Christianity in the Middle Ages*. 2nd ed. Portland, OR: The Littman Library of Jewish Civilization, 2007.

Lazar, Aryeh. "The Structure of the Motivation for Religious Behavior among Jews: A Comparison of Two Structure Models." PhD diss., Bar-Ilan University, 1999.

Lazar, Aryeh and Kravetz, Shlomo. "A Motivational Systems Theory Approach to the Relation Between Religious Experience and Motives." *The International Journal for the Psychology of Religion* 15, no. 1 (2005): 63–72.

Leib, Erin. "God in the Years of Fury: Theodicy and Anti-Theodicy in the Holocaust Writings of Rabbi Kalonymus Kalman Shapira." PhD diss., University of Chicago, 2014.

Lambert, David A. *How Repentance Became Biblical: Judaism, Christianity, & the Interpretation of Scripture.* New York: Oxford University Press, 2016.

Levine, Samuel. "Teshuva: A Look at Repentance, Forgiveness and Atonement in Jewish Law and Philosophy and American Legal Thought." *Fordham Urban Law Journal* 27, no. 5 (2000): 1677–1693

Levitz, Irving N. "Children of Rabbis," *Tradition* 23, no. 2 (Winter 1988): 76–87.

Lichtenstein, Aharon. "Brother Daniel and the Jewish Fraternity," *Judaism* 12, no. 3 (Summer 1963): 260–280.

Lichtenstein, Dovid. *Headlines 2: Halachic Debates of Current Events.* New York: OU Press, 2017.

Lifshitz, Ze'ev Haim. *The Paradox of Human Existence: A Commentary on the Book of Jonah.* Northvale, NJ: Jason Aronson, 1994.

Lightman, Alan. *Einstein's Dreams.* New York: Pantheon Book, 1993.

Litvin, Baruch. *Jewish Identity: Modern Responsa and Opinions.* Edited by Sidney B. Hoenig. New York: Shulsinger Bros. Inc., 1965.

Liwer, Amira. "Oral Torah in the Writings of Reb Zadok ha-Kohen of Lublin." PhD diss., Hebrew University, 2006.

Maccoby, Hyam. *Judaism on Trial.* Portland, OR: The Littman Library of Jewish Civilization, 1993.

Magid, Shaul. *From Metaphysics to Midrash: Myth, History, and the Interpretation of Scripture in Lurianic Kabbala.* Bloomington, IN: Indiana University Press, 2008.

——— "From Theosophy to Midrash: Lurianic Exegesis and the Garden of Eden." *AJS Review* 22, no. 1 (1997): 37–75

"'A Thread of Blue': Rabbi Gershon Henoch Leiner of Radzyń and his Search for Continuity in Response to Modernity," *Polin* 11 (1998): 31–52.

———*Hasidism on the Margin: Reconciliation, Antinomianism, and Messianism in Izbica/Radzin Hasidism.* Madison: University of Wisconsin Press, 2003.

———"Through the Void: The Absence of God in R. Nahman of Bratzlav's 'Likkutei MoHaRan'," *The Harvard Theological Review* 88, no. 4 (October 1995): 495–519.

———"Deconstructing the Mystical: The Anti-Mystical Kabbalism in Rabbi Hayyim of Volozhin's Nefesh Ha-Hayyim," *The Journal of Jewish Thought and Philosophy* 9 (2000): 21–67.

———"Between Zionism and Friendship: The Correspondence between Gershon Scholem and Joseph Weiss," *The Jewish Quarterly Review* 107, no. 3 (Summer 2017): 427–444.

Marcus, Alfred A. and Goodman, Robert S. "Victims and Shareholders: The Dilemmas of Presenting Corporate Policy During a Crisis," *The Academy of Management Journal* 34, no. 2 (June 1991): 281–305.

Mayse, Ariel Evan. "The Sacred Writ of Hasidism: Tanya and the Spiritual Vision of Rabbi Shneur Zalman of Liady," In *Books of the People: Revisiting Classic Works of Jewish Thought.* Edited by Stuart Halpern. Jerusalem: Maggid Books, 2017.

Menninger, Karl. *Whatever Became of Sin?* New York: Hawthorne Books, 1973.

Milton, John. *Paradise Lost* ed. Barbara K. Lewalski. Malden, MA: Blackwell Publishing, 2007.

Mintz, Jerome R. *Hasidic People: A Place in the New World.* Cambridge, MA: Harvard University Press: 1992.

Mondshine, Yehoshua. "The Fluidity of Categories in Hasidism." In *Hasidism Reappraised,* ed. Ada Rapoport-Albert. Portland, OR: The Littman Library of Jewish Civilization, 1996.

Mooney, Richard E. "Editorial Notebook, 'If This Sounds Slippery . . . ' How to Apologize and Admit Nothing." *New York Times,* November 30, 1992.

Morgan, Christopher W. and Robert A. Peterson, eds., *Fallen: A Theology of Sin.* Wheaton, IL: Crossway, 2013.

Pachter, Shilo. "Shmirat Habrit: The History of the Prohibition of Wasting Seed." PhD diss. Hebrew University, 2006.

Peli, Pinchas H. ed. *Al ha-Teshuvah.* Jerusalem: World Zionist Organization, Department for Torah Education and Culture in the Diaspora, 1975.

——— *On Repentance in the Thought and Oral Discourses of Rabbi Joseph B. Soloveitchik.* Northvale, NJ: Jason Aronson, 1996.

———"Repentant Man-A High Level in Rabbi Soloveitchik's Typology of Man," *Tradition* 18, no. 2 (Summer 1980): 135–159.

Pindell, Richard. "Somebody's Son." *American Girl Magazine* 49, no. 9 (August 1966): 28–47

Polen, Nehemia. "Dark Ladies and Redemptive Compassion: Ruth and the Messianic Lineage in Judaism." In *Scrolls of Love: Ruth and the Song of Songs.* Edited by Peter S. Hawkins. New York: Fordham University, 2006.

———*The Holy Fire.* Lanham, MD: Rowman & Littlefield, 2004.

Potter, Matt. *The Last Goodbye: A History of the World in Resignation Letters.* London: Silvertail Books, 2016.

Rabow, Jerry. *50 Jewish Messiahs.* Jerusalem: Gefen Publishing House, 2002.

Rakover, Nahum. "Should Transgression Disqualify One from Public Office?" In *Jewish Law Association Studies XII: The Zutphen Conference Volume.* Edited by Hillel Gamoran. Binghamton: Binghamton University, 2002.

———"Where Penitents Stand, Even the Wholly Righteous Cannot Stand." In *Between Rashi and Maimonides: Themes in Medieval Jewish Thought, Literature and Exegesis.* Edited by Ephraim Kanarfogel and Moshe Sokolow. New York: Yeshiva University Press, 2010.

Ramm, Bernard. *Offense to Reason: The Theology of Sin*. San Franciso, CA: Harper & Row, 1985.

Rapoport-Albert, Ada. "God and the Zaddik as the Two Focal Points of Hasidic Worship." *History of Religions* 18, no. 4 (May 1979): 296–325.

Rapoport, Chaim. *Judaism and Homosexuality: An Authentic Orthodox View*. Portland, OR: Vallentine Mitchell, 2004.

Rembaum, Joel E. "Medieval Jewish Criticism of the Christian Doctrine of Original Sin," *AJS Review* 7/8 (1982–83): 353–382.

Rivlin, Avraham. *Yonah: Nevuah va-Tokhahah*. Israel: Hotzaot Yeshivat Kerem B'Yavneh, 2005.

Rosen, Michael. *The Quest for Authenticity: The Thought of Reb Simhah Bunim*. Jerusalem: Urim Publications, 2008.

Rosenfeld, Jennie. "Talmudic Re-Readings: Toward a Modern Orthodox Sexual Ethic." PhD diss., The City University of New York, 2008.

Rosenthal, Uriel, R. Arjen Boin, and Louise K. Comfort, *Managing Crises: Threats, Dilemmas, Opportunities*. Springfield, IL: Charles C. Thomas, 2001.

Rovner, Jay. "Structure and Ideology in the Aher Narrative (bHag 15a and b)." *JSIJ* 10 (2012): 1–73

Rubin, A. "The Concept of Repentance Among the Hasidey Ashkenaz." *The Journal of Jewish Studies* 16 (1965): 161–176.

Rozen-Zvi, Ishay. *Demonic Desires: Yetzer Hara and the Problem of Evil*. Philadelphia: University of Pennsylvania Press, 2011.

Rubinstein, Jeffrey L. "Elisha ben Abuya: Torah and the Sinful Sage." *The Journal of Jewish Thought and Philosophy* 7 (1998): 139–225.

Sacks, Jonathan. *A Letter in the Scroll*. New York: Free Press, 2004.

———"The Sins of a Leader," In *Covenant and Conversation- Leviticus: The Book of Holiness*. Jerusalem: Koren Publishers, 2015.

Safire, William. "Let a Simile Be Your Umbrella." *New York Times*, February 11, 1996.

———*The Right Word in the Right Place at the Right Time*. New York: Simon & Schuster, 2004.

Schacter, Jacob J. "On the Morality of the Patriachs: Must Biblical Heroes Be Perfect?" In *Jewish Education in Tradition: Proceedings of the First International Conference on Jewish Education*. Edited by Zvi Grumet. Teaneck, NJ: Ben Yehuda Press, 2007

———"Facing the Truths of History." *The Torah U-Madda Journal* 8 (1998): 200–276.

Schachter, Hershel. *B-Ikvei Ha-Tzon*. Jerusalem: 1997.

———*Mi-Pninei Ha-Rav*. Jerusalem: Hotzaot Beit Hamidrash Dflatbush, 2001.

Schochet, Elijah. *The Hasidic Movement and the Gaon of Vilna*. Northvale, NJ: Jason Aronson, 1993.

Scholem, Gershom. *Kabbalah*. Jerusalem: Keter Publishing House, 1974.

———*Sabbatai Sevi: The Mystical Messiah*. Princeton: Princeton University Press, 1973.

———*The Messianic Idea in Judaism: And Other Essays on Jewish Spirituality.* New York: Schocken, 1995.

Schwab, Shimon. "Jewish History." In *Selected Writings.* Lakewood: C.I.S. Publishers, 1988.

Schwarzchild, Steven. "An Introduction to the thought of R. Isaac Hutner." *Modern Judaism* 5, no. 3 (February 1985): 235–277.

Scott, Edgar. "Hermann Cohen." In *The Stanford Encyclopedia of Philosophy.* Edited by Edward N. Zalta. Last modified September 17, 2015. https://plato.stanford.edu/cgi-bin/encyclopedia/archinfo.cgi?entry=cohen.

Severson, Kim. "Mixing Drinks with Work and Staying Sober, Too." *New York Times,* June 23, 2009.

Shapiro, Marc. *Changing the Immutable: How Orthodox Judaism Rewrites its History.* Portland, OR: The Littman Library of Jewish Civilization, 2015.

———*The Limits of Orthodox Theology: Maimonides' Thirteen Principles Reappraised.* Portland, OR: The Littman Library of Jewish Civilization, 2011.

——— "Further Comments." *The Seforim Blog* (blog), May 6, 2010. http://seforim.blogspot.com/2010/05/marc-shapiro-further-comments.html.

———"Scholars and Friends: Rabbi Jehiel Jacob Weinberg and Professor Samuel Atlas." *The Torah U-Madda Journal* 7 (1997): 105–121.

Shemesh, Aharon. *Punishments and Sins: From Scripture to the Rabbis.* Jerusalem: Magnes Press, 2003.

Shenker, Israel. "Responsa: The Law as Seen By Rabbis for 1,000 Years." *New York Times,* May 5, 1975.

Sherwin, Byron L. *Studies in Jewish Theology: Reflections in the Mirror of Tradition.* Portland, OR: Vallentine Mitchell, 2007.

Sherwood, Ben. *The Survivor's Club: The Secrets and Science that Could Save Your Life.* New York: Grand Central Publishing, 2009.

Smith, David L. *With Willful Intent: A Theology of Sin.* Wheaton, IL: A Bridgepoint Book, 2003.

Slansky, Paul and Sorkin, Arleen. *My Bad: The Apology Anthology.* New York: Bloomsbury 2006.

Soloveitchik, Haym. *Collected Essays vol. II.* Portland, OR: The Littman Library of Jewish Civilization, 2014.

———"Rupture and Reconstruction: The Transformation of Contemporary Orthodoxy," *Tradition* 28, no. 4 (Summer 1994): 64–130.

———"Three Themes in the 'Sefer Hasidim,'" *AJS Review* 1, no. 1 (1976): 311–357.

Soloveitchik, Joseph B. *Halakhic Man.* Translated by Lawrence Kaplan. Philadelphia: The Jewish Publication Society of America, 1983.

Soloveichik, Meir. "Rabbi Akiva's Optimism," *Azure* 30 (Autumn 2007).

Stefan, Melanie. "A CV of Failures." *Nature* 468 (November 2010).

Stern, Sacha. *Time and Process in Ancient Judaism.* Portland, OR: The Littman Library of Jewish Civilization, 2007.

Strauch-Schick, Shana. "Intention in the Babylonian Talmud." PhD diss., Yeshiva University, 2011.

Stroumsa, Gedaliahu G. "Aher: A Gnostic." *Proceedings of the Conference at Yale March 1978*, vol. 2, *The Rediscovery of Gnosticism*. Edited by Bentley Layton. Leiden: Brill Academic Publishing, 1997.

Swazo, Norman K. "Rabbi Elisha Ben Abuyah 'At the Mind's Limit': Between Theodicy and Fate." *Philosophy and Literature* 38, no. 1 (2014): 153–168.

Tennant, F.R. *The Sources of the Doctrines of the Fall and Original Sin*. Cambridge: At the University Press, 1903.

Thiem, Annika. "Specters of Sin and Salvation: Hermann Cohen, Original Sin, and Rethinking the Critique of Religion," *Idealistic Studies* 40, no. 1/2 (2010): 117–138.

Tishby, Isaiah. *Messianic Mysticism: Moshe Hayim Luzzato and the Padua School*. Portland, OR: The Littman Library of Jewish Civilization, 2014.

Turing, Alan. "Computing Machinery and Intelligence," *Mind* 59, no. 236 (October 1950): 433–460.

Ulmer, Robert L., Sellnow, Timothy L. and Seeger, Matthew W. *Effective Crisis Communication: Moving from Crisis to Opportunity*, 2nd ed. Thousand Oaks, CA: SAGE Publications, 2011.

Usher, Shaun. *Letters of Note: An Eclectic Collection of Correspondence Deserving of a Wider Audience*. San Fransisco: Chronicle Books, 2014.

Vigoda, Shmuel. "'Be-Hevlei Ha-Zman' Ha-Adam ve-HaZman be-Haguto shel ha-Rav Yitzhak Hutner." In *Be-Darkhe Shalom*, ed. Binyamin Ish Shalom. Jerusalem: Beit Morashah, 2007.

Wilensky, Mordechai L. "Hasidic-Mitnaggedic Polemics in the Jewish Communities of Eastern Europe: The Hostile Phase." In *Essential Papers on Hasidism: Origins to Present*. Edited by Gershon David Hundert. New York: New York University Press, 1991.

Williams, N.P. *The Ideas of the Fall and of Original Sin: A Historical and Critical Study*. London: Longmans, Green and Co., Ltd., 1927.

Weiss, Dov. *Pious Irreverence: Confronting God in Rabbinic Judaism*. Philadelphia: University of Pennsylvania Press, 2017.

Wiesenthal, Simon. *The Sunflower: On the Possibilities and Limits of Forgiveness*. New York: Schocken Books, 1976.

Wiskind-Elper, Ora. *Wisdom of the Heart: The Teachings of Rabbi Ya'akov of Izbica-Radzyn*. Philadelphia: The Jewish Publication Society, 2010.

Wiman, Christian. *My Bright Abyss: Meditations of a Modern Believer*. New York: Farrar, Straus and Giroux, 2013.

Wolfson, Elliot R. "By Way of Truth: Aspects of Nahmanides' Kabbalistic Hermeneutic," *AJS Review* 14, no. 2 (Autumn 1989): 103–178.

Woolf, Jeffrey. "Time Awareness as a Source for Spirituality in the Thought of Rabbi Joseph B. Soloveitchik," *Modern Judaism* 32, no. 1 (February 2012): 1–22.

Yaffe, Gideon. "Criminal Attempts," *The Yale Law Journal* 124, no. 92 (2014): 92–156.

———*Attempts*. Oxford, Oxford University Press, 2012.

Yalom, Irvin D. *Love's Executioner & Other Tales of Psychotherapy*. New York: Perennial Classics, 2000.

Yisraeli, Oded. "Adam's Sin: Its Meaning and Essence." In *Temple Portals: Studies in Aggadah and Midrash in the Zohar*. Translated by Liat Keren. Jerusalem: Magnes Press, 2016.

PERMISSIONS

Sections or ideas within this book have previously appeared as the following articles:

"What to Wear to a Sin." *Torah Musings* (July 21, 2013).
"Life is Full of Failure. Bio Blurbs Should Be Too." *First Things* (May 8, 2014).
"A Radical Theology and a Traditional Community: On the Contemporary Application of Izbica-Lublin Hasidut in the Jewish Community." *Torah Musings* (August 20, 2015).
"Jonah and the Varieties of Religious Motivation." *The Lehrhaus* (October 9, 2016).
"Letters of Love and Rebuke from Rav Yitzchok Hutner." *Tablet Magazine* (October 10, 2016).
"Rabbi's Son Syndrome: Religious Struggle in a World of Religious Ideals." *Jewish Action* (Summer 2017): 38–44.

My appreciation to each of these journals and sites for sharing your platform with me and for the permission to republish the material here.

ACKNOWLEDGMENTS

Any acknowledgment must begin with acknowledging The Source of all Knowledge and Acknowledgment, the Almighty for giving me the resilience and strength to finish this project.

ברוך שהחייני וקימנו והגיענו לזמן הזה

This book, of course, is the product of so many people's patience, advice, and encouragement. If I could, I would publish a second volume just filled with thank yous. My publisher, however, informed me that I cannot. So I would like to thank the following people for their help and support:

Institutional Support:

This book would not have been possible without the institutional support of NCSY, the youth movement of the Orthodox Union, where I serve as Director of Education. Under the leadership of Rabbi Micah Greenland, International Director, the organization has been on the forefront of teen inspiration for over six decades. I am so grateful for their support of my work.

Publisher and Editors:

This book benefited from the able and generous assistance of Alessandra Anzani of Academic Studies Press. She continued to believe in this project when it seemed no one else would. I am also so thankful to Dr. Shaul Magid, Professor of Religious Studies and the Jay and Jeannie Schottenstein Chair of Jewish Studies in Modern Judaism at Indiana University for graciously providing a foreword to this work and for his encouragement and support throughout. I have long been a student of Dr. Magid's writings, so it was truly an honor to have him take such interest in my work. Jason Cohen admirably copy-edited this work and expertly navigated through desultory Talmudic discussions and obscure pop-culture references. Over several months, including several long Sundays, Jonathan Engel sat with me in my office looking over every detail of the manuscript. I could not have asked for a more competent and kind person to work with. Mrs. Joy Bashevkin was my first editor. She began editing my works in fifth grade and put in so much time into ensuring this manuscript did not sound like it was written by my fifth-grade self. The picture on the cover of the book was taken by celebrated photographer Menachem Kahana. From the moment I saw this picture many years ago, I connected with the boy underneath the table. In the room, but not quite at the table. I am honored he allowed his photograph to grace the cover of this volume. And to Mr. Joshua Weinberg, a noted creative director I have worked with for many years, thank you for your friendship, creative vision, and Friday afternoon dips.

Friends:

"The asset I most value," wrote Warren Buffet, "aside from health, is interesting, diverse, and long-standing friends." On the scale of that billionaire, I am a wealthy man. I am so appreciative of all my friends who have helped refine and develop my sensitivities and sensibilities. In particular, thank you to Menachem Butler, who always promotes his friends. In a world of "self-promotion," he is a true "friend-promoter." From our times in the hallways of Toras Chaim in South Shore he is one of my longest standing friends and was an integral part in ensuring the publication of this volume. Deepest admiration to my friend and "sort of" cousin, Altie Karper, for providing much needed guidance. Thank you as well to Rabbi Jake Sasson for your sustained awesomeness, to Rabbi Aryeh Westreich for being a friend and mentor and a constant reminder of what true Torah scholarship is supposed to look like, Rabbi Simcha Willig for making sure I never quit, and Rabbi Mati Diamond for serving as *liban shel yisrael*, the heart of the people. Rabbi Baruch Dov Braun provided much of the substance and direction for my approach to Yonah; I treasure his intellectual generosity. Thank you as well to my friends who taught me about friendship, Rabbi Yoni Sonnenblick and Dr. Akiva Diamond. I am also indebted to the continued belief my friends have had in me, including Rabbi Beni Burstein; Shimon Steinmetz, a true academic rockstar who graciously agreed to read and comment on an early manuscript of this work; Zack and Aharon Schrieber; Alon Amar; Moshe Hager, who showed me the wealth contained in the *machavas*; The Benj Samuels who taught me what it means to be a grown-up; and Duvi Stahler, who taught me the creativity needed for authenticity and the authenticity of true creativity. Special thanks to Rabbi Judah Mischel for his "genuiosity," a rare combination of generosity and genuineness; and to Rabbi Ari Segal, my friend who treats me like family; and to Rabbi Joey Rosenfeld, who showed me the gift of translation. I have many colleagues who have now become friends, all of whom I deeply admire and appreciate, but special thanks to Mr. David Cutler and Mrs. Rina Emerson for their mentorship and friendship navigating the world of professional imperfection. He may not know it, but the friend who first introduced me to the world of resilience and continues to serve as my template for self-acceptance is Mr. Eli Schulman. I am forever grateful for his guidance and insight in the narrow straits. I have also benefited so much from several virtual cohorts including the Twitter Chevra, Egregious, DM Nicorette, Gev-Alt, University of Purim, the Carpool, Taki Stock Chat, and the Bus.

Finally, like the Hebrew volume I published in 2016, many of the ideas in this volume emerged from classes I had the privilege to give at the Young Israel of Lawrence-Cedarhurst. I will never be able to adequately explain how much the 7:30 AM chevra means to me, but האור שבהן מחזירני למוטב. Thank you especially to Mr. Joel Mael for first giving me the opportunity to share Torah to this group and to Dr. Reuben and Mandy Brecher for providing Kiddush on my walk home and opening their heart and home to me.

Teachers:

I am so grateful to the educational institutions in which I have had the privilege to study, including Yeshiva of South Shore, under the leadership of Rabbi Binyamin Kamenetzky zt"l and now his son Rav Mordechai, who in certain pages is really like family. The Menahel Rabbi Chanina Herzberg, zt"l, is still the model of educator I aspire to become. At DRS HALB High School for Boys under the leadership of my Rebbe, Rabbi Yisroel Kaminetsky, I first fell in love with Torah learning and learned the enduring value of having a Rebbe. In Yeshivat Sha'alvim in Israel, I am indebted to Rabbi Ari Waxman who introduced me to the works of Rabbi Yitzhak Hutner and, along with it, the joy of curiosity. I studied for several years at Yeshivas Ner Yisroel Rabbinical College in Baltimore; my rabbeim there still serve as the unaltered standard for committed Torah life. In particular, the Friday

night presentations of Rabbi Ezra Neuberger still echo in the very founda-
tions of my soul. At Yeshiva University I studied in Rabbi Isaac Elchanan
Theological Seminary, and I am so appreciative of the Roshei Yeshiva and
particularly appreciate Rabbi Chaim Bronstein for his care and kindness.
While there I completed my MA at the Bernard Revel Graduate School,
where I was introduced to the academic study of Hasidut by Dr. Yaakov
Elman, of blessed memory, a professor of Talmud at Yeshiva University's
Bernard Revel Graduate School of Jewish Studies, where he held the Herbert
S. and Naomi Denenberg Chair in Talmudic Studies. Together we explored
the writings of Rav Zadok Ha-Kohen of Lublin. His guidance, encouragement, and brilliance will long be remembered. I am also indebted to my
teachers Rabbi Yaakov Glasser, who had faith in me when I did not have
faith in myself, and Rabbi Moshe Benovitz, who first introduced me to the
majesty and sophistication of Torah wedded to experiential life. Over the
years, I have become increasingly close with Rabbi Yossi "Joe" Kanofksy
and his family, with whom I have spent the better half of a decade on Rosh
Hashanah and Yom Kippur. He's been a role model for me in what a contemporary chassidic life and a diverse book shelf should really look like.
Finally, and I know he eschews such superlatives, but my Rebbe Dr. Ari
Bergmann showed me the grandeur of interdisciplinary study and sophisticated academic analysis through the lens of an inspired soul. His ideas
continue to inspire my love of ideas.

Family:

My in-laws present a dilemma and a blessing. They are both friends and
teachers, so they could have rightfully been included within either of
those thank yous. But above all, they are my family who is always there
for me. My deepest gratitude to Dr. Louis and Safta Debbie Flancbaum for
reviewing an earlier manuscript and making me a better person, to Phyllis
Flancbaum for her boundless selflessness for our family, and to Shira,
Jeremy (a.k.a. J-Bone), Meir, Atara, and their entire families for welcoming
me as family and embracing me as a friend.

On September 14, 1997, Fred Rogers, affectionately known as
Mr. Rogers, received the lifetime achievement award at the 24th annual
Daytime Emmy Awards. He asked the audience to take a ten second
moment of silence to think about the "special ones who have loved us into
being." I have always been struck by that phrase. "Loved us into being."

When I think about the people who loved me into being, I always think about my family. Nothing gives me more pride than being a part of the Bashevkin family along with my siblings Sarah, Elana, Rachel, and Elie, as well as their respective spouses, Ian, Shlomo, Dov, and Miriam, and all their children.

My parents, of course, loved me into being. They created a home of learning and prayer. Memories of my parents davening and studying Torah continue to animate my values and ambitions. My gratitude to them is simply ineffable.

Finally, my wife Tova, you brought sweetness into my life and I have so much admiration and appreciation for the home we are building together. We often jokingly say, "You're perfect, even when you're not perfect." It's a fitting phrase given the subject of the book, which I dedicate to you, our Mr. Baby, Zev Moshe, and Baby Kira, Yakira Leeba. For showing me the true meaning of perfection, with enduring love, thank you.

CPSIA information can be obtained
at www.ICGtesting.com
Printed in the USA
JSHW041731170821
17944JS00003B/136